Violence and Understanding in Gaza

Violence and Understanding in Gaza

The British Broadsheets' Coverage of the War

Dávid Kaposi
School of Psychology, University of East London, UK

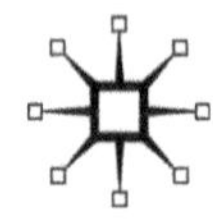

First published 2014 by
PALGRAVE MACMILLAN

Palgrave Macmillan in the UK is an imprint of Macmillan Publishers Limited, registered in England, company number 785998, of Houndmills, Basingstoke, Hampshire RG21 6XS.

Palgrave Macmillan in the US is a division of St Martin's Press LLC, 175 Fifth Avenue, New York, NY 10010.

Palgrave Macmillan is the global academic imprint of the above companies and has companies and representatives throughout the world.

Palgrave® and Macmillan® are registered trademarks in the United States, the United Kingdom, Europe and other countries

ISBN: 978–1–137–43949–9

This book is printed on paper suitable for recycling and made from fully managed and sustained forest sources. Logging, pulping and manufacturing processes are expected to conform to the environmental regulations of the country of origin.

A catalogue record for this book is available from the British Library.

Library of Congress Cataloging-in-Publication Data

Kaposi, Dávid.
Violence and understanding in Gaza : the British broadsheets' coverage of the war / Dávid Kaposi.
pages cm
ISBN 978–1–137–43949–9 (hardback)
1. Gaza War, 2008–2009. 2. Gaza War, 2008–2009 – Press coverage – Great Britain. I. Title.

DS119.767.K37 2014
956.9405′4—dc23 2014024163

For Magda and Stacy

Contents

List of Tables

Acknowledgements

Pictured above is a very small street in Budapest. Short it may be, *Sport utca* is unique nonetheless. It is the only street in the world accommodating two football stadiums, symmetrically sitting side-by-side. Legend has it that when their combined attendance falls below 36, the world shall cease to exist (Scholem, 1995a).

In the past three years, many people (relatives, relative-in-the-making, friends, colleagues and students) have had to put up with revelations of this sort. Everlasting thanks to them. Especially to Vili Frank and Edit Frank-Szigeti, who got a particularly intensive dose at their home in Jaffa/Yaffo, August 2012. Also, many thanks to David Feldman for his confidence in me to ask for a presentation of what is now Chapter 6, and John Richardson for his comments on the final manuscript.

The book would not have been possible without Dávid Szűcs and Georgina Turner, who offered enormous help during various phases of it. It would not have finished as it did without the word processing expertise of Stacy Gandolfi. And it would not have even started, were it not for the financial and moral help of the Vidal Sassoon Center in the Study of Contemporary Antisemitism.

As with everything I write, completing this book as I did would not have been possible without the two academic supervisors with whom I had the luck to work in the past: Anikó Kónya (Budapest) and Mick Billig (Loughborough). They taught me that commitment to the values of the academy is not just a word; it is an idea. I did my utmost to write this book in that spirit.

1
Introduction: Violence and Understanding in the Armed Conflict of Gaza

Introduction

This book presents a case study: it offers an analysis of the British broadsheets' coverage of a war, examining the breadth and depth of their content, and as such, it attempts to examine various ways of understanding violence.

As has been regularly noted, the war of Gaza between 27 December 2008 and 18 January 2009 occupies a special page in the history of the Israeli-Palestinian conflict. It was 'the first major armed struggle between Israel and Hamas, as distinguished between Israel and the PLO and Fatah' (Cordesman, 2009, p. 1), reflecting the new political constellation where the traditional political role of advocating Palestinian interests was overtaken by Hamas from Fatah. It was also an event which not only rendered the highest number of Palestinian casualties and properties destroyed in any Israeli offensive (cf. Amnesty International, 2009, p. 2), but was argued to be 'qualitatively different from any previous military action by Israel in the Occupied Palestinian Territory' (Goldstone Report, 2011, p. 291).

Whilst the major issues of war inevitably concern the places and people directly involved, regarding the Israeli-Palestinian conflict, the role of the Western media and the perception of the population of the main Western stakeholders in the conflict also warrant special attention. In particular, recent debates to be reviewed later in this introduction suggest that another (to be sure, metaphorical) war is taking place in the British media to present and understand the events, with conservative publications taking it upon themselves to advocate Israeli interests and left-liberal ones supporting Palestinians. As any outcome of the conflict will by necessity be predicated on the meanings associated with it, analytic attention must therefore be paid to the 'scene of commentary' in Britain and how the British media engage with the issues occurring in the Middle East.

The first task of this case study is therefore to offer a systematic, multi-method analysis of the ways the British national broadsheets (i.e., *Daily Telegraph, The Times, Guardian, Independent, Financial Times*) engaged with the 'Gaza war' and made sense of violence and the context surrounding it. As such, the book promises to provide insight into dominant *ways of thinking* about the Israeli-Palestinian conflict and makes suggestions regarding how to change these dominant ways of thinking so that they do justice to the terrible tragedies of war and the noble aspirations of peace in the region (Ben-Ami, 2006; Morris, 1999).

Thus, in a broader sense, this book also presents a case study in understanding violence. For war, first and foremost, is an act of violence rendering people (always too many people) dead on its way. It is not evident, and it is not meaningful in itself. It has to be *understood* as such: acts of violence need to be incorporated into a framework of interpretation (Walzer, 2000). This will not nullify the tragedy that is death and glamorize the violence that is war. But it is indeed the only way to create conditions where death does not lead to more death and violence to even more violence. As such, there is nothing inevitable about acts of understanding when it comes to violence. Therefore, the second aspect of this case study is the understanding of the British broadsheets' coverage of the armed conflict of Gaza *as an act of understanding*.

As subsequent chapters of this book will focus on this topic with considerable exclusivity, leaving historical and political facts and insights aside in their pursuit of understanding the broadsheets' texts on their own terms, it is the task of this chapter to set the scene and present relevant details. It will introduce the reader to three aspects of this context. First, the story of the armed conflict itself will be narrated. Then, various reports investigating the legality of the war will be presented. Finally, the status of debates over Israel, Palestine and the media will be engaged with. The introduction will conclude by briefly describing the coming chapters of the book.

Violence: the chronicle of the armed conflict

Mirroring the conflict between Israel and Palestinians (Ben-Ami, 2006; Morris, 1999), the relevant narrative context for the war can be construed from many perspectives. As will be reflected on later in this introduction, any narration of the conflict generates extraordinary tension and has inevitable moral and political dimensions. To construe this story of human relations is itself a story of human relations. For these reasons, no comprehensive attempt will be made to overview the historical details. A brief sketch of events preceding the intensification of the armed conflict as well as the barebones of the war itself will have to suffice.[1]

Events of immediate relevance may be said to have started in the autumn of 2005, when Israel unilaterally abolished its civilian and military presence in the Gaza Strip, which it had occupied (and populated in parts with Israeli civilians) following its war with Egypt, Syria and Jordan in 1967. In notable respects, this was a momentous decision and one without precedent. Israel's stance on war and peace had hitherto been dominated by a doctrine whereby it would only willingly relinquish territory gained in war in exchange for peace (cf. Morris, 1999; Shlaim, 2004). As suggested by the fact that Israel acted *unilaterally*, peace was not a prospect when Israel withdrew its forces from the Strip. From the perspective of its own history and the doctrines evolved to interpret this history, Israel could then be said to have taken an enormous risk to execute an unprecedented plan. Hope and trust, or, to the contrary, desperation, appeared to have overtaken the cautious *realpolitik* that had dominated Israeli political vocabulary. Predictably, the withdrawal caused an extraordinary rift within Israeli society.

From other perspectives, however, its action was seen either as an act of pure self-interest or downright detrimental to the prospects of peace. It was claimed that the decision was prompted merely by matters of convenience, as Israel's pragmatic leaders calculated that the costs of occupying a densely populated territory were simply too high. Others suspected a straightforwardly malicious course of events where not only did Israel not act in the interest of the peace process and a viable two-state solution but, to the very contrary, it simply wanted to put the peace process on hold whilst grabbing more territories from the West Bank (Halper, 2008; cf. Said, 2004).

Indeed, soon enough the very idea of a 'withdrawal' was also contested. For Israel, undeniably, did not completely relinquish its power over the territory and confer sovereignty to its Palestinian authorities. It retained complete oversight and control of the Gaza Strip's borders and airspace, telecommunications, water and electricity networks.[2] It also continued to demarcate so called 'no go areas' even within the Strip itself. Thus, while it is without doubt that a certain amount of real autonomy has been conferred to the authorities of the Strip, critics were quick to point out that no complete transposition of sovereignty can be ascertained, and therefore the occupation must be said to be ongoing (Goldstone Report, 2011, p. 45; Halper, 2008; cf. Operation in Gaza, 2009, pp. 5, 11; Dershowitz, 2006, p. 2). All of this has led to a situation where many people sympathetic to Israel's predicament consider Gaza to be a relatively autonomous territory, whilst others critical of the State of Israel and sympathetic to the miseries of the Palestinians call it but a prison.

In any case, whatever the real (or perceived) risk for the population of Israel and the rift caused within its society were, and whatever the benefits (or otherwise) of a partial autonomy were for the population of Gaza, it may be argued that the events described above led to a 'spiral of violence', ultimately culminating in the war itself. First, the political vacuum left by the Israeli government's *unilateral* decision to withdraw from Gaza was filled by Palestinian militants claiming to have chased away the occupying power. Second, the direct absence of Israelis and the relative autonomy conferred to local authorities meant that these militant organizations could further their 'successful' policy of rejection by launching rockets and mortars into Southern Israel. And third, even if these invectives were mostly homemade and of no overbearing military significance[3], coupled with the ever-ominous and antisemitic rhetoric Islamic militants deployed, they nonetheless constituted acts of military aggression. They terrorized considerable swathes of the Israeli population over the years and contributed to a mentality where the vast military imbalance between Israeli and Palestinian forces was never translated into Israeli citizens' subjective feeling of safety. As a result, renewed rocket fire was met with continuous Israeli military operations in and around Gaza, resulting in anger and desperation on the Palestinian side, too – and of course, renewed bouts of rocket fire.

In January 2006, legislative elections (judged by international observers to have been conducted fairly) were held in the Palestinian Authority (i.e., the West Bank and Gaza), where the militant Hamas won over 70, and the secular-nationalist Fatah 45, of the available 132 seats. This outcome signalled a huge shift in the power balance of Palestinian politics. A radical and Islamist force came into political prominence at the expense of the traditional secular-nationalist vehicle of Palestinian aspirations; Israel's long-time partner in dialogues for peace was replaced by a power that rejected the very idea of peace between the two nations. As a consequence, Israel imposed economic sanctions on the territory. Branding Hamas a terrorist organization, the United States and the European Union followed suit and withheld funds from the Palestinian Authority. Matters hardly improved when in June 2006 groups belonging to Hamas's military wing conducted an incursion into Israeli territory and attacked a military post, capturing an Israeli corporal, Gilad Shalit. Israel duly tightened the economic blockade of Gaza further and conducted military operations in and around the territory.

In early 2007, following an attempt to form a united government of the Palestinian territories, a short civil war broke out between Fatah and Hamas, with the former taking full control of the West Bank, and the latter of Gaza. Accordingly, Gaza was immediately declared a 'hostile entity' by Israel; the Jewish state further intensified its blockade with additional restrictions placed on quantity and quality of food, goods, fuel and electricity permitted to enter the Strip. Meanwhile, Hamas continued to fire rockets into Israeli civilian territory and, by way of partially counterbalancing the blockade, established an underground tunnel system for smuggling goods as well as weapons under the Strip's closed border with Egypt.

This cyclical state of affairs continued until 19 June 2008, when both parties accepted a six-month long Egyptian-sponsored ceasefire – meaning the temporary cessation of hostilities. However, the ceasefire agreement was not without ambiguities, and in fact no text of agreement ever existed. In Hamas's understanding, their ceasing fire would be coupled with the Israeli scrapping of the blockade; in Israel's interpretation, it was only the easing of the restrictions that was required in exchange for Hamas ceasing fire. In turn, Israel expected Hamas to release the IDF corporal Gilad Shalit (held hostage for over two years at this point), and to stop building up its military strength and accumulating weapons through its system of tunnels beneath the Egyptian border.

The months in the aftermath of the ceasefire 'agreement' passed with a very significant reduction of violence on both sides. Yet the real status and value of the ceasefire has been contested ever since, as in retrospect, self-restraint on both sides may have meant little more than covering up actual preparation for war. Hamas duly continued to smuggle weapons into the Strip, expanding its arsenal with weaponry capable of penetrating deeper into Israeli territory. As such, the months of calm may actually have made it a *more dangerous* entity with regard to Israeli strategic objectives and civilian interests. And Israel used the time of relative calm to perfect its coming operation, hoping to banish memories of an ill-planned and ill-executed war against the Lebanese Shia party-cum-militia Hezbollah in 2006. Indeed, it has been argued since that the seeds of the overwhelming military success that the war to come yielded for Israel were sown during these months of careful intelligence gathering (Cordesman, 2009).

The ceasefire itself proved to be less than long-lasting. Following the period of calm, on 4 November Israeli forces conducted an incursion into Gaza. Tanks and infantry entered the Strip in an operation that was stated to be a raid on a tunnel used for smuggling weapons and that ended in the killing of six Hamas gunmen. The Palestinian organization responded with rocket fire of renewed intensity, firing 35 of them into Israel immediately after the incursion and around 200 between November and mid-December. The calm that characterized the first half of the ceasefire was never reached again.

As the by-then nominal ceasefire expired on 18 December, both parties remained ambiguous about their subsequent aims, with action not necessarily corresponding to rhetoric of conciliation.[4] Hamas continued firing rockets and mortars into Israeli civilian territory. Israel continued to carry out limited military action in and around the Strip. In the end, Israel launched full-scale war on 27 December (dubbing it 'Operation Cast Lead'), citing the rocket fire as *casus belli*.

The war started with an aerial phase, just before mid-day on 27 December: the Israeli Defense Forces (IDF) hit around 100 targets within 220 seconds. According to IDF estimates, around 99 per cent of its strikes were accurate, a testimony to the planning and information-gathering that had preceded the offensive. Amongst the early targets were the headquarters of Hamas, the building of the Palestinian Legislative Council, as well as 24 police stations. The first day of the war rendered the highest ever one-day Palestinian casualties (230) in the entire history of the conflict.

The aerial phase of the war lasted until 3 January and was followed by an air-ground phase. In this second and last phase of the war, Israel's main strategic plan was to secure the areas used by Palestinian militants to launch rockets, and to destroy the tunnels used for smuggling weapons into Gaza. To achieve this, the IDF entered Gaza from north and east, dividing the Strip in two. Air attacks continued in the south, whilst ground operations dominated in the more urbanized north. As international pressure was mounting, from 7 January onwards Israel agreed to a daily three-hour ceasefire and the opening of a 'humanitarian corridor' with essential goods supplied to the civilian population of the Strip. Having expanded their ground manoeuvre, entering deeper into the territory, on 15 January Israeli forces started their withdrawal (though with renewed aerial attacks around the border between Gaza and Egypt).

With no official agreement signed, first Israel and then a couple of hours (and rockets) later, Hamas announced unilateral ceasefire on 18

January. Thus the war or 'Operation Cast Lead' ended on the ground and gave place to its evaluation.

Responsibility: investigations in the wake of the conflict

When assessing the war, three types of consideration dominated. The first was of a narrowly *military* kind, concerning simple tactics, implementation, and immediate success on the ground. The second was of a *strategic* kind and concerned the short- or long-term objectives that were met or missed: in short, whether the war was useful. The third was of a more principled kind and concerned whether the parties' conduct of the war conformed to universal *moral and legal* principles: in short, whether the war was just.

As should be clear even from this brief description of the hostilities, the 'war' of Gaza was overwhelmingly dominated, perhaps even *defined* as such, by Israel.[5] As far as the Gaza Strip itself was concerned, Hamas constituted barely any obstacle in the way of the Israeli Defense Forces. Its activity often consisted merely of finding places to hide. Whilst Hamas leaders claimed 'victory' immediately after their declaration of ceasefire, there can be no doubt that the Islamist organization came nowhere near the 2006 achievement of Hezbollah in catching the technically superior forces of Israel by surprise. Likewise, the 800 rockets and mortars that, according to official Israeli sources (Operation in Gaza, 2009, p. 24), it launched into Southern Israel, constituted no military challenge to the Israeli forces as they barely caused any danger or damage – even if their reach was wider than ever before, hitting the towns of Beersheba and Ashdod for the first time. Having killed four civilians and caused very real psychological consequences, these attacks did not alter the narrative of the war, which was written by Israel and composed of Israeli action.

As regards longer term strategic considerations, the picture is somewhat fuzzier: whilst Hamas could certainly claim no other significant success than psychologically terrorizing the Israeli population[6], Israeli gains were not undisputed either. On one hand, a considerable reduction of rocket fire from Gaza followed in the aftermath of the war as official Israeli sources claimed that 80 per cent of the tunnels used for smuggling weapons into Gaza were destroyed. This state of affairs allowed Israeli politicians to claim victory. On the other hand, Hamas was still in power, with some of its weaponry intact and its intention (or indeed, that of the Gaza populace) hardly more favourable to any political solution to the problem. Thus, critics duly claimed that no long-term political aim was reached (or even pursued) by Israel, and no steps were taken towards a comprehensive deal where the Israeli and Palestinian people would live in peace. If anything, causing widespread destruction (of human lives as well as property), anger and consternation, the prospect of any such state of affairs receded considerably from the horizon.

As we can see, the magnitude and composition of fatalities were heavily criticized after the war, even from a purely strategic point of view. Yet it was not simply from a utilitarian angle that questions of life and death were heavily pondered in the international media; the 'Gaza war' prompted unprecedented international investigations as to the parties' compliance with humanitarian law. These debates or investigations did not simply concern the one-sided nature of the conflict, with vastly more Palestinians and, in particular, Palestinian civilians having been killed; they also interrogated the motives on both sides as regarded their attitude towards the fundamental distinction between civilians and combatants.

Unexpectedly in a conflict where virtually all steps leading to the war had been contested from a variety of perspectives, the exercise of allocating responsibility for the deaths of the war created extraordinary controversies in itself.

Not that there has ever been any debate about Israeli casualties. The hostilities resulted in the death of 13 Israeli citizens, nine of them soldiers (four of whom were killed in 'friendly fire') and four of them civilians living in Southern Israel and taking no part in the conflict. 182 Israeli civilians were injured as a result of the rocket fire into Southern Israel.

It was Palestinian fatalities, the total figures and their composition that varied according to different sources. The Gaza-based authority, the Central Commission for Documentation and Pursuit of Israeli War Criminals cites 1,444 Palestinians killed (348 being children and 248 policemen). Palestinian non-governmental organization Palestinian Centre for Human Rights mentions 1,417 Palestinian victims (236 combatants, 235 police, and 926 civilians, with 313 being children and 116 women). Another Palestinian NGO, Al Mezan, reports 1,409 Palestinian fatalities overall (237 combatants and 1,172 civilians, including 342 children, 111 women and 136 members of the police).

Israeli NGO B'Tselem cites 1,387 Palestinians killed (330 active combatants, 243 policemen, 773 civilians with 320 children and 109 women).[7] According to the Israeli Defense Forces, 1,166 Palestinians were killed during the war; 709 of them were 'Hamas terror operatives',

295 'uninvolved Palestinians' (of whom 89 were children and 49 women). A total of 162 men could not be attributed to any organization or category.[8]

Fatality figures thus remained heavily contested, with the main points of contention being as to which category the police belonged; how to define those who were 'involved' in the hostilities; at what age one becomes an adult[9]; and how to categorize a child who is nonetheless taking part in the hostilities. Yet the very asymmetry unanimously conveyed by them meant that what needed to be established was not simply the definite number of fatalities, but the nature of motives and responsibility that led to death in the 'Gaza war'.

Of the various fact-finding inquiries conducted in the wake of the war, the first one was a preliminary inquiry by the United Nations (with its 184-page findings not made available for the public) in May 2009, examining nine specific incidents where UN facilities were attacked.[10] In July of the same year, human rights NGO Amnesty International also published its findings (Amnesty International, 2009), followed by a separate investigation specifically into Israel's use of the chemical material white phosphorous, conducted by Human Rights Watch (Human Rights Watch, 2009).

Whilst these publications led to considerable repercussions, these paled in significance to the most important, comprehensive and controversial report of participants' conduct of the war, the 'Report of the United Nations Fact-Finding Mission on the Gaza Conflict' or Goldstone Report (Goldstone Report, 2011). As early as 12 January 2009, the UN Human Rights Council commissioned an investigation of Israeli acts during the war. In April, prominent South African judge Richard Goldstone accepted the mandate, though only after it was expanded to examine *all* (that is, those of Hamas as well) activities concerning the armed conflict.[11] Neither Hamas nor the State of Israel cooperated with the commission. The report's findings were released on 15 September 2009, to predictably intense public scrutiny not short of recriminations, innuendos and *ad hominem* arguments (Slater, 2011). Briefly after its publication, the UN General Assembly endorsed a resolution which called for independent investigations on both Israel's and Hamas's part in the incidents unearthed by the report.

Meanwhile, Israel also published updates of the proceedings of internal investigations. Initiated independently yet in parts responding to the international probes, in a succession of three papers it reported 161 command investigations into some 400 allegations/complaints about the war, 47 of them having been referred to criminal investigations

(Operation in Gaza, 2009; Gaza operation investigations: update, 2010; Gaza operation investigations: second update, 2010). It also distributed information of the six (initially five) broader *special command investigations* that the IDF Chief of General Staff commissioned on 20 January 2009, shortly after the hostilities concluded. These concerned not simply individual acts but whole areas of the 'most serious allegations of wrongdoing' (Gaza operation: update, 2010, p. iii; cf. Operation in Gaza, 2009, pp. 117–156):

- incidents in which a large number of civilians not directly participating in the hostilities were harmed;
- incidents where UN and international facilities were fired upon and damaged;
- incidents involving shooting at medical facilities, buildings, vehicles and crews;
- destruction of private property and infrastructure by ground forces;
- the use of weaponry containing (white) phosphorous;
- additional investigation into three incidents covered in the Goldstone Report.

What did these various investigations conclude? As far as its rockets fired into Southern Israel were concerned, Hamas was of course unambiguously condemned in all of these reports. As the Goldstone mission asserted, '[w]here there is no intended military target and the rockets and mortars are launched into civilian areas, they [i.e., actions by Palestinian militants] constitute a deliberate attack against the civilian population. These actions would constitute war crimes and may amount to crimes against humanity' (Goldstone Report, 2011, p. 311). Debates may persist as to the amount of condemnation or its structural place in reports, but none of the other reports, including the Israeli investigation, came to any different conclusions in any different style (cf. Amnesty International, 2009, pp. 67, 74; Operation in Gaza, 2009, pp. 52–76).

Another aspect of Hamas's conduct, arguably of equal significance in terms of moral and legal responsibility for the dead, became heavily contested, however. This was the organization's conduct *with respect to* Gaza itself. Namely, just as in disclaimers of Israeli politicians and advocates during the war, the Israeli military's subsequent investigations laid emphasis on Hamas using Palestinian civilians as human shields as well as using nominally non-military objects (e.g., mosques) or even UN buildings to launch attacks on Israelis (Operation in Gaza, 2009, pp. 52–76). In stark contrast, neither Amnesty International (2009, pp. 75–77) nor the Goldstone Report (2011, pp. 72–80) found much evidence of Palestinian civilians having been forced into providing cover for Hamas militants or Hamas fighters using civilian or UN premises to launch attacks.[12] Acknowledging the inconclusive nature of its inquiries into the matters, the Goldstone Report also noted its lack of evidence for Hamas booby-trapping civilian homes, or using mosques to store weapons or launch attacks on Israel.

These were obviously controversial findings in that they rendered a different picture of Hamas from the Israeli one, and one that did not necessarily fit the image of an evil creature impossible to negotiate with. Likewise, they indicated a significant re-allocation of legal responsibility regarding the death of Palestinian civilians. Yet nothing could have foreshadowed the *diametrically* opposite conclusions the human rights organizations' reports, as well as that of the Goldstone commission, arrived at from the IDF investigation, as far as Israel's responsibility was concerned.

Whilst identifying 'some operational errors and mistakes' as well as 'violations of rules of engagement' resulting in disciplinary actions (Gaza operation: update, 2010, p. 29), the IDF papers reported of no criminal investigations initiated in any of the incidents covered by their 'special investigations', duly concluding that 'the IDF [...] did its best to minimize civilian casualties and damages to civilian property and sensitive sites' (Operation in Gaza, 2009, p. 156).[13] In line with the Israeli army's self-image as a *moral* force though, these words of summary could not be more different from those of the fact-finding reports.

The UN Board of Inquiry concluded that seven of the nine attacks it investigated were committed by the Israeli army (with at least one being committed by Palestinian groups) and involved 'varying degrees of negligence or recklessness with regard to United Nations premises' (UN Board of Inquiry, 2009, p. 21). In a similar vein, the comprehensive Goldstone Report claimed that Israel's Operation Cast Lead constituted 'a deliberately disproportionate attack designed to punish, humiliate and terrorize a civilian population' (Goldstone Report, 2011, p. 295), whilst Amnesty International ascertained that 'much of the destruction was wanton and resulted from direct attacks on civilian objects as well as indiscriminate attacks that failed to distinguish between legitimate military targets and civilian objects. Such attacks violated fundamental provisions of international humanitarian law' (Amnesty International, 2009, p. 1). Likewise, in its investigation of Israel's use of white phosphorous, Human Rights Watch declared that '[t]he unlawful use of white phosphorous was neither incidental nor accidental. It was repeated over time and in different locations' and as a consequence was indicative of 'criminal intent' (Human Rights Watch, 2009, p. 60) and 'war crimes' (p. 65).

How are we to understand the emergence of such startlingly different formulations? How can honest investigations equally conclude that the IDF's effort to avoid civilian casualties was 'extensive' and that it lived up to its own 'stringent ethical and legal requirements' (Gaza operation: second update, 2010, p. 32), *and* that there was an IDF 'military doctrine that views disproportionate destruction and creating maximum disruption in the lives of many people as legitimate means to achieve military and political goals' (Goldstone Report, 2011, p. 195)?

These questions point to the very heart of this book. They concern the existence of radical opposite versions of responsibility and how such opposite versions may have surfaced.

To be sure, questions pertained to some factual aspects of the war. There was some dispute over the use of weaponry, bullets and shells found on the ground and the like. Yet what the framework of the Israeli argument consisted of was demonstrating how war against a terrorist organization is by its nature inimical to war as traditionally understood, and why apparently inadmissible action therefore is necessary if such an organization is to be tackled in war. As the distinction between Hamas's military and political or social arms came to be negated, so traditional perceptions of the civilian-combatant distinction were problematized: Israel considered policemen as legitimate targets, just as it did buildings such as the Palestinian Legislative Council.

A case in point is the evaluation of the IDF's deployment of the chemical substance white phosphorous as an obscurant during the operation.[14] There was no disagreement between the reports that Israel used the chemical material in munitions in the war. There was also little disagreement about the facts: that there is no blanket international ban on the use of white phosphorous; that Israel did not use it as a direct weapon against civilians but rather as an obscurant; and that it was used in densely populated areas. Surprisingly, perhaps, there was even relatively little disagreement as to what was hit by white phosphorous shells or parts of them. The real point of debate concerned not so much facts but indeed ideas; not execution but policy and the perspectives underlying policy.

The IDF summary on the special command investigation of white phosphorous noted that

> international law does not prohibit use of smoke projectiles containing [white] phosphorous. Specifically, such projectiles are not 'incendiary

> weapons' [...] because they are not primarily designed to set fire or to burn. The Military Advocate General [i.e., the IDF's independent legal authority] further determined that during the Gaza Operation, the IDF used such smoke projectiles for military purposes only, for instance to camouflage IDF armour forces from Hamas anti-tank units by creating smoke screens. (Gaza operation: second update, 2010, pp. 32–33)

What is revealing about this quote is that there is next to nothing in it with which the Goldstone Report, Amnesty International or the Human Rights Watch would not have agreed. They did not claim that white phosphorous was used by Israel as an incendiary weapon. What they claimed was that with the chemical substance being used within heavily built-up areas, the unintended corollary effects of smoke-screening could not (and should not have) be(en) decoupled from whatever effect the Israeli authorities consciously used white phosphorous for. Their claim was not that Israel intended to kill civilians with white phosphorous but that Israel did not convincingly demonstrate *an active intention not to kill civilians* as they used white phosphorous in heavily built-up areas: 'Even if intended as an obscurant rather than a weapon, the IDF's firing of air-burst white phosphorous shells from 155mm artillery into densely populated areas was indiscriminate or disproportionate, and indicates the commission of war crimes' (Human Rights Watch, 2009, p. 65).

The enormity of this gap of understanding was revealed nowhere so clearly as in the IDF probe, which directly engaged with the idea that the usage of white phosphorous amidst urban warfare is willy-nilly bound to lead to indiscriminate military conduct:

> Some have suggested that air-burst white phosphorous munitions are by nature indiscriminate because they are designated to scatter over a wide area and therefore cannot be targeted precisely at a military objective. However, smoke projectiles are not designed or intended to be lethal or destructive, and as a result they are not used for targeting purposes. Rather, they are intended to disorient and neutralise the enemy by creating obscuration of the enemy's field of view (and therefore the objective in using them depends to a large degree on achieving a wide area of effect). Indeed, white phosphorous smoke screen projectiles worked well in serving their intended objective of protecting Israeli troops during the conflict. Therefore, smoke obscurants containing white phosphorous were not used for targeting

> purposes and cannot be classified as an indiscriminate weapon; otherwise, any smoke-screening means would be prohibited, in contrast to the well established practice of militaries worldwide. (Operation in Gaza, 2009, p. 148)

As we can see, the proposition that white phosphorous is 'by nature indiscriminate' is countered by the argument that such munitions are 'not used for targeting purposes' and 'are intended [for] obscuration' by the IDF. Even as the idea of inevitable or natural consequences is raised, the Israeli perspective is still couched in terms of direct intention. Alongside the reiteration of the lack of a formal ban on white phosphorous, it is this active intention that is negated. The fact that responsibility may involve not simply lack of intention to kill but also the positive intention not to kill civilians and, in the words of moral philosophers Michael Walzer and Avishai Margalit, 'that active intention can be made manifest only through the risk the soldiers themselves accept in order to reduce the risk to civilians' (Margalit & Walzer, 2009, p. 22) hardly surfaced with any substance in Israel's argumentation.

Thus, the reason for the shocking difference in conclusions between the investigations was not the existence (or not) of Israeli 'bad apples' or their number. Likewise, it was not a mundane matter of fact and procedures. But nor was it to be found at a simple level of command and the actual origin of orders. The international investigations seem to have been right in intuiting that what they understood as Israel's flouting the legal principles of proportionality and distinction was at its core not derivative of individual wrongdoing but of a different institutional understanding of core elements of the conflict (Goldstone Report, 2011, p. 293). As the Amnesty International report noted, Israel's were 'overly broad interpretations of what constitutes a military objective or military advantage' (Amnesty International, 2009, p. 65) and its 'definitions of legitimate targets and proportionality [were] not consistent with the requirements of international humanitarian law' (Amnesty International, 2009, p. 64; cf. Goldstone Report, 2011, p. 194). More ominously, the Goldstone Report asserted that '[t]he repeated failure to distinguish between combatants and civilians appears to the Mission to have been the result of *deliberate guidance* issued to soldiers, as described by some of them, and not the result of *occasional lapses*' (Goldstone Report, 2011, p. 293 – emphases mine).

Indeed, it is true that the disagreement between the IDF and the human rights investigations derived from deeper differences of perspectives as to what the principles of discrimination and proportion imply: a matter of dispute was not merely *who* counts as civilian and *what* as civilian objects, but *what civilian status as such entails.*[15]

At the same time, acknowledging the enormity and depth of these differences does not mean that the interpretations guiding them would be incommensurable with each other, or that the Israeli authorities would have been guided by some intention to cause evil. Indeed, in the second and last update of its legal proceedings concerning alleged wrongdoings during its operation, the following unexpected sentence creeps into the Israeli treatise concerning the summary of the special command investigation of the use of white phosphorous:

> [...] the policy of using such munitions was consistent with Israel's obligations under the Law of Armed Conflict. Nonetheless, following that investigation, the Chief of General Staff ordered the implementation of the lesson learned from the investigation, particularly with regard to the use of such munitions near populated areas and sensitive installations. As a consequence, the IDF is in the process of establishing permanent restrictions on the use of munitions containing white phosphorous in urban areas. (Gaza operation: second update, 2010, p. 22)

More than 'permanent restrictions', in April 2013 the IDF announced that it would stop using white phosphorous in populated areas (Human Rights Watch, 2013).

Understanding: the British media and the Israeli-Palestinian conflict

The account of the war and its aftermath offered above appears to throw up a series of vexing questions. Was Israel's pull-out from Gaza an honest withdrawal of the occupying force or the practical consolidation of the occupation? Was it a difficult act that had genuinely torn Israeli society apart? Or was it an act of mere convenience, nay, malice? Did it confer considerable autonomy to the local authorities? Or did it merely create a prison? Did the IDF conduct itself by admirable moral principles in the ensuing armed conflict? Or did it commit heinous crimes?

If historical and legal representations of the conflict are highly contested and predicated upon values of political and moral kinds (cf. Morris, 1999), one would expect narratives provided in the (daily) media to be even more controversial and debates even more heated.

After all, procedures leading to the composition of a news story or an opinion piece in a newspaper tend to be far less rigorous and circumspect then those of (quasi)-legal reports or academic documents like historiographies. The daily media operate synchronously with events in the world; their reflections and the intensity of their scrutiny is not *intrinsically* determined. Their coverage does not so much come after the events but alongside them.

In line with this, it comes hardly as a surprise that the conflict in Israel/Palestine is notoriously 'one of the most problematic with which journalists need to deal' (Philo & Berry, 2011, p. 1) and where 'journalists feel compelled to watch every single word they write and broadcast' (Richardson & Barkho, 2009, p. 619). This is not simply due to an ever-present public scrutiny of unprecedented intensity; rather, there is a special quality to the context in which the media operate. As in its commission to investigate the BBC's impartiality regarding its coverage of the Israeli-Palestinian conflict the BBC panel concluded: 'much of our evidence in effect sought to recruit the Panel to support one side or the other in the conflict' (Report of the independent panel for the BBC governors, 2006, p. 5). The consensus was (contrary, in fact, to the conclusions of the Panel) that the BBC was biased. Where stakeholders differed, and differed staggeringly, was simply on whose side it was biased. Thus, scrutiny in the case of the Israel-Palestine conflict somehow inevitably entails not so much the more effective detection of mistakes: it reflects an atmosphere of suspicion where coverage will always already be expected to contain inaccuracies and where inaccuracies will always already be expected to be the expressions of systematic and motivated bias (Klug, 2003, 2009).

Indeed, one of the hallmarks of the discourse of the Israeli-Palestinian conflict is that it exists in the presence of *meta*-discourses, which are monitoring not so much the veracity but the very legitimacy, benevolence and genuineness of alternative accounts. Their *raison d'être* is not so much to say something meaningful or true about the conflict as such, but to uncover sinister motives lurking behind undesirable accounts of the conflict. It is in the context of these *meta*-discourses, acts of purification, that the British media operate.

The most important of them is that of the theory of 'new antisemitism'. Originating in the 1970s (cf. Foster & Epstein, 1974) with a revival that dates to the 2000s (Foxman, 2004, 2007; Markovits, 2006), it makes a twofold claim (cf. Foster & Epstein, 1974; Foxman, 2004, 2007; Markovits, 2006). First, it contends that contemporary antisemitism operates in disguise. Antisemitism, as a form of racism, has been categorically banished from politics in the aftermath of World War II and, in particular, the emergence of the discourse of universal human rights. Presenting an argument or an identity recognizable as antisemitic constitutes political and moral suicide. As a result, contemporary antisemitism does not dare to speak its name openly. Instead, it operates in the mask of apparently legitimate political criticism: that of Israel or Zionism.

Second, the theory also claims that the source and forms this ultimately antisemitic discourse takes have also radically changed in the past decades (Julius, 2010; Laqueur, 2006). Not only does contemporary antisemitism often not use the language of traditional (and thus honest) racism against Jews, but it presents itself as honest political criticism instead. It actually uses concepts developed precisely to counter antisemitism as well as other forms of racism: antifascism, human rights and humanitarian law. And as the language antisemitism uses has changed, so has its source. Instead of the familiar sweaty (extreme) right-wing corners, it is now surfacing in supposedly progressive, left-wing enclaves. As David Cesarani notes in a special volume dedicated to the topic, 'a convergence of anti-Zionism and anti-Jewish discourse occurred not at the fringes, but at the centre of British political and cultural life' (Cesarani, 2006, p. 155).

Indeed, these arguments are often presented in the context of the British media. Publications or broadcasts associated with the left or liberal-left are often seen as vehicles for anti-Israeli views, thus accelerating anti-Jewish hostility on the left (Wistrich, 2011, pp. 9, 15; cf. Davis, 2003). To continue with Cesarani, 'doctrinaire hostility to Israel is confined to niche publications of the left, such as the *New Statesman*, and the relatively small-circulation papers of the liberal-left such as the *Guardian* and the *Independent*' (Cesarani, 2006, p. 155; cf. Baram, 2004). The eminent British historian's ideas are fairly uncontroversial as far as treatises on the 'new antisemitism' are concerned. In fact, what distinguishes them from the usual formulations is their relatively calm tone and lack of overblown rhetoric:

> During the last decade Britain, led by its liberal-left elite has been sleepwalking into a morass of anti-Israel and anti-Jewish bigotry, while vehemently denying that anything is amiss. Even more appalling is to witness the nihilistic folly of 'progressive' Jews – driven by self-congratulatory narcissism as much as self-loathing – assuming prominent roles in directing the suicidal charge into the abyss. For that particular malady, there may be no treatment, only a post-mortem. (Wistrich, 2011, p. 22; cf. Chesler, 2003; Taguieff, 2004)

So, is there a resurgent antisemitism where its vicious content is disguised as simple political criticism? And are representatives of the (left-)liberal British media at the forefront of this puzzling and disturbing phenomenon? It will come as no surprise that in the wake of the theory of the 'new antisemitism', ideas firmly countering those exposed above have also emerged. True to fashion, conservative disparagement of the British media is met here with equally unequivocal praise as we read about the *Guardian*'s and the *Independent*'s 'astute objectivity and refreshing outsider's perspective' (Beller, 2007b, p. 220; Bourne, 2006).

In fact, many thinkers associated with the political left came to the conclusion that the 'theory of new antisemitism' is little more than a mere ploy to deflect and choke criticism of Israel (Finkelstein, 2005, p. xxxii; Kustow, 2008, p. 215; Lerman, 2008, p. 159; Mearsheimer & Walt, 2008, p. 189). In their reading, invectives directed at (left-)liberal segments of the (British) media are not exposing deeply problematic political-moral actions but trying to immunize the State of Israel against legitimate and valid public dissent (Cockburn & Clair, 2003; Karpf et al., 2008). Far from contributing to antisemitic agendas by intent or consequence, these liberal publications actually reveal something true about Israel's conduct and its dispossession of Palestinian. Far from contributing to anti-racism, the 'exposure' of these dissenting voices as antisemitic actually reveals a repressive and ultimately quasi-totalitarian agenda to choke public dissent and criticism of the State of Israel (Finkelstein, 2005).

Who, then, is right? It is undeniable that both of the positions in this debate (could) have something important to say about antisemitism, Israel and the limits of criticism (Fine, 2009; Hirsh, 2007; Laqueur, 2006; Julius, 2010). It appears perfectly reasonable to say that present day antisemitism will not advertise itself overtly and will instead make its unhelpful contribution to the heated debate on Israel undercover. The 'criticism' of the Jews raises eyebrows; the humanitarian 'criticism' of the Jewish state does not necessarily do so. It is also perfectly reasonable to say that zealots wishing to defend the State of Israel at all costs will not advertise overtly this inclination of theirs, and will seek instead to immunize their cherished state by using the obvious conversation stopper of 'antisemitism'. Uncritically supporting Israel raises eyebrows; trying to eradicate racism from discourse does not necessarily do so.

The upshot of this should be the acknowledgment of the enormous gravitas of the issues at hand. In Israel/Palestine, people are suffering, and the human community's preferred method of dealing with such things is to discuss them. In whatever form, antisemitism cannot be helpful to those discussions: if it is present in a piece of argument, then for that reason; if it is only present in the judgment of that piece of argument, then for that reason. Yet, the upshot should also be that both the detection of present day antisemitism (i.e., what an antisemitic piece of discourse is and what a simply critical one is) and of unjustified uses of the term antisemitism (i.e., which judgment of antisemitism is legitimate and which merely a motivated conversation stopper) requires, essentially, a *hermeneutical* activity: the unpacking of meaning not visible at face value (Fine, 2009). Beyond any doubt, there is a dire need for critical judgment and the application of that critical judgment with the utmost care.

Yet those taking a step back from the debate inevitably reflect on its fiercely 'partisan' (Judaken, 2008, p. 533) nature where 'jeering and sneering substitute for the give and take of argument, disagreement degenerates into abuse' (Klug, 2008, p. 287). Indeed, historian Steven Beller tellingly dubs the debate a 'literary tennis match' (Beller, 2007b, p. 217; cf. Fine, 2009, p. 461; Judaken, 2008, pp. 533–534; Peace, 2009, p. 112), and anthropologist Matti Bunzl terms it a zero-sum contest between the polar position of 'alarmists' and 'denialists' (Bunzl, 2007).[16]

From the perspective of this state of the debate, the relevant question may therefore not be: who is right? It may instead be what the reasons are for underlying assumptions and interpretative frameworks to differ to an extent where not only the veracity of alternative accounts but their very legitimacy and genuineness are questioned. Why is it that disagreements are pushed to the very extreme as arguments are not so much countered as characters assassinated? And why do appraisals whose main message would nominally be to carefully scrutinize accounts end almost inevitably in the absence of any activity resembling reading, interpretation and understanding?

Rather than weighing in, this book's task will be to weigh things up. For, it would appear, when it comes to Israel and Palestine, the task is not simply to interpret the conflict but to interpret those very interpretations of the conflict that seem to make any genuine understanding impossible.

Chapters to come

This introductory chapter has reviewed three areas of debate concerning the Israeli-Palestinian conflict in general and the 'Gaza war' (or Operation

Cast Lead) in particular. In narrating the story of the region leading up to the intensification of the armed conflict and that of the fact-finding investigations in the aftermath of the war, it revealed vastly different versions of the same events. In reviewing currently dominant explanations for the existence of diametrically opposite versions for virtually every aspect of the conflict, it revealed diametrically opposite accounts where not simply the veracity of the opponent was thrown in doubt but their very legitimacy and right to speak.

It is in such an overcharged public atmosphere that the present book seeks to find a place and a voice. Yet its task will not merely be to claim a place in the discourse but, ultimately, to provide an account for it. As such, this book will, hopefully, not only be a case study *of* understanding, but a case study *in* understanding.

This understanding is attempted through the focus on different conceptual areas and the utilization of different methods of inquiry. Action and death in war, historical context, criticism as well as the vexed question of antisemitism, and the dilemma of the just-ness of war will be examined in turn on these pages. They will be scrutinized to uncover divergences (or otherwise) the broadsheets exhibited when engaging with them. Quantitative analysis will be deployed to do this in the first half of the book; qualitative inquiry will help to uncover arguments in the second half.

Having reviewed the basic methodological procedures and the composition of the database in Chapter 2, Chapter 3 looks at the coverage of the basic 'building blocks' of the war. It will start with comparing the broadsheets on the issue of fatalities and analyse which categories of death were prioritized by them. In contradistinction to much existing literature, not only will the nationalities of the dead be taken into consideration but also their humanitarian status: were they civilians or combatants?

Following this, the analysis will try to understand how newspapers *accounted* for death. As such, the book will be concerned with widening narrative and argumentative contexts presented. This will already start in Chapter 3, as distribution of fatalities will be followed by the presentation of the immediate context to them. Actions of the participants, Israel and Hamas, in war will be analysed as delivered by the broadsheets. Chapter 4, then, examines how the newspapers engaged with a still broader framework of interpretation, that of historical context, and how historical events were deployed to help the understanding of immediate events and tragedies happening on the ground.

In the following chapters, different aspects of the argumentative context will be examined. As has been argued in the sections above, when it comes to the conflict of Israel-Palestine, criticism as such becomes a very dilemmatic concept. Not simply because any such act will immediately find itself amidst a fierce debate where counter-criticisms are overwhelming and plenty, but because the act of criticism *as such* is often cause for suspicion. Mere opinions are scrutinized not simply as concerns their validity, but also their very honesty and legitimacy. Therefore, Chapters 5 and 6 will examine the broadsheets' columnists' direct engagement with acts of criticism and antisemitism.

The concluding empirical chapters (7 and 8), in turn, will analyse the conservative and liberal newspapers' arguments for and against war. Traditional questions will be encountered here as the broadsheets tackle the question of *ius ad bellum* (law to war) and *ius in bello* (law in war). It is these dilemmas that will reveal the British newspapers' take on the identity of participants of the conflict as well as their ultimate account for the war.

As will be shown throughout the course of empirical chapters in this book, against all expectations perhaps, coverage of facts or 'building blocks' of narratives (Chapter 3) shows no great deal of difference, regardless of the source of publications. No black-and-white ideological divide will be recognizable when accounting for them, as differences will be haphazard, non-systematic and, occasionally, downright contradictory of what we would expect of conservative (i.e., allegedly pro-Israeli) and (left-)liberal (i.e., allegedly pro-Palestinian) newspapers. As analysis will move beyond facts and focus on narrative context (Chapter 4) and argumentative perspective (Chapters 5 and 6), however, an ever-widening divide will unfold. In fact, arguments about war will reveal two incommensurable critical perspectives as we reach the end of the book (Chapters 7 and 8): a conservative one where blame for the war falls exclusively on Hamas, with Israel being kept above the very possibility of criticism, and a (left)-liberal one, where it is Israel that is to be blamed, with Hamas presented as essentially unproblematic in terms of negotiations to be conducted.

Final reflections in Chapter 9 ponder such a split state of affairs. As will be argued, however, there is more in common in these perspectives than would immediately appear. Namely, instead of asking crucial questions of political-moral-legal responsibility, broadsheets ask the simplistic question of who is to be blamed: who is the perpetrator and who is innocent? Who is manifesting the essence of Evil and who that of

Innocence? Instead of assessing various shades of grey, broadsheets only see black-and-white when it comes to Israel/Palestine.

Such logic, as will be argued, might derive from a *metaphysical* conception of the events in Israel/Palestine where, against the appearance of political-moral discourse and criticism, it is not human agents who are pitched against each other in the imagination but non-human essences, and where the ultimate questions are not couched in the secular vocabulary of responsibility but in the sacred one of purity and impurity. Whilst the book will offer an account as to why this might be the case, it will also argue for a change of critical discourse in terms of which the conflict is assessed. For the prevailing discourse, from right to left, instead of advancing the prospect of negotiated peace, overwhelmingly replicates the very logic of war. As such, it contradicts the newspapers' avowed aim to advance a negotiated solution to the conflict.

2
Method of the Analysis and General Characteristics of the Newspapers

Introduction

This is the first of three (and a half) chapters where the broadsheets' coverage will be *quantitatively* analysed. Certain topics will be selected, and we will have a look at how frequently they occurred in the broadsheets' paragraphs. Thereby, we will learn, for instance, how many times the *Guardian* mentioned the Israeli occupation of Palestinian territories in its coverage, and how often the *Telegraph* mentioned Palestinian civilian death. We will learn how important each of the topics was for the newspapers in general. And we will also learn whether there is any important divergence between newspapers with regard to either specific codes or meaningful clusters of them (such as fatalities or historical context, for instance). Breaking down the newspapers' coverage into codes is a useful exercise that can help us to characterize the British reception of the 'Gaza war' in broad strokes (Richardson, 2007).

This relatively short chapter serves a threefold purpose. First, it will introduce the reader to the sample of newspaper articles that formed the basis of the analysis, and answer some basic questions. Where were they found? How were they arrived at? How were they selected? Second, it will briefly explain the procedures that lead to quantitative analysis of the data. How were the articles broken down to analysable units? What were the codes assigned to those units? And finally, what calculations were done to those codes? Third, quantitative analysis to come in subsequent chapters will be demonstrated with regard to the general characteristics of the sample. How many paragraphs did broadsheets devote to the conflict? What types of articles did those paragraphs feature in (i.e., editorials, news articles, etc.)? And what can we learn about the broadsheets' coverage in general and the divergences between specific outlets via analysing the distribution of paragraphs?

Subsequent chapters shall interrogate more specific conceptual areas using the same principles, whilst from the second half of the book, more in-depth investigations will focus on the underlying perspectives of the broadsheets.

Construction of the sample

The period of the intensified armed conflict between the State of Israel and Hamas in the Gaza strip stretched from 27 December 2008 to 18 January 2009; the parameters of the sample were set at 20 December 2008 and 25 January 2009 in order to capture coverage immediately before, during and after the war. It was decided that data would be collected from the publications displayed in Table 2.1.

In common parlance, these newspapers are dubbed as 'conservative' (*Daily Telegraph* and *The Times*) and 'liberal' (*Financial Times*) or 'left-liberal' (*Guardian, Independent*). Though such categorization is rather simplistic and, in some sense, possibly invalid, the newspapers will be referred to by these terms throughout the book.

Quantitative analysis in this as well as subsequent chapters will focus on the daily newspapers. To incorporate Sunday editions, it was found, would have made the quantitative data too heterogeneous to be captured within the remit of the present investigation. At the same time, later chapters in the book, looking at arguments and the construction of context by close reading, will make use of Sunday editions as well.

A single search term – 'Gaza' – was selected to produce an original sample. This, it was felt, would be sufficient to identify articles concerned with the conflict and turn up minimal irrelevant data. Initially, all articles with at least one mention of 'Gaza' were included, but as they were manually filtered, those that made only passing reference to the conflict, and were in fact otherwise focused, were removed. For instance, several

Table 2.1 Publications included in the case study

National broadsheets	Sunday editions of national broadsheets
Daily Telegraph	*Sunday Telegraph*
The Times	*The Sunday Times*
Guardian	*Observer*
Independent	*Independent on Sunday*
Financial Times	

Table 2.2 Illustration of data cataloguing

Item	Headline	Source	Date	Type	Page	Words
3	Israel masses troops...	Daily Telegraph	29 December 2008	News article	1	781
555	Why Israel is united: Disdain for the tactics and ideology of Hamas has led to wide support for the Gaza operation	Guardian	7 January 2009	Comment	34	629

diary columnists wrote about personal and/or light-hearted matters, but used Gaza as a simple reference point for 'more important things'. Likewise, 'Gaza' made its way into some economic analysis of no relevance whatsoever to the war. To keep track of the 'original' sample and its reduction, though, numbers allocated to articles were kept as they were in the 'unfiltered' sample.

Each article was assigned a unit number, and catalogued in a spreadsheet along with the publication, date, headline, type/genre, page number and word count.

The Nexis UK electronic news archive was used as the primary source due to its relatively comprehensive scope and in order to collect data most efficiently. Copy from all of the national broadsheet newspapers was collected from the Nexis database.[1]

Quantitative analysis

The construction of the codebook and coding

Once the database was collected, the task was to analyse its main features. To do that, first a codebook was developed containing relevant topics and their definitions; then the codebook was applied to the database. This codebook was used to ascertain what topics (if any) were occasioned by each paragraph of the database. The codebook used for quantitative analysis was developed via 'bottom-up' reading of the newspapers and gaining a sense of what is relevant for them, as well as consulting other sources both about the war and the wider historical context (e.g., The Goldstone Report, 2011; Operation in Gaza, 2009; Philo & Berry, 2011).

This latter exercise was done due to the possible importance of information theoretically relevant yet practically missing from the material.

Much like numbers, neither codes nor the decision of a paragraph in the database being coded one way or another come out of nothing. They depend on decision. That decision is sometimes easy: for instance, when what needs to be decided is whether a given paragraph features the topic of the 1967 or Six Day war between Israel and Arab states, or that of the total number of Israeli civilian fatalities in the Gaza war. Most of the coding decisions were of this kind. Yet there were certain cases where the definition of a code and its recognition in a paragraph was more difficult and perhaps even counter-intuitive.

To give a brief illustration, the status of Gazan police officers being killed was a dilemmatic issue: should they be categorized as civilian or combatant casualties? The issue may not at first be apparent, but as subsequent debates catalogued in the previous chapter established, there is an overlap in the case of some/most policemen between the two categories (cf. Goldstone Report, 2011, pp. 60–70; Operation in Gaza, 2009, pp. 89–95). Wherever possible, the question was treated as an empirical one: that is, when the paragraph coded explicitly stated whether the police officer was civilian or combatant, the paragraph was coded as such. However, in cases where such a decision could not be made on a narrow empirical basis, a decision had to be made as to what the 'default' code for police would be. Both theoretical and wider empirical considerations suggested that in these cases police should be coded as civilian. Theoretically, because, as noted above, it is the basic perspective of western societies, and if differences between this perspective and those of the society where these policemen operate are not explicitly occasioned, it is fair to assume that it is the western perspective of the newspapers that would operate. And in a wider empirical sense, for in the majority of cases where there were explicit cues as to the nature of the Gaza police, these cues suggested civilians. As such, it could be taken for granted that even in the absence of explicit cue, police can be assumed to be understood to be 'civilian'.

Once established and defined, codes were applied to the database. A decision was made regarding each paragraph: whether or not it features the topics contained in the codebook. Naturally, a paragraph usually featured more than one topic and was consequently coded in more than one way. As a result, there are more occurrences of codes/topics than paragraphs coded.

Finally, the decision was made to cluster the codes into meaningful conceptual areas for the purpose of analysis. A small cluster, to be examined in the present chapter, concerned 'general characteristics' of the broadsheets' coverage. Then, to learn more about what might, from a moral aspect, be the most crucial outcome of the war, its fatalities were clustered into a conceptual area (7 codes). Subsequent conceptual areas were identified so that the broadsheets' *account* for death would be approached. The first conceptual area concerned 'action in war' (20 codes) where the aim was to understand the events as well as explanations of the war; 'historical context' then concerned a broader layer to help explain facts on the ground (28 codes). Analysis in the chapters to follow shall proceed along these lines.

Quantitative concepts used in analysis

Once the coding exercise was completed, codes were entered in the SPSS statistical package, and data were subsequently analysed regarding the frequency of individual codes (of respective conceptual areas). Differences between patterns of frequencies *within* (i.e., the distribution of topics within a specific newspaper) and *between* (i.e., the distribution of one specific topic between the newspapers) the newspapers were equally calculated. On the basis of these calculations, a good deal of information can be gathered. These will be introduced here. The remainder of the chapter, analysing 'general characteristics' of the newspapers, will duly showcase them.

First, the point of departure in each chapter is the general frequency of topics within all paragraphs in the sample. A table composed of them shows how much attention newspapers in general devoted to each code within a conceptual area and what, therefore, the overarching preferences were. In addition, we will also learn how much of the data had been covered by the conceptual area. These calculations tell us the *empirical importance of a topic or a conceptual area (i.e., action, fatalities, historical context) within the entire database.*

Second, the prevalence of specific topics in each newspaper can likewise be identified. This gives us a picture of which codes and conceptual areas were important for each individual newspaper and what the priorities were within newspapers. There are two methods to do this. One is simply to compare the coverage of a code or conceptual area to the newspaper's own coverage of other codes and conceptual areas. We can, for instance, assert the importance for the *Guardian* to write about fatalities when writing about the war as such (cf. Table 3.2); and the importance for the same newspaper to mention the specific category of Palestinian civilians when writing about fatalities as such (cf. Table 3.3). This way, we can establish *the empirical importance of a topic for a specific newspaper, relative to that newspaper's own coverage.*

Another way to gain a picture of the distribution of individual topics in each newspaper is to compare their prevalence not to the given newspaper's own coverage but to the topic's coverage in the full database. We can, for instance, assert not just how important it was for the *Daily Telegraph* to write about historical context when compared to other newspapers (cf. Table 4.2) but also how important it was for this newspaper to write about the specific code of the occupation when compared to that single code's overall prevalence in the full database (cf. Table 4.3). To detect priorities, a specific figure will be recruited: each newspaper will be allocated a *benchmark figure* on the basis of its overall presence in the database (cf. Table 2.3). Namely, as we shall see shortly, *Daily Telegraph* paragraphs comprise 16.3 per cent of the entire sample. Thus, we would expect that, randomly picking a paragraph from the subsample comprised of paragraphs coded with a specific code, we have a 16.3 per cent chance that it is a paragraph from the *Daily Telegraph.* If this is not the case, then it means that for some reason the *Telegraph* attributes more/less importance to the particular code, relative to all the newspapers, than what we would expect. The *weighted divergence*[2] from the benchmark figure helps us to understand the *empirical importance of a topic for a specific newspaper, relative to the full database's (i.e., all the newspapers') coverage of the same topic.*

Having reviewed basic information about the way the database and the codebook were constructed, and what numerical information was calculated on the basis of coding, let us now turn to a 'live' example of analysis.

General characteristics of the broadsheets' coverage

Characterizing newspaper coverage may well start with very basic information: who published how many and what types of paragraphs? Such information will be rudimentary, but, *as a point of departure,* it can prove to be useful. It may point to characteristics to be explored later. It may provide explanations for later findings. It may even point to conclusions of sorts. It will have to be followed up by more fine-grained quantitative analysis (which, in turn, has to be followed up by close reading of certain aspects of the sources), but for a start, it will certainly do.

The chapter will proceed very slowly. This is for two reasons. First, because a relatively small amount of information will be reviewed here, in comparison to later chapters. Second, because this allows us conveniently to showcase some of the details of quantitative analysis that characterize later chapters as well: what numerical information was used? How was it organized into the tables used?

Concepts described in the previous section will be revisited here: the empirical importance of a code within the entire sample; empirical importance of a code within a specific newspaper; and empirical importance of any particular code relative to other newspapers (i.e., weighted divergence from the benchmark figure). As subsequent chapters utilize the same concepts, it is useful to review them here.[3]

To gain some preliminary understanding of the patterns of coverage of the broadsheets, as well as differences between them, certain basic information is presented here, beginning with figures indicating the extent of coverage of the Gaza armed conflict in each sampled newspaper.

Table 2.3 shows that the *Guardian* wrote the most paragraphs about the war, with the *Independent* some way behind in second. Indeed, the *Guardian* wrote nearly as much about the war as the entire conservative broadsheet press (i.e., the *Telegraph* and *The Times*) together.

Does this very first piece of information, then, confirm some of the judgments reviewed in Chapter 1: that the left-liberal media deals with the Israel/Palestinian conflict obsessively and out of all proportion? Is there a conclusion to be jumped at? Certainly not.

First, even the statement that left-liberal newspapers wrote more about the war must be qualified. The circulation of this type of broadsheets is considerably smaller than that of their conservative peers.[4] If we multiply the number of their paragraphs by their actual circulation number, the differences will be significantly altered.[5]

Second, the fact that singular physical pieces of left-liberal newspapers wrote more paragraphs about the war will not in itself tell us why they wrote more about the war. This may well be because of the circulation statistics and a felt need to adjust what they perceive to be imbalanced coverage of the conflict in the first place. Likewise, it may well be that left-liberal papers attribute more importance to foreign affairs in general. This can only be known if the newspapers' coverage of the conflict is

Table 2.3 Overall coverage of the war in the newspapers

	Guardian	*Independent*	*Daily Telegraph*	*The Times*	*Financial Times*	Total
Paragraphs	2460	1595	1276	1276	1223	7830
% of Total	31.4	20.4	16.3	16.3	15.6	100

Note: '% of Total' will form the benchmark figures for any subsequent analysis. Benchmark figures are the percentage with which we would hypothetically expect a newspaper to write about anything, relative to other newspapers.

Table 2.4 Article types in the full database

	News	*Feature/ eyewitness*	*Comment*	*Analysis*	*Letter*	*Editorial*	Total
Paragraphs	2867	2429	1229	787	279	239	7830
% of Total	36.6	31.0	15.7	10.1	3.6	3.1	100

compared to their coverage of other conflicts abroad. Alternatively, the left-liberal newspapers may generally write more about issues involving war crimes. This, again, needs to be tested.

Third, and correspondingly, even if left-liberal papers wrote more about the armed conflict, the real question of importance is not answered simply by how much, but *in what way* newspapers covered the conflict.

It is the third of these considerations that the present book attempts to deal with. To answer it, we may start by looking at the newspapers' general priorities in deploying article types to convey the war's events.

From Table 2.4 we can gather that, overall, it is news and feature articles that dominated the coverage. That is, articles whose main purpose is to report facts, events and narratives; there are considerably fewer argumentative or analytic paragraphs. What is more, editorials come last – after, even, letters.

At the same time, such bare calculations may not in themselves answer what significance newspapers attributed to different article types. For different spaces in newspapers do not carry the same weight. Front pages are certainly to be distinguished from page 13 in their significance, and editorials, no matter how many of them were published, are quite possibly the most important of the article types analysed here. They carry weight inasmuch as they communicate the main perspective of the newspaper: facts and events may gain their meaning precisely from that perspective. Indeed, the significance of editorials may precisely be derived from the fact that newspapers publish so few of them.

Moving on from Table 2.4, we can consider the distribution of paragraphs in certain types of articles. Tables 2.5 and 2.6 are composed on the basis of these two pieces of information mentioned above: the prevalence of paragraph types within each newspaper; and the prevalence of paragraph types relative to other newspapers (i.e., weighted divergence from benchmark figures).

First, Table 2.5 and *empirical importance within a specific newspaper.* Here, the percentage of the number of paragraphs in a newspaper is calculated with regard to *that specific newspaper's* entire coverage

Table 2.5 Article types across the newspapers: within each newspaper (i.e., relative to all the article types' use in the particular newspaper)

	Telegraph		*The Times*		*Guardian*		*Independent*		*Financial Times*	
	N	Within paper %	N	Within paper %	N	Within paper %	N	Within paper %	N	Within paper %
News article	802	62.9	508	39.8	753	30.6	429	26.9	375	30.7
Feature/eyewitness	145	11.4	414	32.4	973	39.6	504	31.6	393	32.1
Comment	172	13.5	195	15.3	325	13.2	454	28.5	83	6.8
Analysis	124	9.7	70	5.5	218	8.9	117	7.3	258	21.1
Letter	14	1.1	51	4.0	153	6.2	40	2.5	21	1.7
Editorial	19	1.5	38	3.0	38	1.5	51	3.2	93	7.6
Summa	1276	100	1276	100	2460	100	1595	100	1223	100

Table 2.6 Article types across the newspapers: within each article type (i.e., relative to the article type's use in the full database)

	Telegraph (16.3%)		*The Times (16.3%)*		*Guardian (31.4%)*		*Independent (20.4%)*		*Financial Times (15.6%)*		Summa
	Within code %	Weighted divergence from benchmark %	Within code %	Weighted divergence from benchmark %	Within code %	Weighted divergence from benchmark %	Within code %	Weighted divergence from benchmark %	Within code %	Weighted divergence from benchmark %	Within code % (weighted divergence from benchmark)
News article	28.0	4.3	17.7	0.5	26.3	–1.9	15.0	–2.0	13.1	–0.9	100 (0)
Feature/Eyewitness	6.0	–3.2	17.0	0.2	40.1	2.7	20.7	0.1	16.2	0.2	100 (0)
Comment	14.0	–0.4	15.9	–0.1	26.4	–0.8	36.9	2.6	6.8	–1.4	100 (0)
Analysis	15.8	–0.1	8.9	–0.7	27.7	–0.4	14.9	–0.6	32.8	1.7	100 (0)
Letter	5.0	–0.4	18.3	0.1	54.8	0.8	14.3	–0.2	7.5	–0.3	100 (0)
Editorial	7.9	–0.3	15.9	0.0	15.9	–0.5	21.3	0.0	38.9	0.7	100 (0)

(i.e., all the paragraphs of that newspaper). Thus, if the *Guardian* devoted 2460 paragraphs to the war, and if it devoted 753 paragraphs to the war in news articles – then within this newspaper, 30.6 per cent of paragraphs are of the 'news article' type. This can be compared to 39.6 per cent of 'eyewitness/feature' of the newspaper, which expresses that the *Guardian*'s coverage was characterized by considerably more paragraphs in 'eyewitness/feature' types of articles than 'news' articles. Of course, empirical importance of codes *within newspapers* will vary, and we can then compare their coverage to each other.

Second, *empirical importance for a newspaper, relative to other newspapers* (as captured by the *weighted divergence from benchmark*) can also be calculated (cf. Table 2.6). The basis of calculating the percentage here is not all the paragraphs one specific newspaper devoted to the war, but the sum of paragraphs in all newspapers coded with a specific code. Given the overall distribution figures, all things being equal we would expect the *Guardian* to publish 31.4 per cent of all news articles/features/editorials/etcetera paragraphs, the *Telegraph* 16.3 per cent and so on (see Table 2.3). This, of course, happens very rarely. But if there is tendency in divergences from these benchmark figures, we may be able to make some interesting inferences.

To give an example, the *Financial Times* wrote 93 editorial paragraphs. All newspapers wrote a total of 239 editorial paragraphs, of which, then, 38.9 per cent featured in the *Financial Times*. The newspaper's benchmark figure is 15.6 per cent: of the entire sample of paragraphs devoted to the armed conflict of Gaza, 15.6 per cent appeared in the *Financial Times* and, as such, all things being equal, we would expect the newspaper to have the same 15.6 per cent share regarding the sub-sample consisting of all newspapers' editorial paragraphs. As it is, however, the *Financial Times*' share of all newspaper editorial paragraphs is 38.9 per cent – a staggering 23.9 per cent higher than what its benchmark is (i.e., what we would expect). Thus, *relative to other newspapers*, the *Financial Times* attributed far more importance to editorial coverage.

At the same time, as can be seen from Table 2.2, editorials were the least frequent of the articles the newspaper wrote. Numerically speaking, this code is of the least importance and can therefore easily yield wild differences in divergences from benchmark figures.[6] It was for this reason that *weighted* (rather than absolute) divergences from the benchmark were introduced, where the importance of a code was also accounted for – in the case above, the *Financial Times*' weighted divergence from its benchmark, as far as editorials go, is 0.7 per cent. This is still an impressive divergence, but with the relative numerical unimportance of the code factored in now.

Undoubtedly, there are some interesting patterns emerging from the tables above. Both conservative newspapers wrote more news paragraphs than feature paragraphs, with all of the liberal papers the other way round. Indeed, the *Telegraph* wrote considerably more news paragraphs than any other type of paragraphs. Not only do the newspaper's own priorities confirm this, where over 60 per cent of all paragraphs are classed as featuring in news articles. Its weighted divergence is 4.7 per cent: a singularly high figure, akin to which we will not find throughout this book. Thus, we may expect that, due to their focus on news, conservative newspapers will write more about action and perhaps fatalities in war (see Chapter 3); and liberals will contextualize the issues more (see Chapter 4).[7]

At the same time, that contextualization may not always come through arguments or analysis of arguments. It is not only true of the *Telegraph* and *The Times*, but also of the *Guardian* that explicitly argumentative/analytic types of paragraphs featured relatively rare in the coverage. Whilst (in contrast to conservative papers) the left-liberal paper contains far more feature/eyewitness paragraphs and news article paragraphs, both within itself and relative to other newspapers, it puts a lesser emphasis on comments, analysis and editorials – in line with conservative papers.

In stark contrast, the *Independent* was comprised of far more comment articles than any other newspaper. Not only does, uniquely, the percentage of comment paragraphs exceed those of news paragraphs in the same newspaper, but their weighted proportion relative to other newspapers' comment paragraphs exceeds the left-liberal newspaper's benchmark by 2.6 per cent. Likewise, the *Financial Times* devoted far more editorial and analysis paragraphs to the conflict relative to its other article types when compared to other newspapers. What is more, its weighted divergence from its benchmark is 0.7 per cent in the case of editorial paragraphs, and 1.7 per cent in the case of analysis paragraphs. We may then conclude that, of the broadsheets, the *Financial Times* attributed by far the most importance to these argumentative and analytic genres.

Discussion and the way forward

On the basis of this intriguing yet rather rudimentary information, we may be able to form some tentative conclusions. More importantly, we are able to point towards areas of interest whose importance may later be fully revealed.

First of all, there are visible similarities and divergences between newspapers in terms of the paragraphs of a certain type of article they devoted to the armed conflict. Talking of a conservative 'pole' may perhaps be meaningful in these terms. The conservative newspapers exhibited similar characteristics in their coverage: they both were dominated by news articles (with the *Telegraph* staggeringly so), thus putting more emphasis on news than on context; as for context, they seem to be less interested in arguments or analysis (comments, analyses, letters, editorials) than in narrative (feature/eyewitness). This, of course, may be because their arguments or analyses are deemed to be consensual, or that they will express them in no uncertain terms, anyway. This we can only learn later. What is for sure is that we may expect the conservative papers uniformly to provide us with more of a factual and less of a compassionate, victim-centred account of the war.

At the same time, even at this early point, it appears to be rather meaningless to talk about a liberal 'pole' – even of a *left*-liberal one, in fact (i.e., the *Guardian* and the *Independent*). First, of all the newspapers, it was the *Financial Times* that devoted the fewest paragraphs to the conflict. Second, though all liberal papers devoted more quantitative importance to feature/eyewitness paragraphs than news, their coverage was otherwise rather divergent. The *Guardian* was on par with the conservative newspapers in its relative neglect (both within the newspaper and relative to the other newspapers) of paragraphs published in explicitly argumentative or analytic articles. The reasons for this are as unclear as with the conservative newspapers, but it is certainly an interesting feature to keep in mind.[8]

So it was the *Independent* and the *Financial Times* that showcased the most paragraphs in articles of an explicitly argumentative and analytic nature, with the difference being that whilst the *Independent* featured an extraordinary amount of comments, the *Financial Times* attributed more (quantitative) importance to analysis and editorials. Such a feature may prove to be interesting when reading about arguments offered in the war in the latter chapters of the book. The *Financial Times*' editorials will be of special interest as (in addition to the editorials' heavy status by definition) it appears to have carried the most quantitative weight amongst all newspapers. And the *Independent*'s comments will be of special interest when positions on criticism and antisemitism are analysed.[9]

By the time we reach those chapters, however, the analytical strategy of the book will have changed. Whilst quantitative analysis is best suited to come up with a general description of the data, to understand arguments and narratives the newspapers marshalled in the war, a close and attentive reading of those relevant arguments is required. Gone will be by then the difference that lies in broad patterns; it is the devil in the details which will form the focus of our analytical interest (Richardson, 2007).

3
Action and Death in War

Introduction

As we saw in Chapter 1, there are many outcomes of a war. There will be arguments about who won, who is better placed for future political developments. And there will be people mourning. This chapter will start with the analysis of what this book finds to be the only ultimate and unalterable outcome of war: the people dead. It will examine how the national broadsheets made reference to different categories of fatalities and what their coverage might imply.

Death is a tragedy, but its public meaning might only be determined with respect to different contexts of accounts around it. What it was that led to a violent death is a question that can be answered from many angles. In this chapter, this angle will be the main protagonists' action in war. Hamas as well as the Israeli Defense Forces will be scrutinized as to their conduct during the 22 days of the conflict and what their action, in turn, implies as to the responsibility for the fatalities of the war. As such, the chapter examines the basic 'building blocks' of the newspapers' coverage of the armed conflict, laying out the groundwork for further chapters investigating the wider context from the perspective of which these basic elements were presented.

Coding for fatalities proceeded from two straightforward dimensions. What was coded was, first, whether the fatalities mentioned were of Palestinian or Israeli nationality; second, another dimension was added, as it was felt that no understanding of death can be comprehensive without knowing their 'humanitarian' status in war: were they civilians or combatants?

Coding for action, on the other hand, was more complicated. Broadly speaking, it concerned two sub-areas: first, the general or iterative action of the participants – Hamas and the State of Israel. This mostly includes general tactics and strategy in war. Respective general actions were defined in a way that one code covered fairly neutral military actions, and another code referred to action that might be considered problematic from a humanitarian perspective; such as allegations of Hamas firing rockets from neighbourhoods densely populated by civilians, or Israel hitting *prima facie* non-military objects such as hospitals. The paragraphs were also coded for Israel's highly dilemmatic use of the chemical material white phosphorous.

Hamas's deeply problematic general conduct was captured in their repeatedly firing rockets into Southern Israeli civilian territories and reaching further into Israel with their rockets than ever before. At the same time, in distinction to Hamas, Israel aspired to distinguish itself by its moral conduct (cf. Operation in Gaza, 2009, pp. 1–51). To capture this, humanitarian tactics by Israel were also coded, as was its decision to open daily three hour-long 'humanitarian corridors' for the delivery of food and goods. Beyond these clear instances of action, the conceptual area also includes official explanatory statements (quoted directly or indirectly) as these interpretations were deemed to qualify as action-done-by-words: they tried to sell an image of the war that either official Israeli or Palestinian agents would favour.

Second, specific events were also incorporated into the conceptual area of action in war. These incidents were all legally and morally dilemmatic, and as such formed the subject of subsequent investigations into Israel's conduct of the war. They all resulted either in significant civilian casualties or in considerable material damage to apparently civilian objects. That these events all concern Israeli action derive from the fact, already remarked upon in Chapter 1, that the armed conflict of Gaza was a thoroughly asymmetrical event where Hamas's efforts were, mostly, notable by their absence.

Code	Description of code
The mid-day start of the Israeli offensive	Israel's offensive started on 11.30 am, 27 December.
Attack on police headquarters	On the first day of the IDF military operations, the Arafat City Police Headquarters were attacked, where members of the police were taking part in a training exercise (on alternative account: in a graduation ceremony) with 48 of them being killed immediately (cf. Goldstone Report, 2011, pp. 60–62).

Continued

Code	Description of code
al-Maqadma mosque incident	On 3 January, a projectile struck the al-Maqadma mosque (on the outskirts of the Jabaliya area, close to Beit Lahiya), killing 15 people (probably civilians) (Goldstone Report, 2011, pp. 133–137).
Zeytoun incidents	On 5 January, the house of Wa'el al-Samouni was hit. At the time, around 100 members of the extended family resided in the house, having following instructions by the IDF to go there. Twenty-one of them, all civilians, were killed in the attack. Subsequent attempts of the Red Cross to attend to the dead and injured were thwarted by the IDF for a number of days. On 6 January, 22 members of the al-Daya family (12 of the children under the age of ten) were killed when their home was struck by a projectile fired by an F-16 aircraft. The IDF probe later described the event as an 'operational error'. Both incidents happened in the area of Zeytoun (Goldstone Report, 2011, pp. 115–124, p. 48).
UN al-Fakhura school incident	On 6 January, the al-Fakhura street in Jabaliya was hit several times with high-explosive mortar shells, including the surroundings of the UNRWA elementary school, temporarily functioning as a shelter for civilians. There were 35 civilian fatalities, none in the school itself (Goldstone Report, 2011, pp. 106–113).
Attack on UNRWA compound	On 15 January, the UNRWA field office compound (Rimal neighbourhood, Gaza City) was struck with at least three explosive shells and seven white phosphorous container shells, causing considerable damage and ensuing fire. At the time, 600–700 civilians were sheltering in the compound. No fatalities but significant material damage resulted from the ensuing fire (Goldstone Report, 2011, pp. 88–98).
Attack on al-Quds hospital	On 15 January, the al-Quds hospital (Tal el-Hawa, Gaza city) was directly hit by a number of shells containing white phosphorous, as well as at least one high-explosive shell. The hospital housed 50 patients as well as around 500 civilians sheltering amidst the premises. The building had to be evacuated. No fatalities but considerable physical damage resulted from the ensuing fire (Goldstone Report, 2011, pp. 98–105).
UN Beit Lahiya school incident	On 17 January, white phosphorous shells hit the UNRWA elementary school (Beit Lahiya neighbourhood), which at the time provided shelter for 1600 people. Two fatalities.

In what follows, analysis of these conceptual areas will be conducted. In both the cases of fatalities and action in war, we will first have a look at the general frequencies of the topics regarding the entire database. This will be followed by a breakdown with respect to specific newspapers.

Fatalities

One thousand three hundred and fifty-nine occurrences of the conceptual area 'fatalities' were found in 1057 paragraphs. This means that 13.5 per cent of all of the database's paragraphs (7830) were coded as containing some reference to death of participants or non-participants in the conflict.

Unsurprisingly, Palestinian deaths far outweigh Israeli deaths, by a ratio of around 5.5:1.[1] More than that, the predominance of the *category* of Palestinians is not simply captured by this ratio. It is also reflected by the fact that any category of Palestinian death (i.e., civilian, combatant, uncategorized) outweighs any of the Israeli deaths. Nonetheless, previous research tended to ask whether such representation is proportionate to that found on the ground. Indeed, examining the ratio of Palestinian versus Israeli fatalities in the BBC's coverage of the war, researchers Greg Philo and Mike Berry found a ratio of 5:1 (7:1 in the case of the ITV). As they noted, with the actual ratio of casualties being 100:1, '[t]here is a disproportionate representation of Israeli casualties' (Philo & Berry, 2011, p. 363).

Table 3.1 Individual 'fatalities' codes in the full database

Name of code	**Occurrences**	**% within all daily paragraphs (7830)**	**% within all fatalities occurrences (1359)**
Palestinian civilian fatalities	624	8.0	45.9
Palestinian uncategorized fatalities	372	4.8	27.4
Palestinian combatant fatalities	117	1.5	8.6
Israeli civilian fatalities	75	1.0	5.5
Israeli uncategorized fatalities	73	0.9	5.4
Israeli combatant fatalities	69	0.9	5.1
Other fatalities	29	0.4	2.1
SUMMA	1359	–	100

Whether the 'proper' way of representing death should be that of proportional representation will not be pursued here. The morally dubious fallacy of conflating various categories of fatalities is worth mentioning, though. Namely, it makes an enormous difference in the evaluation of war whether those fatalities were civilians or combatants. As we can see above, when this category was explicitly occasioned, civilians outweighed the mentioning of combatants by 4.2:2; perhaps not as dominantly as in the case of Palestinians versus Israelis, but still to a rather considerable extent.[2]

Indeed, the status of Palestinian *civilians* is clearly of special nature in the database. Whilst different categories within Israeli fatalities are all around the same figure, references to Palestinian civilian fatalities far outweigh the other two categories of Palestinian fatalities. Thus, the Palestinian civilian might be said to symbolize the war and feature with singular prominence when it comes to its evaluation.

Let us now look beyond these general figures and see how individual newspapers diverged from the ones on display in Table 3.1. To this end, we shall first examine individual newspapers' overall take on fatalities and then turn to their rendering of specific codes.

Table 3.2 helps us to get an overall picture of the newspapers' respective coverage. It tells us the percentage of a newspaper's paragraphs referring to fatalities, of all the particular newspaper's paragraphs. As such, it tells us the empirical importance of fatalities within the particular newspaper. For example, 204 paragraphs in the *Telegraph* occasioned topics coded as fatalities. This means that 16.0 per cent of all of the *Telegraph*'s paragraphs (1276) contained reference to fatalities, a percentage higher than generally across newspapers (13.4 per cent). It might be ascertained, then, that fatalities constituted a conceptual area that was of relatively high importance for the conservative newspaper, compared to other newspapers.

Table 3.2 'Fatalities' across the newspapers

	Telegraph	*The Times*	*Guardian*	*Independent*	*Financial Times*	SUMMA
Fatalities paragraphs (occurrences)	204 (253)	156 (202)	333 (436)	261 (327)	99 (141)	1053(1359)
Empirical importance within newspaper	204/1276 16.0%	156/1276 12.2%	333/2460 13.5%	261/1595 16.4%	99/1223 8.1%	1053/7830 13.4%

Interestingly, perhaps, it is clear that based on these figures there is no indication of some overarching right–left divide in the database. Most concerned with fatalities were the *Independent* and the *Telegraph*, least the *Financial Times* and *The Times*. At the same time, this lack of tendency along ideological lines might, actually, disguise some very firm tendencies where conservatives focus exclusively on Israeli death and left-liberals on Palestinian ones. Thus, we clearly need to look beyond this table and investigate the full distribution of fatalities codes in detail.

Table 3.3 on the next page shows us the empirical importance of specific fatalities codes to newspapers, within their own coverage of fatalities (i.e., column 1) and relative to all the other newspapers' (i.e., weighted divergences in column 2). The *Telegraph*, for instance, devoted 40.7 per cent of its codes of all fatalities to Palestinian civilian fatalities. Within the newspaper, this was the most frequent topic. Yet, its weighted divergence is a mere 0.1 per cent, indicating that relative to the other newspapers' coverage of Palestinian civilian fatalities, the *Telegraph* wrote barely a little more than what would be expected (i.e., its benchmark figure: 16.3 per cent). Indeed, *The Times* devoted the vast majority of its fatalities coverage to Palestinian civilians (45.4 per cent), a proportion that is higher than that of the *Telegraph* – yet its weighted divergence is actually *negative*. How can it be? Because weighted divergences are also influenced by the overall importance a newspaper devotes to a conceptual area. And, as we saw above in Table 3.2, whilst the *Telegraph* was shown to be interested in fatalities, *The Times* was most decidedly not. As a consequence, even if the *Telegraph* attributes less importance to a particular fatalities topic *within its own coverage*, its coverage of that particular topic might still be considerable, *relative to all other newspapers*. And with *The Times*, vice versa: as the newspaper tended to neglect the topic of fatalities as such, high empirical importance of a code within the newspaper might still go hand-in-hand with relatively small weighted divergence relative to all the other newspapers' coverage of the particular code.

Scrutinizing Table 3.3 now, the first thing to notice is that those who expect some clear-cut, black-and-white picture of the national broadsheets' coverage of the conflict must once again be disappointed. Whilst we do find many differences in the table and even, as will be argued shortly, some tendentious ones, there are certainly no incommensurable mirror-images to be found there. By and large, the coverage of fatalities is similar for all the newspapers. Contrasting Palestinian to Israeli casualties, all but one of the newspapers present a ratio not dissimilar to the one on average, 5.5:1; and, with minor (if not unimportant) differences, newspapers are all characterized by their focus on Palestinian

Table 3.3 Individual 'fatalities' codes across the newspapers: within each newspaper (i.e., relative to the particular newspaper's own coverage of all 'fatalities' codes) and within each 'fatalities' code (i.e., relative to the full database's coverage of the particular 'fatalities' code)

	Telegraph		***The Times***		***Guardian***		***Independent***		***Financial Times***		**SUMMA**	
	Within paper %	**Within code % weighted divergence %**	**Within paper %**	**Within code % weighted divergence %**	**Within paper %**	**Within code % weighted divergence %**	**Within paper %**	**Within code % weighted divergence %**	**Within paper %**	**Within code % weighted divergence %**	**Within paper %**	**Within code % weighted divergence %**
Palestinian civilian fatalities	40.7	16.5 *(0.1)*	45.4	14.7 *(–0.7)*	51.1	*35.7* (2.0)	49.2	25.8 *(2.5)*	31.9	7.2 *(–3.9)*	–	100 *(0)*
Palestinian uncategorized fatalities	25.7	17.5 *(0.3)*	30.2	16.4 *(0.0)*	24.7	29 *(–0.7)*	27.0	23.7 *(0.9)*	35.4	13.4 *(–0.6)*	–	100 *(0)*
Palestinian combatant fatalities	16.2	35 *(1.6)*	9.4	16.2 *(0.0)*	6.7	24.8 *(–0.6)*	6.4	17.9 *(–0.2)*	5.0	6 *(–0.8)*	–	100 *(0)*
Israeli civilian fatalities	6.3	21.3 *(0.3)*	3.5	9.3 *(–0.4)*	5.3	30.7 *(0.0)*	6.7	29.3 *(0.5)*	4.9	9.3 *(–0.3)*	–	100 *(0)*
Israeli uncategorized fatalities	4.7	16.4 *(0.0)*	4.4	12.3 *(–0.2)*	3.7	21.9 *(–0.5)*	4.6	20.5 *(0.0)*	14.9	28.8 *(0.7)*	–	100 *(0)*
Israeli combatant fatalities	4.7	17.4 *(0.1)*	5.4	15.9 *(0.0)*	5.5	34.8 *(0.2)*	3.7	17.4 *(–0.2)*	7.1	14.5 *(–0.1)*	–	100 *(0)*
Other fatalities	1.6	13.8 *(–0.1)*	1.5	10.3 *(–0.1)*	3.0	44.8 *(0.3)*	2.4	27.6 *(0.2)*	0.7	3.4 *(–0.3)*	–	100 *(0)*
SUMMA	100	–	100	–	100	–	100	–	100	–		

civilian, Palestinian uncategorized, and Palestinian combatant fatalities, and in that order.[3] Whilst there is some more divergence concerning Israeli fatalities, they still concern divergences of smaller details. Thus, whatever differences we find as regards different newspapers' coverage of fatalities, they are *relative* ones drawn by shades of grey, *not categorical* ones of black and white.

Acknowledging all this, it is highly interesting to note that the *Telegraph* wrote far more about Palestinian *combatant* fatalities than any other newspaper. The category's empirical importance within the newspaper is 16.2 per cent (nearly 10 per cent more than that of the liberal newspapers), and its weighted divergence is 1.6 per cent. Likewise, *The Times'* coverage of Palestinian combatants is high for a newspaper that generally neglected the area of fatalities. The *Guardian* and the *Independent,* in contrast, by and large ignore Palestinian *combatant* fatalities and emphasize *civilian* ones. Their weighted divergence figures are whopping 2.0 per cent (*Guardian*) and 2.5 per cent (*Independent*). Are we witnessing here the emergence of a conservative-left-liberal division in covering fatalities?

To answer this question, the first thing to note is that the figures in the preceding paragraph are rather ambiguous in themselves. It is either that the *Telegraph* presents a somewhat pro-Israeli take on the issue of fatalities, or that its coverage emphasizes the *military* (as opposed to humanistic) aspect of the conflict. Likewise, the *Guardian* and the *Independent* might wish to draw their readers' attention either to the suffering of Palestinians as such, or to the *humanitarian* aspects of the conflict. Not that these distinctions are necessarily and categorically either-or: a military-oriented coverage might in and of itself favour the Israeli side, and a humanitarian one might present events from a perspective that will tend to favour the Palestinians. Yet the primary tendency needs to be established.

For instance, *The Times* wrote relatively little about Palestinian civilian and more about Palestinian combatant fatalities. No preference either way might be ascertained, though, with respect to its coverage, as it equally wrote little about Israeli civilians' and more of Israeli combatants' deaths: what mattered for the newspaper was professional death on the battlefield.

Of the *Independent,* the exact opposite can be said. Its coverage of Palestinian civil fatalities is very high, and that of Palestinian combatants low. Yet, this pattern is repeated with regard to Israeli fatalities. According to both measures, it was the left-liberal newspaper that wrote the most about Israeli civilian fatalities and the least about Israeli combatant fatalities. Thus, what appears to have been the overriding concern for the *Independent* was not the nationality of those dead but the civilian status of those who died.[4]

No such logic might be found as regards the *Telegraph* and the *Guardian*. For the *Telegraph*, civilian fatalities appear to be of more importance only if they are *Israeli*, and combatant fatalities if they are *Palestinian*. And for the *Guardian*, the focus it paid to Palestinian civilians is nowhere to be seen when it comes to writing about Israeli civilians, and its relative neglect of Palestinian combatants is not replicated in its coverage of Israeli combatants.

Thus, it would appear that whilst both the *Guardian* and the *Independent* mentioned Palestinian civilian fatalities a lot, they had different reasons for doing that. And whilst *The Times* and the *Telegraph* equally paid relatively more attention to Palestinian combatants, their respective focus might have been motivated by different factors.

To find out more, a comparison between selected ratio figures is presented below. Ratios are displayed in a way that, crudely, the higher the ratio is, the more pro-Palestinian the coverage might be termed; the smaller it is, the more pro-Israeli it is. Where such comparison was deemed to make no sense, no figures are on display.[5]

Table 3.4 Ratios of selected 'fatalities' codes across the newspapers

	Telegraph	***The Times***	***Guardian***	***Independent***	***Financial Times***
Israeli combatant: Israeli civilian	12/16 0.75	11/7 1.57	24/23 1.04	12/22 0.55	10/7 1.43
Palestinian civilian: Palestinian combatant	103/41 2.51	92/19 4.84	223/29 7.69	161/21 7.67	45/7 6.43
Palestinian civilian: Israeli civilian	103/16 6.44	92/7 13.14	223/23 9.70	161/22 7.32	45/7 6.43
Israeli combatant: Palestinian combatant	12/41 0.29	11/19 0.58	24/29 0.83	12/21 0.57	10/7 1.43
Palestinian uncategorized: Israeli uncategorized	65/12 5.42	61/9 6.78	108/16 6.75	88/15 5.87	50/21 2.38

Looking at Table 3.4, a picture is discernible that reinforces the tentative conclusions offered above. Namely, in all of the cases, the *Telegraph*'s coverage (i.e., ratio) is either the most or the second most supportive of Israel, and in four of the five cases, the *Guardian*'s is amongst the top two pro-Palestinian ratios. Nor do we find any instance above where these two newspapers would be seen to support the other side. Such tendency is completely lacking as regards any of the other newspapers.[6] In fact, the *Independent* further appears to systematically focus on civilians and neglect combatants, with *The Times* doing the opposite. Whilst their coverage looks rather confusing if one attempts to understand it from the point of view of the relevance of nationality, it becomes quite clear when approached from a humanitarian status perspective.

Indeed, such findings present some of the figures in an interesting light. That both the *Telegraph* and *The Times* neglected the category of 'other' fatalities like UN workers or volunteers is no surprise. They shed less than appealing light on Israel's conduct of war (for the *Telegraph*) and are of no major relevance from a professional militaristic point of view (for *The Times*). Yet the left-liberal newspapers' seemingly shared focus on the category also hides crucial differences. The prominence the *Guardian* accords to casualties that are neither Palestinian nor Israelis might be understood as an indication of the indiscriminate or savage nature of Israel's conduct of war. It is only from the perspective that seemed to emerge from the coverage of the *Independent* that a genuine humanitarian concern can be established to motivate the coverage of these non-national deaths.

Thus, we might tentatively conclude that the primary tendency discernible from the figures points not towards a uniform conservative-left-liberal dimension. It would appear that the main dimension motivating the *Telegraph*'s and the *Guardian*'s coverage of fatalities is nationality: the conservative paper was prone to a tendency supportive of Israel and the left-liberal one to one supportive of Palestinians. In the case of the *Independent* and *The Times*, what is of primary relevance is the humanitarian status of the victim, with the former broadsheet focusing on civilians and the latter on combatants.

Action in war

Death is a tragedy, but in war it is not supposed to come without a 'reason'. It is terrible, but its *meaning* might not be established until it is clear why it happened and how it happened. The present section will examine what in Gaza directly led to death, as it will look at the action that characterized the armed conflict. We will look into the distribution across the pages of general military action, explanations given for action, as well as specific events in the war. Analysis of the ways broadsheets covered fatalities came up with findings coloured by shades of grey. Will the analysis of action present us with something more definite?

In the broadsheets, 5251 occurrences of the conceptual area 'action in war' were found in 3673 paragraphs. This means that 46.9 per cent of all (7830) paragraphs were coded as containing some reference to action done by the participants of the armed conflict. This is a predictably high percentage: the gist of war for the daily media cannot really be anything other than the action they are supposed to report.

As we can see from Table 3.5 on the next page, vastly dominant amongst these topics were those concerned with Israel: the two most prevalent codes cover more than 50 per cent of all codes referring to action in war. Again, this much is hardly a surprise: as reviewed in Chapter 1, the war was indeed dominated by Israeli action and Israeli terms. More interesting, perhaps, is the finding that neither of these two codes as such implies the problematic nature of that action of Israel's. One concerns neutral Israeli action, whilst the other covers instances where the official Israeli perspective on the events is aired. Whilst each individual newspaper's divergence from these aggregate figures will be interesting, previous findings of the British media as dominated by Israel's concerns appear to be replicated here (Philo & Berry, 2011, p. 340). This means that whilst Palestinian civilian fatalities dominated virtually all the newspapers' columns (if with varying degrees), the dominant representation of Israeli action suggested no Israeli moral responsibility for civilian death; whatever it did or did not do, Israel had ample opportunity to offer its official version of events and responsibility.

Correspondingly, as a direct military and interpretative agent, Hamas was far less prevalent than Israel. Its actions, however, are far more problematic *intrinsically* than those of Israel. The most frequent code related to the Islamic organization – its shelling rockets into civilian territories in Southern Israel – straightforwardly implies war crimes. In fact, it is in a mere 4.1 per cent of codes related to action in war that Hamas acts on the battlefield in a way that would not be found automatically problematic from a moral or legal point of view. It appears, then, that whilst Hamas was mostly characterized by its lack of action, the moment it acted, it became gravely problematic from a humanitarian perspective. It is from this viewpoint that Hamas's relative lack of official explanation is noteworthy.

Yet, further examination suggests that the picture is not as simple as these findings would imply, and that it would be difficult indeed

Table 3.5 Individual 'action in war' codes in the full database

Name of code	Occurrences	% within all daily paragraphs	% within all 'action in war' occurrences
General Israeli military action	1736	22.2	33.1
Direct/indirect official Israeli explanations	1141	14.6	21.7
Hamas rockets directed into Southern Israel	472	6.0	9.0
Direct/indirect official Hamas explanations	451	5.8	8.6
Israel's use of white phosphorous	228	2.9	4.3
General Hamas military action	214	2.7	4.1
Problematic Israeli military tactics/action	196	2.5	3.7
Zeytoun incidents	176	2.2	3.4
UN al-Fakhura school incident	141	1.8	2.7
Problematic Hamas military tactics/action	108	1.4	2.1
Hamas rockets capable of reaching distant Israeli towns	93	1.2	1.8
Israel killing Hamas leaders	84	1.1	1.6
Attack on UNRWA compound	64	0.8	1.2
Israeli humanitarian corridor	63	0.8	1.2
Israeli humanitarian tactics	29	0.4	0.6
Attack on Gaza police headquarters	26	0.3	0.5
The mid-day start of the Israeli offensive	18	0.2	0.3
Attack on al-Quds hospital	9	0.1	0.2
UN Beit Lahiya school incident	2	0.0	0.0
al-Maqadma mosque incident	0	0	0
SUMMA	5251	–	100

to conclude on the basis of the table that the media in general presented a systematically pro-Israeli or anti-Hamas picture. For the topic occasioned most frequently following the ones mentioned above was the IDF's use of the highly incendiary chemical material white phosphorous as an obscurant on the battlefield. As has been reviewed in Chapter 1, this was a very controversial development of the war that many took as an indication of the less than humanitarian motives Israel harboured.

Furthermore, the dominance of the official Israeli perspective (at the expense of either Hamas or a general Palestinian one) might also be tempered if looking at topics newspapers utilized infrequently. These are, of course, mostly topics relating to specific incidents in the war. But they also contain codes of a general nature. Namely, none of the two codes that might imply humanitarian gestures from Israel gained much coverage; that the Israeli military deployed so-called 'humanitarian tactics', and opened as of early January a daily humanitarian corridor to let food and goods into Gaza, were of no interest for newspapers whatsoever, just as the utterly new and rather ominous development of Hamas being capable of firing rockets deeper inside Israeli territory than ever before received relatively little coverage.

Thus, with the highly important exception of Israel's use of white phosphorous, it might be argued that the overall coverage's main feature is not simply a reliance on the Israeli perspective, but a general lack of responsivity and reflectivity to the conflict and its novelties. It is from this perspective that the fact should be mentioned that Israel banned all media presence in Gaza during its operations and, as a consequence, newspapers lost a considerable source for their independence and were significantly exposed to official versions. (Incidentally, the media ban was mentioned on 96 occasions in the sample, featuring far more in the *Guardian* [on 40 occasions] and the *Independent* [on 30 occasions] than in the other newspapers.)[7]

The general picture gathered from Table 3.5 is of obvious interest and has already shown some curious findings. Yet, given the supposed rift between British broadsheets alongside a conservative-left-liberal dimension, it is equally important to examine how the coverage of individual newspapers' varied with regard to the codes. Where was it that newspapers differed from each other? Which codes were deployed more/less frequently in the conservative newspapers? Can we perhaps clearly see a conservative-left-liberal divide as regards codes specifically implying Israeli or Palestinian/Hamas responsibility? Can we perhaps see the deployment of generally neglected codes in specific publications?

These questions will be pondered first by looking at the variations of the coverage of action in war across the newspapers. Following this, first specific events and then general (i.e., iterative) action as deployed in the newspapers will be examined.

Table 3.6 'Action in war' across the newspapers

	Telegraph	*The Times*	*Guardian*	*Independent*	*Financial Times*	SUMMA
Action in war occurrences (paragraphs)	952 (681)	1034 (671)	1622 (1157)	942 (646)	701 (518)	5251 (3673)
Empirical importance within newspaper	681/1276 53.4%	671/1276 52.6%	1157/2460 47.0%	646/1595 40.5%	518/1223 42.4%	3673/7830 46.9%

If not an outrageous one, a clear conservative versus liberal tendency appears to be shown by Table 3.6. The general message is that action was uniformly more important for conservative newspapers than for liberal ones. This conservative tendency to write more of action and events is more moderate in respect to the *Guardian*'s coverage; it is over 10 per cent, though, when compared to the *Independent* and the *Financial Times*. Not that such a distribution is entirely unexpected: the predominance of news articles for the conservative papers entailed the predominance of the field of action and events.

Yet whilst there is a conservative tendency to attribute more importance to action, a further and equally important question that needs to be answered is whether this quantitative tendency is translated into a 'qualitative' one as well. Does the conservative coverage of action entail differences in detail? Or does it mean more of the same? To examine this, first the coverage of specific events, then that of general action will be reviewed.

Based on the figures on display in Table 3.7 next page, it is difficult to find any systematic difference between the newspapers – let alone alongside the supposedly dichotomous conservative versus liberal axis. Looking first at the specific incidents (see in the upper half of the table), we can ascertain that the *Guardian* and the *Independent* devoted somewhat more coverage to the incidents in Zeytoun and at the al-Fakhura street UN school, both resulting in massive civilian casualties. Yet this interest indicates no real tendency to comprehensively report events of humanitarian import, as neither of the newspapers wrote much more than their conservative counterparts (or indeed the *Financial Times*) of other humanitarian incidents.

What is more, it is the *Telegraph*'s coverage of the Zeytoun events that is the single outstanding figure of the upper half of Table 3.7. Not that the conservative broadsheet would nurture some overriding preoccupation with incidents of humanitarian concern: the attention it devoted

Table 3.7 Individual 'action in war' codes across the newspapers: within each newspaper (i.e., relative to the particular newspaper's own coverage of all 'action in war' codes) and within each 'action in war' code (i.e., relative to the full database's coverage of the particular 'action in war' code)

	Telegraph		*The Times*		*Guardian*		*Independent*		*Financial Times*		SUMMA	
	Within paper %	**Within code % weighted divergence %**	**Within paper %**	**Within code % weighted divergence %**	**Within paper %**	**Within code % weighted divergence %**	**Within paper %**	**Within code % weighted divergence %**	**Within paper %**	**Within code % weighted divergence %**	**Within paper %**	**Within code % weighted divergence %**
Zeytoun incidents	6.2	33.5 *(0.6)*	1.9	11.4 *(−0.2)*	3.9	35.8 *(0.1)*	3.6	19.3 *(0.0)*	0.0	0 *(−0.5)*	–	100 *(0)*
UN al-Fakhura school incident	1.4	9.2 *(−0.2)*	1.8	13.5 *(−0.1)*	3.5	40.4 *(0.2)*	3.6	24.1 *(0.1)*	2.6	12.8 *(−0.1)*	–	100 *(0)*
Attack on UNRWA compound	1.5	21.9 *(0.1)*	1.3	20.3 *(0.0)*	1.2	31.2 *(0.0)*	1.6	23.4 *(0.0)*	0.3	3.1 *(−0.2)*	–	100 *(0)*
Attack on Gaza police headquarters	0.4	15.4 *(0.0)*	0.3	11.5 *(0.0)*	0.8	50 *(0.1)*	0.2	7.7 *(−0.1)*	0.6	15.4 *(0.0)*	–	100 *(0)*
The mid-day start of the Israeli offensive	0.4	22.2 *(0.0)*	0.4	22.2 *(0.0)*	0.3	27.8 *(0.0)*	0.2	11.1 *(0.0)*	0.4	16.7 *(0.0)*	–	100 *(0)*
Attack on al-Quds hospital	0.2	22.2 *(0.0)*	0.1	11.1 *(0.0)*	0.1	22.2 *(0.0)*	0.4	44.4 *(0.0)*	0.0	0 *(0.0)*	–	100 *(0)*
UN Beit Lahiya school incident	0.1	50 *(0.0)*	0.1	50 *(0.0)*	0.0	0 *(0.0)*	0.0	0 *(0.0)*	0.0	0 *(0.0)*	–	100 *(0)*
al-Maqadma mosque incident	0	0 *(0)*	0	0 *(0)*	0	0 *(0)*	0	0 *(0)*	0	0 *(0)*	–	100 *(0)*
General Israeli military action	31.2	17.1 *(0.3)*	34.4	20.5 *(1.4)*	33.0	30.8 *(−0.2)*	33.2	18 *(−0.8)*	33.7	13.6 *(−0.7)*	–	100 *(0)*
Direct/indirect official Israeli explanations	20.6	17.2 *(0.2)*	16.6	15 *(−0.3)*	23.9	34 *(0.6)*	18.8	15.5 *(−1.1)*	29.8	18.3 *(0.6)*	–	100 *(0)*

Hamas rockets directed into Southern Israel	10.6	21.4 *(0.5)*	8.3	18.2 *(0.2)*	6.8	23.5 *(−0.7)*	10.9	21.8 *(0.1)*	10.1	15 *(−0.1)*	–	100 *(0)*
Direct/indirect official Hamas explanations	7.3	15.5 *(−0.1)*	7.6	17.5 *(0.1)*	9.1	32.6 *(0.1)*	9.2	19.3 *(−0.1)*	9.7	15.1 *(0.0)*	–	100 *(0)*
Israel's use of white phosphorous	2.8	11.8 *(−0.2)*	10.3	46.9 *(1.3)*	3.6	25.4 *(−0.3)*	2.7	11 *(−0.4)*	1.6	4.8 *(−0.5)*	–	100 *(0)*
General Hamas military action	4.6	20.6 *(0.2)*	7.3	35.5 *(0.8)*	3.1	23.4 *(−0.3)*	2.7	11.7 *(−0.4)*	2.7	8.9 *(−0.3)*	–	100 *(0)*
Problematic Israeli military tactics/action	2.8	13.8 *(−0.1)*	2.2	11.7 *(−0.2)*	4.6	37.8 *(0.2)*	4.5	21.4 *(0.0)*	4.3	15.3 *(0.0)*	–	100 *(0)*
Problematic Hamas military tactics/action	3.2	27.8 *(0.2)*	2.7	25.9 *(0.2)*	1.8	26.9 *(−0.1)*	1.7	14.8 *(−0.1)*	0.7	4.6 *(−0.2)*	–	100 *(0)*
Hamas rockets capable of reaching distant Israeli towns	2.2	22.6 *(0.1)*	1.5	17.2 *(0.0)*	1.4	23.7 *(−0.1)*	2.7	26.9 *(0.1)*	1.3	9.7 *(−0.1)*	–	100 *(0)*
Israel killing Hamas leaders	3.3	36.9 *(0.3)*	0.8	9.5 *(−0.1)*	1.2	22.6 *(−0.1)*	2.0	22.6 *(0.0)*	1.0	8.3 *(−0.1)*	–	100 *(0)*
Israeli humanitarian corridor	1.1	15.9 *(0.0)*	1.0	15.9 *(0.0)*	1.2	30.2 *(0.0)*	1.7	25.4 *(0.1)*	1.1	12.7 *(0.0)*	–	100 *(0)*
Israeli humanitarian tactics	0.1	3.4 *(−0.1)*	1.3	44.8 *(0.2)*	0.6	34.5 *(0.0)*	0.4	13.8 *(0.0)*	0.1	3.4 *(−0.1)*	–	100 *(0)*
SUMMA	100	–	100	–	100	–	100	–	100	–	–	–

to the al-Falkhura UN school incident is, for example, the lowest of all newspapers. But its coverage of the Zeytoun events, where 43 civilians were killed, with 6.2 per cent of all action in war codes devoted to the event, far outweighs those of any other newspaper. This is also reflected by the 0.6 per cent weighted divergence figure which, given the unimportance of the code in general, is relatively speaking very high.

It is perhaps no exaggeration to state therefore that the newspapers' concerns seem rather unpredictable as far as incidents of humanitarian import are concerned. Will this perhaps change if we turn our attention to the codes that weigh more as far as action is concerned – those of general action?

On the basis of the lower half of Table 3.7, the answer to this question is a resounding no. There is not a great deal of systematic difference that can be discerned as regards the broadsheets' coverage of general or iterative action in war. Table 3.7 showcases similar priorities of topics and weighted divergences mostly close to zero. Whatever systematic difference we may find between newspapers, it will only show rather small tendencies.

Even such small tendency might only be discernible in the coverage of the *Telegraph*. The newspaper generally wrote more about action than its liberal counterparts. Its highest weighted divergence percentages relate to topics that appear to favour the Israeli side (i.e., Hamas rockets being capable of reaching further down in Israel and Israel's targeted killing of Hamas notables). And when, according to the weighted divergence figures, it writes *less* about a topic, it is virtually always done from a position that favours Israel as opposed to the Palestinian side. Thus, if a small one, and if with the caveat that it is the *Telegraph* that wrote the most (and by some distance) about the Zeytoun incidents, there is some pro-Israeli tendency discernible in the newspaper's account.

Even on this small scale, however, hardly any tendency can be ascertained as regards the other newspapers. It is difficult to decipher any coherent message from the *Independent*'s and the *Financial Times*' statistics, other than their general lack of interest in action. With regard to some topics, the *Guardian* appears to offer a coverage which might be taken to favour the Palestinian side: its rendering of Israel's questionable tactics is relatively high, as is the space it gives to the official Hamas perspective of explanation. Yet, it also occasions one of the highest proportions of the exposition of the official Israeli position.

Most importantly, the newspaper that appears to have made Israel's use of the chemical substance white phosphorous the popular topic it proved to be (cf. Table 3.4) is the conservative *The Times*. White phosphorous in this newspaper is the single most outstanding code within the conceptual area of action in war, with 10.3 per cent of *The Times'* paragraphs devoted to the topic: a figure far higher than that of the combined total of all the liberal newspapers. Likewise, its weighted divergence percentage is 1.3. This is a very high figure indeed.

Just as was the case with the *Telegraph*'s coverage of the Zeytoun incidents, of course, *The Times'* focus on white phosphorous is not indicative of a general tendency to focus on those aspects of the war which might show Israel in a problematic light: it wrote the most of neutral Israeli action, and was in fact the only newspaper that devoted some non-negligible focus to Israel's humanitarian tactics. Yet the case remains that the most outstanding topic of the entire conceptual area, and one with potentially damning consequences to Israel, that of the IDF's use of white phosphorous, was covered by the conservative *The Times*.

Taken all this together, the only unambiguous message to be taken from the broadsheets' coverage of action in war is the lack of unambiguous messages. The conservative tendency to write more about action veiled no straightforward and strong tendency to write more about different topics as newspapers tended to render action in a rather uniform way. This was only offset in a relatively major way with regard to isolated topics (Zeytoun, white phosphorous) – and then not from the sources that would have been assumed, as it was conservative newspapers that deployed these topics with surprising frequency, potentially implying the problematic nature of Israel's war effort.

Discussion

Having examined the newspapers' coverage of the basic 'building blocks' of the armed conflict in Gaza, this chapter reviewed a fair amount of information. Two large conceptual areas came under scrutiny as similarities and divergences were investigated as regards action and death in war.

First and foremost, and against expectations of a rigid ideological divide between conservative (i.e., pro-Israeli) and (left-)liberal (i.e., pro-Palestinian) poles, analysis showed that whatever specific or systematic differences may be found across the newspapers, they are characterized by the shades of grey, rather than black and white.

To be sure, differences were found regarding both the attention paid to broad conceptual areas as well as specific codes. But these were differences of degree, not of kind. And they did not necessarily conform to a preconceived ideological conservative-liberal axis. Covering fatalities, it was the *Independent* and the *Telegraph* that devoted the most attention to the area, *The Times* and the *Financial Times* the least. What is more, the tendencies recovered from the coverage of specific codes of fatalities indicated similarities between newspapers supposedly at different ends of the ideological spectrum. Showcasing a tendency to support one side or the other, it was the *nationality* of the victim that appeared to motivate both the *Telegraph*'s and the *Guardian*'s coverage. The *Independent* and *The Times*, to the contrary, appeared to be more interested in the *humanitarian status* of the victim.

Other than the conservative propensity to write more about action, no kind of tendency appeared to characterize the newspapers' coverage when it came to the action that resulted in the fatalities. Just as virtually all newspapers were dominated by Palestinian civilian fatalities, they now devoted more than half of their coverage of action to mostly neutral Israeli manoeuvres and the official Israeli perspective explaining those manoeuvres and indeed the reasons why those Palestinian civilians died. If there was systematic difference between the newspapers' references to the dead, systematic divergences disappeared from their accounts when it came to explaining how the dead actually died. With one outstanding difference, that is: *The Times'* coverage of the IDF's use of the highly incendiary chemical material white phosphorous as obscurant weapon potentially raised important dilemmas in a unique fashion not discernible anywhere else in the database as regarded action in war.

Yet this very finding indicates the necessity of further analysis.

To begin with, *The Times'* utilization of the topic of white phosphorous, much like the *Telegraph*'s of the Zeytoun incidents, was rather isolated and idiosyncratic, even as far as the newspapers' own coverage was concerned. It indicated no broader and systematic critical engagement with the Israeli conduct of war. As such, whilst it pointed toward the relevance of Israel's potential responsibility in Palestinian civilian death, it did not appear to proceed with any such investigation at this point.

Indeed, further analysis would suggest the necessity to take a closer look on *The Times'* engagement with white phosphorous. Examining the code not simply in itself but *in conjunction* with the topic of Israeli war crimes (i.e., when not only the chemical substance was mentioned in a paragraph but also the possibility of Israeli war crimes was also made explicit), we find that in only 3.4 per cent of *The Times'* paragraphs occasioning 'white phosphorous' did reference to 'Israeli war crimes' occur as well. This is not only in stark contrast with the coverage of the left-liberal papers[8], it is actually less than half of even that of the *Telegraph* (7.4 per cent).[9] What this would suggest, then, is that 'building blocks' need to be examined in the argumentative context they feature.

What is more, it might even be the case that difference is where *no difference appeared to have been found* in this chapter. Thus, the entire database was found uniformly wanting in occasioning the controversial mid-day timing of the start of the Israeli offensive. Yet lack of quantitative difference should not be confused with that of quality. Namely, the *Guardian* made note of the timing in one of its editorials in a way concerning directly the dilemma of law in war (*Guardian*, 441) – just as it did, on two occasions (*Guardian*, 441, 520) of the targets of the first attacks (i.e., a police ceremony).

All of this points to the necessity of further analysis. To understand the *meaning of war and death*, further layers of accounts need to be investigated. This will start in the next chapter with the examination of the newspapers' accounts of historical context, and conclude with their arguments about law to and law in war (cf. Extracts 8.14 and 8.15 on white phosphorous). And as the analytic scope of this book will broaden to scrutinize the historical and argumentative context, so will the investigation reveal ever-broadening divergence between British broadsheets in their coverage of the war.

4
Engagements with History

Introduction

The previous chapter started with what may be regarded as the ultimate, unalterable outcome of war. It was the newspapers' representation of death as a result of the conflict that was first engaged with. Subsequently, the chapter went on to examine how the broadsheets accounted for death: what the sequence of events directly leading to people having died was, and who or what might have been responsible for that. Thus, the previous chapter examined basic facts, events, acts, and acts of explanation. In the main, it was found that whilst representation of death differed between publications, no such systematic difference could be found when it came to provide an account for it. For this reason, it was concluded that further investigation of different contexts is required. This is the first in a succession of chapters that occasion such investigation.

Context may be understood here in two senses. The traditional account values context inasmuch as it gives more information to the reader, and contributes to their understanding of the importance of facts reported. It is context in this sense that recent examination of media coverage of the Israeli-Palestinian conflict focused on (Philo & Berry, 2004, 2011). However, the concept may also be understood to refer to something more fundamental. Namely, in line with post-structuralist philosophical (Rorty, 1999), literary (Fish, 1980), historical (White, 2010), anthropological (Geertz, 2001) and psychological (Billig, 1996; Engel, 2000) explorations, we may conceive of context not as something additive but constitutive to the report of facts and events. This would mean that instead of adding something more to already available building blocks of facts, examining them in context reveals that it is this very context or perspective that lends the 'building blocks' their meaning.

As the book progresses, these two senses of context will be accounted for in turns. The present chapter will take more of an 'additive' view on context, whilst Chapters 7 and 8 take a nearly exclusively 'constitutive' one. What will be of interest, in both cases, is similar though. The question that these chapters will engage with is how the relative consensus manifest in the newspapers' coverage of facts, events, and acts of explanations changes as we learn more and more about their *(critical) perspectives*: will the general agreement between conservative and liberal newspapers as to what matters and how it matters hold? Or will differences in degree become differences of kind?

To tackle these questions, 28 topics were identified, and the newspapers' paragraphs coded for them. By their nature, some of these codes may be more political than historical. Some reach back to a distant past, others (such as the Israeli elections that were held after the war) even refer to a near future. As such, the conceptual area is by nature a rather heterogeneous one. Still, it was found that to account for everything that might go under historical context, considerably more codes would be needed. The code 'other historical events' was thus created to capture every topic that is historical but is not pre-determined in the codebook.

As in the previous chapter, at first historical context in the entire database will be analysed, with details pertaining to specific newspapers to turn to afterwards.

Historical context

In general, 1949 paragraphs were coded with 2744 occurrences of 'historical context' codes. Historical context featured in 24.9 per cent of the database's paragraphs: a smaller percentage than of action but considerably more than that of fatalities. Due to the *daily* character of the publications, the newspapers' foremost task is to cover news, with, arguably, only the second being to contextualize them. (Fatalities, at the same time, feature mostly in introducing some action or context, but not in the main body of the articles.) Besides, though numerically less frequent, historical context had a tendency to occur in editorials, comments and analysis: in spaces, that is, which may be argued to carry more weight for readers, as it is there that the political-moral perspective of the publications is communicated.

As can be seen, historical context is a more heterogeneous area than either of the two engaged with in the previous chapter. Topics are

Table 4.1 Individual 'historical context' codes in the full database

Name of code	Occurrences	% within all daily paragraphs	% within all historical context occurrences
Other historical events	400	5.1	14.6
Hamas rockets fired into Southern Israel (before the war)	372	4.8	13.6
The Israeli blockade on Gaza	335	4.3	12.2
The 2006 Lebanon war	216	2.8	7.9
Palestinian smuggling of weapons through tunnels under the Gaza–Egyptian border	201	2.6	7.3
Israeli elections (February 2009)	149	1.9	5.4
Israel's occupation of Palestinian territories (1967–)	139	1.8	5.1
Palestinian legislative elections (2006)	108	1.4	3.9
Palestinian 'civil war' (2007)	106	1.4	3.9
Six-month ceasefire between Hamas and Israel (2008)	91	1.2	3.3
Israeli withdrawal from Gaza (2005)	76	1	2.8
The end of the six-month ceasefire (2008)	76	1	2.8
Palestinian terror	50	0.6	1.8
The 'Six-Day War' (1967)	49	0.6	1.8
The Iraq war	49	0.6	1.8
The Palestinian 'nakba' (1947–1949)	48	0.6	1.7
Palestinian intifadas (uprisings)	44	0.6	1.6
The first Arab–Israeli war (1948–1949)	42	0.5	1.5
The war in Afghanistan	32	0.4	1.2
Other Arab–Israeli wars	31	0.4	1.1
Israeli military incursion into Gaza (4 November 2008)	26	0.3	0.9
Holocaust	24	0.3	0.9
Camp David peace negotiations between Yasser Arafat and Ehud Barak (2000)	22	0.3	0.8
The Oslo peace process	22	0.3	0.8
Palestinian violations of the six-month ceasefire (2008)	20	0.3	0.7
The Arab League's peace initiative (2002–)	12	0.2	0.4
Israel's 'war of independence' (1948–1949)	3	0.0	0.1
Peace agreement between Israel and Egypt (1979)	1	0.0	0.0
SUMMA	2744	–	100

clearly more 'spread out' with none of them dominating the conceptual area anywhere near the way Palestinian civilian deaths did 'fatalities', or general Israeli military action did 'action'. What is more, the most frequent category was actually defined to be a heterogeneous one: it was designed to comprise all the topics that represented historical context, yet were neither on theoretical nor on empirical ground deemed worthy of being independent codes.

As represented in Table 4.1, the general coverage is clearly dominated by events that occurred in the relatively recent past. Indeed, given the overall diversity of the table representing a considerable distribution of concerns, the topics of the Hamas rockets fired into Southern Israel, as well as Israel's economic blockade of Gaza, are by all means outstanding. Yet close analytic scrutiny in their case is also warranted by the fact that they exhibit a largely *homogenous critical perspective* as well.

Topics such as the Lebanon war of 2006, the coming Israeli elections in February 2009, or the Israeli pull-out from Gaza in 2005 can cover a wide variety of moral/political judgments and as such be presented from a perspective critical or supportive of Israel/Hamas/both. As seen previously, the Israeli withdrawal from Gaza is to this day often couched as a magnanimous gesture in the interest of peace, or a self-interested action, perhaps even committed to hinder peace. Elections in Israel were occasionally taken as a display of Israel's democratic credentials and other times to argue that the war taking place just before the elections proves it was a mere outcome of Israeli domestic propaganda. The Lebanon war between Israel and Hezbollah in 2006 was often presented in an unequivocally critical perspective, yet what was criticized was often simply Israel's military strategy or its leaders' political competence.

In contrast, there is virtually no instance of mentioning the topic of the Israeli economic blockade of Gaza that does not imply some sort of substantial political-moral criticism of Israel. And there is no instance of mentioning Hamas rockets fired into Israeli civilian territory that does not imply some sort of serious criticism of Hamas. The kind or the degree of criticism implied will, of course, vary. Yet, in addition to them being the two most frequent codes, their undoubted *homogeneity of critical perspective* makes them especially interesting for the purposes of this analysis. Their distribution amongst newspapers will be highly noteworthy.

Similar considerations prompt analytic interest in references to the tunnel system connecting Gaza and Egypt where Hamas continued to smuggle weapons (as well as other goods) into the Strip during the six-month ceasefire, and to the continuing Israeli occupation of Palestinian territories (some would argue, Gaza itself). They are not only relatively prevalent amongst the topics utilized by the newspapers to construct the historical events surrounding the war, but also betray a marked critical perspective in relation to one or the other of the conflict's protagonists.

One last comment is in place before turning to the specifics of newspapers' individual renderings of historical context. As noted above, details of a more distant past rarely made their way into the newspapers' coverage and, given the daily character of the publications, there can be no real surprise here; their perspective is inescapably limited and focuses closely on the here and now. Yet, more surprisingly perhaps, even some events of the relatively recent past, and ones with immediate relevance to the escalation of the conflict, appear to be underrepresented. For example, the relative lack of mentioning Israel's pull-out of the territory in 2005 might be rather surprising. No real understanding of the war is possible without the historical details surrounding Israel's decision to terminate its military and civilian presence within the Strip, yet only confer partial autonomy to it. As mentioned in Chapter 1, any narration of the story of the war seems to account for this event in one way or another. Yet it features in a mere 1 per cent of all paragraphs and 2.8 per cent of historical context ones. Equally, the six-month long ceasefire that immediately preceded the armed conflict, violations of it, and its eventual cessation are, by and large, missing from the newspapers' general account.

Taken together, the impression created by the prevalent topics simply appears to be one of ongoing, everlasting, perhaps even inevitable lethal conflict: a 'cycle of violence', as newspapers occasionally put it. The point here, of course, is not to deny that the Israeli-Palestinian conflict has been long and bloody, with very few moments of hope. Rather, it is to argue that by overlooking events that were integral to the narrative of the war, it is presented not simply as bloody but as *naturally* bloody: as if it were not composed of human events and human decisions.

Looking at Table 4.2 on the following page now, it is clear that historical context featured uniformly higher on the (left-)liberal papers' agenda. Without exception, they deployed a greater proportion of paragraphs referring to historical context in their coverage than what characterized the database as a whole (i.e., 25 per cent). For both conservative newspapers, this frequency is lower than 25 per cent. Thus, whilst conservative newspapers were dominated by factual coverage in accounting for

Table 4.2 `Historical context' across the newspapers

	Telegraph	*The Times*	*Guardian*	*Independent*	*Financial Times*	SUMMA
Historical context paragraphs (occurrences)	242 (306)	286 (383)	667 (1003)	443 (641)	318 (411)	1956 (2744)
Empirical importance within newspaper	242/1276 19%	286/1276 22.4%	667/2460 27.1%	443/1595 27.8%	318/1223 26%	1956/7830 25%

war (and death), liberal ones appear to have attempted to make sense of these issues with regard to historical context.

Let us not forget, of course, that these differences are merely relative. *All* newspapers devoted more attention (around 45 per cent) to action in war than historical context (around 25 per cent). It is only within that basic similarity that differences surface, and it is in this sense that differences are relative and not categorical. And let us also not forget that the left-right tendency that was indicated by the differences in the coverage of action disguised no such tendency when it came to the distribution of specific topics within that coverage. It is an open question whether quantitative difference between conservative and left-liberal historical coverage hides (or is motivated by) deeper-lying, qualitative differences as well.

It is with these caveats in mind that we shall examine the distribution of specific historical topics in each of the newspapers.

Table 4.3 is considerably more heterogeneous than any of the previous ones. This can be gathered from the fact that, first, the priority rank of historical topics diverges a great deal between newspapers, and second, the weighted divergences are far more extravagant than anything witnessed hitherto.

As may be expected, other than the 'omnibus' category of other events, it was the topic of Hamas rockets fired into Israeli civilian territory before that war to which both conservative newspapers attributed the most empirical importance. Of note is, however, not so much this but the extent to which they have done so. In the *Telegraph*, of all historical context codes, 16.0 per cent referred to the rockets, with the economic blockade coming as a distant second with 8.8 per cent. In *The Times*, the rockets accounted for 16.7 per cent of the paragraphs of historical context, with the Lebanon war coming second at 10.2 per cent and the economic blockade only fourth at 7.8 per cent. On the

Table 4.3 Individual 'historical context' codes across the newspapers: within each newspaper (i.e., relative to the particular newspaper's own coverage of all 'action in war' codes) and within each 'action in war' code (i.e., relative to the full database's coverage of the particular 'action in war' code)

	Telegraph		***The Times***		***Guardian***		***Independent***		***Financial Times***		**SUMMA**	
	within paper %	**within code % weighted divergence %**	**within paper %**	**within code % weighted divergence %**	**within paper %**	**within code % weighted divergence %**	**within paper %**	**within code % weighted divergence %**	**within paper %**	**within code % weighted divergence %**	**within paper %**	**within code % weighted divergence %**
Other historical events	14.4	11 *(−0.8)*	16.5	15.8 *(−0.1)*	16.3	40.8 *(1.4)*	13.9	22.2 *(0.3)*	9.9	10.2 *(−0.8)*	–	100 *(0)*
Hamas rockets fired into Southern Israel (before the war)	16.0	13.2 *(−0.4)*	16.7	17.2 *(0.1)*	14.4	38.7 *(1.0)*	10.9	18.8 *(−0.2)*	11.0	12.1 *(−0.5)*	–	100 *(0)*
The Israeli blockade on Gaza	8.9	8.1 *(−1.0)*	7.9	9 *(−0.9)*	14.0	41.8 *(1.3)*	10.9	20.9 *(0.1)*	16.5	20.3 *(0.6)*	–	100 *(0)*
The 2006 Lebanon war	6.2	8.8 *(−0.6)*	10.2	18.1 *(0.1)*	5.8	26.7 *(−0.4)*	8.6	25.5 *(0.4)*	10.9	20.8 *(0.4)*	–	100 *(0)*
Palestinian smuggling of weapons through tunnels under the Gaza-Egyptian border	8.1	12.4 *(−0.3)*	9.7	18.4 *(0.2)*	5.7	28.4 *(−0.2)*	6.4	20.4 *(0.0)*	10.0	20.4 *(0.4)*	–	100 *(0)*
Israeli elections	6.5	13.4 *(−0.2)*	4.7	12.1 *(−0.2)*	3.4	*22.8* (−0.5)	7.0	30.2 *(0.5)*	7.8	21.5 *(0.3)*	–	100 *(0)*
Israel's occupation of Palestinian territories	4.3	9.4 *(−0.3)*	2.1	5.8 *(−0.5)*	6.9	49.6 *(0.9)*	3.8	17.3 *(−0.2)*	6.1	18 *(0.1)*	–	100 *(0)*
Palestinian legislative elections	1.3	3.7 *(−0.5)*	3.9	13.9 *(−0.1)*	5.0	46.3 *(0.6)*	4.1	24.1 *(0.1)*	3.2	12 *(−0.1)*	–	100 *(0)*
Palestinian 'civil war'	3.9	11.3 *(−0.2)*	4.7	17 *(0.0)*	2.6	24.5 *(−0.3)*	3.4	20.8 *(0.0)*	6.8	26.4 *(0.4)*	–	100 *(0)*
Six-month ceasefire between Hamas and Israel	2.9	9.9 *(−0.2)*	2.4	9.9 *(−0.2)*	4.7	51.6 *(0.7)*	2.5	17.6 *(−0.1)*	2.4	11 *(−0.2)*	–	100 *(0)*
Israeli withdrawal from Gaza	2.6	10.5 *(−0.2)*	3.9	19.7 *(0.1)*	3.2	42.1 *(0.3)*	1.4	11.8 *(−0.2)*	2.9	15.8 *(0.0)*	–	100 *(0)*
The end of the six-month ceasefire	3.3	13.2 *(−0.1)*	2.9	14.5 *(0.0)*	2.9	38.2 *(0.2)*	2.5	21.1 *(0.0)*	2.4	13.2 *(−0.1)*	–	100 *(0)*

Palestinian terror	2.9	18 *(0.0)*	2.1	16 *(0.0)*	1.6	32 *(0.0)*	1.7	22 *(0.0)*	1.5	12 *(−0.1)*	–	100 *(0)*
The 'Six-Day War'	1.3	8.2 *(−0.1)*	0.5	4.1 *(−0.2)*	2.3	46.9 *(0.3)*	2.8	36.7 *(0.3)*	0.5	4.1 *(−0.2)*	–	100 *(0)*
The Iraq war	3.3	20.4 *(0.1)*	2.1	16.3 *(0.0)*	1.8	36.7 *(0.1)*	2.0	26.5 *(0.1)*	0.0	0 *(−0.3)*	–	100 *(0)*
The Palestinian 'nakba'	1.0	6.2 *(−0.2)*	1.6	12.5 *(−0.1)*	1.4	29.2 *(0.0)*	3.3	43.8 *(0.4)*	1.0	8.3 *(−0.1)*	–	100 *(0)*
Palestinian intifadas	2.0	13.6 *(0.0)*	1.3	11.4 *(−0.1)*	1.2	27.3 *(−0.1)*	1.9	27.3 *(0.1)*	2.2	20.5 *(0.1)*	–	100 *(0)*
The first Arab-Israeli war	1.0	*7.1* (−0.1)	1.0	9.5 *(−0.1)*	1.5	35.7 *(0.1)*	3.1	47.6 *(0.4)*	0.0	0 *(−0.2)*	–	100 *(0)*
The war in Afghanistan	2.9	28.1 *(0.1)*	1.3	15.6 *(0.0)*	1.2	37.5 *(0.1)*	0.9	18.8 *(0.0)*	0.0	0 *(−0.2)*	–	100 *(0)*
Other Arab-Israeli wars	0.0	0 *(−0.2)*	0.3	3.2 *(−0.1)*	0.6	19.4 *(−0.1)*	3.1	64.5 *(0.5)*	1.0	12.9 *(0.0)*	–	100 *(0)*
Israeli military incursion into Gaza	0.7	7.7 *(−0.1)*	0.5	7.7 *(−0.1)*	1.1	42.3 *(0.1)*	1.2	30.8 *(0.1)*	0.7	11.5 *(0.0)*	–	100 *(0)*
Holocaust	0.3	4.2 *(−0.1)*	2.6	41.7 *(0.2)*	0.5	20.8 *(−0.1)*	1.2	33.3 *(0.1)*	0.0	0 *(−0.1)*	–	100 *(0)*
The Oslo peace process	0.3	4.5 *(−0.1)*	0.5	9.1 *(−0.1)*	0.5	22.7 *(−0.1)*	0.9	27.3 *(0.1)*	1.9	36.4 *(0.2)*	–	100 *(0)*
Camp David peace negotiations between Yasser Arafat and Ehud Barak	4.6	63.6 *(0.4)*	0.5	9.1 *(−0.1)*	0.0	0 *(−0.3)*	0.8	22.7 *(0.0)*	0.2	4.5 *(−0.1)*	–	100 *(0)*
Palestinian violations of the six-month ceasefire	1.0	15 *(0.0)*	0.3	5 *(−0.1)*	1.2	60 *(0.2)*	0.6	20 *(0.0)*	0.0	0 *(−0.1)*	–	100 *(0)*
The Arab League's peace initiative (2002-)	0.0	0 *(−0.1)*	0.0	0 *(−0.1)*	0.4	33.3 *(0.0)*	0.6	33.3 *(0.1)*	1.0	33.3 *(0.1)*	–	100 *(0)*
Israel's 'war of independence'	0.3	33.3 *(0.0)*	0.0	0 *(0.0)*	0.1	0 *(0.0)*	0.2	33.3 *(0.0)*	0.0	0 *(0.0)*	–	100 *(0)*
Peace agreement between Israel and Egypt	0.0	0 *(0.0)*	0.0	0 *(0.0)*	0.0	0 *(0.0)*	0.2	100 *(0.0)*	0.0	0 *(0.0)*	–	100 *(0)*
SUMMA	100	–	100	–	100	–	100	–	100	–	–	–

basis of these frequencies, we can unequivocally establish that within the conservative newspapers' coverage of historical context, considerations of rockets (and the resulting criticism of Hamas firing rockets into Israeli civilian territory) came to be attributed the most importance.

This is compounded by further characteristics. References to illicit Palestinian underground smuggling (of weapons) featured very prominently on both conservative newspapers' agendas. And the issue of Israeli occupation was nearly completely neglected, with the coverage in the *Telegraph* constituting only 4.2 per cent of the historical coverage and in *The Times* an even smaller percentage, 2.1 per cent.

Indeed, further illustration of the conservative newspapers' tendency to prioritize events which tend to support the Israeli perspective may be gathered from the few instances in newspapers where a topic of general quantitative unimportance features relatively frequently in a specific newspaper's coverage. The *Telegraph* was the only newspaper to refer with any kind of meaningful frequency to peace negotiations: the 2000 Camp David negotiations between Israeli Prime Minister Ehud Barak and President of the Palestinian Authority Yasser Arafat. Whilst these negotiations can be framed from a left-wing angle as well (cf. Halper, 2008; Said, 2004), it was inevitably presented in the conservative newspaper as the occasion where Israel made an unprecedentedly generous offer to which Arafat's response was simply to cut short negotiations and launch the second intifada (*Daily Telegraph*, 9, 37, 75). So even when the prospect of peace and the actuality of peace negotiations were mentioned, it was mostly done to argue against the reasonability of the Palestinian side, past or present.

Likewise, the newspapers generally neglected the historical event of the Holocaust. *The Times* was the exception, as the conservative newspaper found that symbol of the immense historical suffering of the Jewish people relevant to the war in 2.6 per cent of its own historical coverage. This is a figure that easily exceeds the combined total of the topics' coverage of all other newspapers.

So far, so clear, we may say. Conservative newspapers tend to be branded in the UK as pro-Israel. Indeed, the *Telegraph* explicitly tagged itself this way in a succession of editorials (*Daily Telegraph*, 43, 76). Not that they would be blind to any piece of historical reality that may contradict their overall framework: the Israeli economic blockade was still a prominent topic in their coverage. In that sense, the picture evolving is still one of relative rather than absolute, black-and-white differences. Yet those differences appear to be rather systematic ones, with no information to overly contradict them: a distinct picture appears to emerge from the conservative newspapers where historical events that can be assumed to be critical of Hamas are attributed more space, and events that may imply the historical responsibility of the State of Israel are, comparatively speaking, neglected.

However, introducing results from the calculations of newspapers' attention to specific codes *relative to other newspapers* alters this smooth and unsurprising picture quite radically. Namely, not only did conservative newspapers write less in general about historical context when compared to the space the liberals devoted to the area (cf. Table 4.2), this relative neglect even pertains to the particular topics that, taking the newspapers in themselves, appeared to be important for them. That both of them wrote less than would be expected of codes such as the occupation and the issue of the blockade is of no surprise, of course. What is of surprise is that the *Telegraph* wrote considerably less than its benchmark figure even of Hamas rockets (–0.4 per cent), with *The Times* exceeding its benchmark by a mere 0.1 per cent. The pattern can be seen repeated as regards illicit Hamas smuggling of weapons through its underground tunnel system.[1]

As a consequence, it appears that the ultimately distinctive feature of conservative newspapers, when compared to all other dailies, is not so much their tendency to over-report events that might be construed to provide support for Israel's cause and criticism to that of Hamas/Palestinians, but their general tendency to underreport historical aspects of the conflict.[2] And whilst this tendency certainly pertains more to codes that represent critical arguments towards the conduct of Israel, it is not overly contradicted by their invocation of the main topics of the rockets or that of smuggling, both used to unequivocally condemn Hamas.

Turning now to the analysis of the coverage of (left-)liberal newspapers, the first thing to notice is that they uniformly wrote far more of the Israeli economic blockade when compared to Hamas rockets than the conservative publications. In fact, the *Independent*'s blockade coverage matches and the *Financial Times*' even exceeds that of the rockets (cf. Table 4.3). Does this mean that with the treatise of history we have finally found a (left-)liberal *pole* opposed to a conservative one? And does it mean that the (left-)liberal feature of writing more about history (cf. Table 4.2) is due to some liberal predisposition, nay, 'obsession', to criticize Israel (Harrison, 2006; Rosenfeld, 2006)?

The answer is no to both questions.

To begin with, the *Independent*'s coverage appears rather inconsistent as regards historical events depicting Israel in a less than favourable light. Whilst in the *Financial Times* the topic of the Israeli occupation featured prominently (6.1 per cent) and, uniquely amongst newspapers, the *Guardian*'s fourth most frequent code was occupation (6.9 per cent); its empirical importance was less for the *Independent* than even for the *Daily Telegraph* (3.8 per cent). Likewise, whilst the newspaper wrote less of the rockets than would be expected (–0.2 per cent), it equally wrote less of the occupation (–0.2 per cent) and only slightly more of the economic blockade (0.1 per cent). If anything, the reason why the *Independent* devoted more paragraphs to history than its conservative counterparts appears to be that it dwelt on topics which, in themselves, connote no substantial political-moral critical perspective (i.e., Israel's 2006 war in Lebanon).

In contrast, the *Financial Times* did look to apply a consistently critical perspective to the actions of the State of Israel. As mentioned, of all newspapers, it was the one that wrote the most of the economic blockade of Gaza (exceeding its benchmark considerably) and the critical perspective implied in this was equally matched up by its prominent coverage of the Israeli occupation. Is the reason therefore that the *Financial Times* devoted significant attention to historical issues due to its predilection to criticize Israeli action and Israeli action only? Here the picture becomes rather fuzzy: whilst the Palestinian smuggling of weaponry and Hamas's violent takeover of Gaza from its secular rival featured in the newspaper with some prominence, it virtually neglected the all-important issue of Hamas rockets.

To turn now to the last of the (left-)liberal publications, the *Guardian* appears to have consistently deployed a perspective critical of Israel: both the blockade and the occupation feature with singular prominence in its account of the war. Yet the newspaper can be accused of an anti-Israeli bias even less than the *Financial Times*. With a weighted average of +1.0 per cent, it was the *Guardian* that mentioned the Hamas rockets *in the most historical paragraphs relative to all the other papers*. Full 38.7 per cent of all paragraphs referring to Hamas rockets in the database featured in the *Guardian*. In other words, and with the caveat that it appears to have somewhat neglected the issue of Palestinian smuggling of weapons, the reason why the *Guardian* devoted considerable attention to historical context appears to be a consistently deployed critical perspective towards not just one but *both* participants of the war.

It would appear, then, that the general tendency of liberal newspapers to write more about historical context than conservative newspapers may not simply be attributed to the fact that they would be 'obsessed' with those aspect of the context that are bound to be seen as critical of Israel. It is not a partisan tendency that appears to have motivated their historical accounts. What it was, though, is more difficult to ascertain, as the only important feature that applies to all of the liberal newspapers (but to neither of the conservative ones) is that they wrote more, *relative to all other newspapers*, about the blockade than rockets. As we have seen above – as regards the attention devoted to blockade versus rockets within a particular newspaper, the attention devoted to the occupation both within a newspaper and relative to others, the relative attention devoted to rockets when compared to conservative newspapers – the picture remains somewhat inconsistent, pertaining to both the homogeneity of the liberal end of the spectrum of newspapers and an unequivocal line demarcating them from those on the conservative end.

Discussion

Historical context was invoked less frequently by newspapers than action in war but more frequently than fatalities: understanding war and death was therefore subordinated to the flow of daily events and general characteristics. To repeat, this can probably be attributed to the daily character of the papers and their primary role in distributing authoritative original information for the general public. At the same time, the organization of this quantitatively less frequent cluster of codes nonetheless indicates their relative importance. Whilst information about facts, events, and casualties were by and large confined to the news and feature articles in the newspapers, historical context was overwhelmingly reflected on in editorials, comments and analyses. As noted above, these are articles carrying more weight than other (and longer) types of articles. This is because they convey more straightforwardly the newspapers' perspective (i.e., the *reason* why people buy them) and provide the reader with a *framework* to interpret information provided elsewhere.

Whilst perspective, of course, may be detectable in other, ostensibly more factual, sections of the papers, it never is so explicit as in the argumentative articles that predominantly featured historical context.[3] Thus, even if of relative quantitative unimportance, historical context and its coverage matters a great deal.

For this reason, the chapter's finding that *each* of the (left-)liberal newspapers attributed more importance to historical context relative to all the other newspapers than *either* of the two conservative ones is of some interest. Indeed, as analysed above, conservative newspapers did not even 'over-report' the one code that featured most prevalently in their own publication. The *Telegraph*'s share of the code 'rockets' relative to the other newspapers was still lower than what was expected and even matched that of the *Independent*; and whilst *The Times*' relative share was slightly higher than expected, it was still far lower than that of the *Guardian*.

As was the case in the previous chapter, too, however, as we looked beyond this initial difference, the picture became somewhat blurry. Whilst no unequivocal pro-Palestinian trend was discernible with the liberal newspapers, neither was it entirely clear what might explain the high overall proportion of historical interest. Indeed, no meaningful pattern was showcased in the *Independent*, and whilst the *Financial Times* appeared to have critiqued both sides on important accounts, it flatly neglected the issue of Hamas rockets fired into Israeli civilian territory.

Arguably, it was only in the case of the *Guardian* where some genuine parity could be noted. Whilst the newspaper unequivocally disparaged the State of Israel on account of its policy of the occupation and the economic blockade, it also wrote the most relative to all other newspapers about the Hamas rocket-fire into Southern Israel. Thus, in the *Guardian*'s case, emphasis put on historical context appeared to reflect a substantial critical perspective, not just on one but on *both* participants of the conflict.

Of course, whether this tentative conclusion is acceptable depends on a number of factors, though. First, due to the rhetoric generally adopted by Israeli politicians as well as their temporal immediacy, it may be that the rockets fired at Israeli civilian territories by Hamas were events in the foreground, whilst the occupation and the blockade were in the background. This is not to say that they were less important, only to raise the possibility that they may have been, metaphorically speaking, *discursive affordances* (Engelbert & McCurdy, 2012; cf. Gibson, 1979). In other words, the consensual interpretation of events made it simply impossible to neglect them, even if one may not have attributed the significance to them that, say, the Israeli government did. If this is so, the hypothetically more critical propensity of the liberal newspapers (and the *Guardian* in particular) may simply stem from the fact that they talked more about issues they would be inclined to talk about anyway (i.e., occupation and blockade), but also talked about issues that they simply *had to address* (i.e., Hamas rockets).

Second, as with the previous two chapters, importance in this chapter was equated with simple numerical frequency. The more paragraphs a newspaper referred to a topic in its columns, the more important the topic was judged to be. Yet things might not be this straightforward. For instance, though the *Financial Times* wrote fewer paragraphs containing reference to the occupation either in absolute or relative terms than the *Guardian*, those occurrences tended to be exhibited in a space with undoubtedly special status: in editorials. Of all its editorial paragraphs (40), the *Financial Times* referred to the occupation in 30 per cent (i.e., 12 times). The respective figures for the other newspapers are: *Telegraph* 0, *The Times* 0, *Guardian* 4.3 per cent (1), *Independent* 6.3 per cent (1). This means that of all the editorial paragraphs in the newspapers, a whopping 85.7 per cent appeared in the *Financial Times* (well above not only the newspaper's overall share of paragraphs in the sample (15.6 per cent) but even its share of editorial paragraphs in the entire sample (40.0 per cent)). On the basis of the statistics reported in this chapter, then, the *Guardian* attributed more significance to the occupation than did the *Financial Times*. On the basis of the statistical considerations introduced in this paragraph, the picture may not be so clear-cut.

Third, the analysis in this chapter proceeded on the assumption that four topics in particular (Hamas rockets and the smuggling of weapon, the Israeli occupation and economic blockade) were not just thematically homogenous but also inevitably implied a critical perspective towards either the State of Israel or Hamas. As we shall see in Chapters 7 and 8, it is true that writing about Hamas rockets is impossible without at least implying criticism of Hamas's conduct. But we will also see that it is possible to talk about them with far more varying degrees of criticism than, say, of the Israeli occupation and the economic blockade of Gaza.

The *Financial Times*, for instance, not only mentioned the Israeli occupation in its editorials with relative frequency, but featured the following assessment:

> It must be remembered that the root cause of the Israeli-Palestinian conflict is the Israeli occupation – which Israel's 2005 withdrawal from Gaza was meant to consolidate, through its subsequent expansion of Jewish settlements in the West Bank and Arab east Jerusalem. (*Financial Times*, 1039)

No paragraph like this has appeared anywhere in the newspapers' editorials. As such, no such forceful and deep criticism of the Israeli position has been occasioned by using the topic of the occupation anywhere else. Whilst all mention of the occupation implied a critical perspective, not every one of these perspectives was the same.

What is more, an even more remarkable divergence regarding the rockets Hamas fired into Israeli civilian territory might be discernible in broadsheets' editorials. To cite the *Guardian*, the newspaper's first editorial on the war stated that: 'The death toll by last night had climbed to nearly 290, with more than 700 wounded. This in reply to hundreds of rockets from Hamas militants which killed one Israeli in six months. But the equation is always like this' (*Guardian*, 441). Its last editorial referred to Hamas 'continuing to fire rockets at the civilian population in southern Israel.' (*Guardian*, 661) The first quotation visibly downplays the importance of the rockets, at least in comparison to the destructive conclusion of Israel's attack. The second quotation, in turn, pinpoints what may be their horrific *differentia specifica*: they directly and exclusively aim at civilians. The first quotation concerns relatively insignificant material effect. The second concerns the worst possible intention according to morality and international law. How this and other newspapers navigate between these two poles will make incredible reading – not simply adding to the findings of this chapter, but subtly creating the very meanings (here, of 'rockets') that were largely taken for granted so far (cf. Richardson, 2007).

In the concluding chapters of this book, we shall return to these issues. Death, action and history will be analysed as they were deployed in forming the broadsheets' overall perspectives on the war.

5
Engagements with Criticism

Introduction

The previous chapters addressed the newspapers' explicit engagements with death, action and historical context. Not only were pieces of data (i.e., paragraphs) identified explicitly, quantitative analysis accounted for what may be termed their explicit, manifest, evident content. From the present chapter on, the course of analysis will progressively become more and more interpretative: concerning more and more implications of engagements with criticism, antisemitism and war.

Dealing with explicit engagements with criticism, this chapter will be something of a hybrid in this sense. Data were still identified explicitly, and the first half of the analysis will be quantitative, examining broad trends in the broadsheets. But the second half of the chapter will consist of purely qualitative analysis of certain aspects of criticism.

It will not simply be the method of analysing the texts that changes from this chapter onward, however. Whilst the concern of previous chapters was more bottom-up, working predominantly with what the newspapers offered, from this chapter on certain crucial theoretical concepts will guide the analysis. Thus, as we have seen in Chapter 1, the act of criticism is a focal point of the (meta-)debate on Israel/Palestine. What can be said and who can say it were dilemmas both proponents and opponents of the 'new antisemitism' theory pondered heavily. It therefore promises to be a fertile ground from which to understand some deeper aspects of the coverage.

For the purposes of this chapter, all utterances in the database concerning acts of either explicit criticism or explicit support of one of the warring sides were collected from the newspapers' comment pieces.[1] The interest will lie in what authors thought of *other stakeholders'* relevant positions and how they engaged with them. Thus, of prime interest here is the fact that explicit occasioning of the act of criticism in most cases means engagement with the position of some 'other' agent. Via their criticism, and the newspapers' evaluation thereof, we will learn who the 'other' side in the debate on Israel/Palestine is, and what 'we' disagree with them on, how 'we' debate the dilemmas with 'them', and what the chances are for 'us' or 'them' to settle our dissensus.

For the purposes of quantitative analysis, the *agent* and the *position* of an utterance of criticism was first coded. It was decided whether they are neutral, supportive/critical of Israel/Hamas or Palestinians, or expressing overlapping values. At the same time, it was quickly realized that another dimension needed to be introduced: an author may express approval as to a particular critical/supportive position or signal his/her distance. To account for this, coding would not simply account for what the position of those 'others' who expressed criticism/support was, but also what the author's position was *vis-à-vis* the occasioned act of criticism/support: was the *evaluative perspective* distancing, synoptic or neutral?

Whilst it may look straightforward enough, such a system of coding presented the analysis with a number of revealing dilemmas. First of all, the book's choice of the coding values does not necessarily indicate agreement as to the categorically distinct nature of these values. Namely, the idea of being critical or supportive of an agent may arguably not be a meaningful position in itself. What does it mean to be pro-Israeli or supporting Israel? Does it mean to support the idea of Greater Israel? To support the idea of the two-state solution based on the pre-1967 borders? To support the idea of the two-state solution based on the borders ratified by the UN General Assembly in 1947? To support the idea of a bi-national state upholding equal rights to every one of its citizens? To justify certain Israeli military/political actions unrelated to the above? To justify any Israeli military action? This list could go on with positions that are subscribed to by relevant agents, and that represent such vast variability as to make the simple values of 'supportive of Israel' or 'pro-Israel' borderline-meaningless – even if they actually *fitted the data* very well.

Second, a unique problem presented itself in the collapsing the 'State' and its populations. Whilst rarely acknowledged, this is an issue even in the case of Israel: a sizeable number of its citizens may not warrant being treated contiguously with the State of Israel, especially when it comes to an armed conflict with Palestinians. Yet it is even more of a problem when it comes to the relationship between Hamas and the

Palestinians. Whilst Hamas first gained power in 2006 through free and fair democratic elections, it later ousted its rival Fatah, in what is sometimes described as a civil war, in 2007. The question of contiguity in this case therefore does not simply concern dissent (as in Israel) but violence and coercion. Nonetheless, for the sake of methodological clarity, as well as the fact that war creates distinct poles of entities otherwise displaying features of heterogeneity and homogeneity, it was decided that the values of dimensions would reflect two poles, and thus convey (the illusion of?) homogeneity.

Third, to assess a columnist's 'evaluative perspective' on an utterance is clearly not without its practical problems either. For a start, there are many aspects of evaluation. There is the issue of truth (is an utterance true or false?), the issue of morality (is it right or wrong?), the issue of practicality (does it work?), or even the perspective of one's prioritized agent (is it good for the State of Israel/Hamas/Palestinians?). Any evaluation may be given from one rather than another of these aspects, and there may or may not be harmony between these aspects. Then, there is a scale of evaluation, even in qualitative (let alone quantitative) terms. Obviously, one may explicitly or implicitly endorse a statement; it is possible to explicitly or implicitly be against it. These may represent different intensities of (dis)engagement (although the intensity of engagement also depends on the actual statement one endorses/opposes and what the consensual stance regarding that may be). Yet a newspaper could equally report on an utterance without further comment, explicitly or implicitly. Whilst such constructions mostly imply endorsement, questions remain again as to what extent *this* type of endorsement can be treated similar to a clearly phrased, ringing piece of support.

As may be gauged from these considerations, assigning values to the dimensions of agent, position and evaluative perspective proved to be a somewhat paradoxical exercise. Empirically speaking, they fitted the data nicely. Theoretically speaking, they occasionally conveyed rather dilemmatic assumptions. It was for this reason that a more in-depth, close engagement with some aspects of the data was felt necessary. Such engagement will be showcased in the second half of the chapter, where utterances conveying *overlapping political-moral positions* will be examined.

Quantitative analysis of content

To start with, the distribution of utterances explicitly oriented to criticism in the four remaining newspapers is as follows:

Table 5.1 'Criticism' utterances across the newspapers

	Telegraph	*The Times*	*Guardian*	*Independent*	*Financial Times*	Total
Occurrences	44	35	92	82	19	272
% of all 'criticism' utterances	16.2	12.9	33.8	30.1	7.0	100

As can be seen, left-liberal newspapers occasioned more utterances referring to explicit criticism. In fact, the frequency is extraordinarily high as concerns the *Independent*. To remember, the newspaper occasioned an outstanding number of comment pieces. These pieces are more adversarial in a newspaper and hence house the most of constructions this chapter analyses. Likewise, both *The Times* and the *Financial Times* featured a relatively smaller number of comments than would have been expected given its overall share which explains why in Table 5.1, too, their share is relatively low.

Of course, these general figures tell a very limited story. In what follows, the interest will be in *how* the newspapers represented the critical or supportive position they occasioned. As first and general steps, we shall examine what agents they found relevant in these debates, and what positions these agents subsequently took up.

As can clearly be seen in Table 5.2, the relevant agents were not only overwhelmingly neutral (69.5 per cent), but homogenously so across the spectrum of newspapers. Likewise, there appears to be consensus amongst the newspapers regarding the relative irrelevance of agents supportive and, *especially*, critical of Hamas or the Palestinians. Inasmuch as agents were relevant, they were (overwhelmingly) neutral or, to a considerably lesser degree, concerned with Israel.

Where difference does surface is the cluster of agents that were (perceived to be) critical towards Israel. Thus, for the left-liberal newspapers, positions supportive of Israel were rather more of concern. For conservative newspapers, this is not true: both the *Telegraph* and *The Times* found critical and supportive positions towards Israel more or less of equal importance. Subsequently, their relative share of agents predisposed to be critical of Israel was considerably higher than that of the left-liberal newspapers.

Nonetheless, we ought to repeat that agents featured in news reports in all newspapers sampled were, overwhelmingly, coded as being neutral

Table 5.2 Individual 'agent' values across the newspapers

		Telegraph	*The Times*	*Guardian*	*Independent*	*Financial Times*
	Total %	Within paper %	Within paper %	Within paper %	Within paper %	Within paper %
Neutral	69.5	63.6	71.4	69.6	70.7	73.7
Supportive of Israel	15.1	13.6	14.3	15.2	14.6	21.1
Critical of Israel	8.8	15.9	11.4	6.5	8.5	0
Supportive of Hamas/ Palestinians	4.8	4.5	2.9	5.4	4.9	5.3
Critical of Hamas/ Palestinians	0.7	2.3	0	1.1	0	0
Overlap	1.1	0	0	2.2	1.2	0
SUMMA	100	100	100	100	100	100

with regards to Israel and Hamas/Palestinians. They were not predisposed to take one side or the other. In principle, they were open to argument and persuasion, and able to turn their minds one way or the other. If this is acceptable, then it may be of interest to note that the consensus of British newspapers was that the prevalent subject position of agents commenting on or having a stake in the conflict is *not a predisposition.* Even if they exhibit a tendency (as they, indeed, will) towards one position or another, this position bears no mark on their identity. Political-moral thought does not become human identity. In a debate where positions are often entrenched and debate is often reduced to catchphrases and identity politics, the agents presented here are open to persuasion.

Though this is of importance, the other main feature to characterize the sample punctuates this (admittedly abstract) conclusion as the openness cherished in the previous paragraph quickly disappears when we focus on the overall position of the utterance in Table 5.3.

That the value 'neutral' disappears when it comes to the actual action and object of criticism is no surprise: criticism implies some judgment of value. What is of interest is that for *each* newspaper, the most relevant position becomes that which is critical of Israel. Inasmuch as criticism is an explicit issue, it is mostly criticism of Israel that makes it so.

Where considerable divergence can be detected is the share of these positions in each newspaper. Here, a polarized picture starts to emerge.

Table 5.3 Individual 'position' values across the newspapers

		Telegraph	*The Times*	*Guardian*	*Independent*	*Financial Times*
Value	**Total %**	**Within paper %**	**Within paper %**	**Within paper %**	**Within paper %**	**Within paper %**
Supportive of Israel	30.1	27.3	20.0	30.4	36.6	26.3
Critical of Israel	46.0	59.1	60.0	39.1	39.0	52.6
Supportive of Hamas/ Palestinians	6.6	9.1	8.6	8.7	2.4	5.3
Critical of Hamas/ Palestinians	14.7	4.5	11.4	15.2	20.7	15.8
Overlap	2.6	0	0	6.5	1.2	0
SUMMA	100	100	100	100	100	100

Both conservative newspapers occasioned positions critical of Israel far more frequently than those supportive of Israel's stance. For left-liberal newspapers, this ratio is a considerably more balanced one.[2] Almost a mirror image to this emerges when positions taken towards Hamas/Palestinians are taken into account. Here it is liberal newspapers (including the *Financial Times*) that found positions critical of Hamas/ Palestinians disproportionately more relevant than those supportive ones. And it is *The Times* where some balance might be detected, with the *Telegraph* actually occasioning twice as many 'pro' than 'anti'-Hamas/ Palestinian utterances.

Interestingly, then, the majority of newspapers appeared to detect a formally balanced position on *either* Israel (in the *Guardian* and the *Independent*) *or* Palestinians/Hamas (in *The Times*). Exceptions to this pertained to the *Telegraph*, where a rather black-and-white picture emerged with agents simply and overwhelmingly criticizing Israel and supporting Hamas/Palestinians, and to the *Financial Times* where both Israel and Hamas/Palestinians were overwhelmingly critiqued.

In other words, beyond some uniform features across newspapers, a more polarized picture starts to emerge. Though most of the agents appeared to be neutral initially, this might by now be regarded as a mere facade as newspapers subsequently took these neutral agents to adopt tendentious positions. In fact, the only conspicuous similarity between conservative and left-liberal newspapers might be the uniform neglect of overlapping positions: that is, precisely those stances where different values and perspectives might merge in judgments of the war.

To investigate this further, two other aspects of the data will now be examined. First, we shall look at what specifically happened to neutral agents. What position did they adopt subsequently? Second, and most importantly, the author's 'evaluative perspective' will be analysed. Thus, a take on the newspapers' perspective on the positions they engaged with can only be comprehensive if we consider what *the newspapers'* evaluation of those positions was.

For the sake of clarity, presentation of the data will now proceed by collapsing the complementary positions into two poles: critical of Israel and supportive of Hamas/Palestinians *versus* supportive of Israel and critical of Hamas/Palestinians.

What Table 5.4 shows us is that, for example, in the *Guardian*, of its 60 originally neutral agents, 29 adopted a position critical towards Israel or supportive of Hamas/Palestinians. In *The Times*, of the 25 neutral agents, 6 adopted a position supportive of Israel or critical of Hamas/Palestinians.

Thus, we can see that neutrals for the conservative papers became critical of Israel or supportive of Hamas/Palestinians. The opposite is true of the *Guardian* and the *Independent*. However, we can also see that these poles are pushed afar from each other. As far as criticism was concerned and defined in this chapter, not only did the conservative papers and the *Independent* disagree on what the relevant positions of those neutral agents eventually became – they *radically* disagreed. Indeed, conservative

Table 5.4 The positions occupied by neutral agents across the newspapers

	Telegraph	*The Times*	*Guardian*	*Independent*	*Financial Times*
Critical of Israel and supportive of Hamas/ Palestinians	20	19	29	22	8
Supportive of Israel and critical of Hamas/ Palestinians	8	6	31	36	6
Ratio	2.5	3.17	1:1.07	1:1.64	1.33

newspapers wrote what might technically be termed disproportionately more about positions broadly favourable to Hamas/Palestinians or critical of Israel than the opposite ones.

The disparity is not this pronounced with the left-liberal papers; in their case, whilst neutrals became more supportive of Israel or critical of Hamas/Palestinians, they did not overwhelm the number of those who shifted to the other direction. In fact, in the case of the *Guardian*, the progressive polarization of newspapers may not be detected at all as yet.

So how does this dynamic of polarization look if we account for the evaluative perspective the newspapers displayed with regard to each of these positions? After all, it is perfectly possible that, say, the *Independent* would actually distance itself from positions critical of Israel, and the *Telegraph* from those supporting it. To calculate this, perspectives *synoptic* with positions critical of Israel or supportive of Hamas/Palestinians were clustered together with perspectives *distancing from* positions critical of Israel or supportive of Hamas/Palestinians – and vice versa. The newspapers' tendencies can be gathered from the Table 5.5.

Table 5.5 Evaluative perspectives across the newspapers

	Telegraph	*The Times*	*Guardian*	*Independent*	*Financial Times*
Distancing with critical of Israel and supportive of Hamas/Palestinians positions; *and* synoptic with supportive of Israel and critical of Hamas/Palestinians positions	28	21	24	17	1
Synoptic with critical of Israel and supportive of Hamas/Palestinians positions, *and* distancing with supportive of Israel and critical of Hamas/Palestinians positions	14	5	62	58	5
Ratio	2	4.2	1:2.58	1:3.41	1:5

Once again, of interest is not simply that the perspective of the liberal newspapers would be, broadly, critical of Israel or supportive of Hamas/ Palestinians, and the perspective of conservative newspapers the other way round. Rather, of interest is the extent to which these preferences became so polarized as to constitute a rigid *dichotomy*.

In the case of *The Times* and the *Independent*, they did so to a staggeringly large extent. *The Times* occasioned 4.2 times more often a broadly 'pro-Israel' perspective than a 'critical of Israel' one. As a mirror image to this, a broadly 'critical of Israel' perspective was occasioned 3.41 times more frequently in the *Independent* than a 'pro-Israel' one. In the *Telegraph*, the difference is somewhat less pronounced but still amounts to two in three utterances (in favour of the 'pro-Israel' perspective, of course). And at this stage, the relative balance previously perceived in the *Guardian* disappears too, with the papers' ratio of perspective becoming somewhat more polarized than that of the *Telegraph*.

The only exception is the *Financial Times*. We have already noted that the liberal newspaper showcased significantly fewer utterances of explicit criticism/support than any other paper. As Table 5.5 indicates, it also showcased a minuscule number of evaluative perspectives different from neutral. Thus, the *Financial Times* might be said to be interested far less in partisan affairs and a distinct *other* to agree or disagree with than any of the other broadsheets.

Other than this exception, however, the general perspective of the newspapers' coverage starts to display a categorical, either-or picture that was distinctly absent when 'building blocks' were investigated.

Yet, polarization is not merely detectable in the codes that featured in the sub-sample. There is clearly more to this story, and there is another crucial issue to be addressed here. It concerns the simple yet often neglected question of what the newspapers *did not* write about (cf. Billig, 1996, 1999; Richardson, 2007). What was it that was considered irrelevant, but that could, by common sense, have been relevant? And in what way may it be relevant for *us* what the British broadsheets neglected in their coverage? Critical mass, the topic of the previous subsection, is clearly of importance. The crux of the matter, however, may actually be found in the critical 'miss'.

Interpretation of (lack) of content: the fusion of perspectives

Hitherto overlooked, the generally polarized picture that the newspapers offered as far as explicit criticism is concerned is equally and powerfully expressed in the nearly complete lack of the value of *overlap*: that is, the fusion *of political-moral perspectives*. In terms of both 'agent' and 'position', only a very negligible number of utterances were coded as representing an overlap between categories, and taking into account the 'author's evaluative perspective', the picture became further polarized. Utterances were, overwhelmingly, either-or and as such offered no promise of dialogue between different political-moral perspectives.

At face value, this most certainly should not be so. Indeed, one may argue that the most plausible position to deploy in the context would be that of 'overlap': one does not have to be a zealot of any persuasion to criticize the policies of the State of Israel as well as those of Hamas. To repeat, the latter fired rockets to areas where their sole possible targets could be civilians. The former, for all the declared humanitarian intentions, killed hundreds of civilians within a couple of weeks. These positions are, of course, not outcomes of sustained legal-moral deliberations, merely plausible – yet perhaps the most plausible – starting points. Undoubtedly, though, they show that there *is* room for criticism there all round, much like there certainly is something to support regarding the predicament of the State of Israel and, at the very least, the Palestinian people.

Yet, according to the coding just reported, they have rarely been expressed simultaneously. What theoretically appear highly reasonable positions barely surfaced empirically in the data, in any given newspaper. How are we to account for this?

To better understand this state of affairs, it is timely now to have a closer look at the data. Doing this, the most plausible counterargument must be considered first. Namely, lack of overlap in positions/perspectives may simply be the artefact of the coding system that broke down articles and arguments to single units of meaning. Overlap may be difficult to be found in single utterances. It may, however, be detected if *sequences of utterances* (and their assorted codes) are examined. Thus, in what follows, rather than making calculations on the basis of coded utterances, both single utterances coded as 'overlap' and sequences of utterances that show the characteristics of 'overlap' between perspectives will be scrutinized.

Interestingly, the vast majority of cases of fusion of perspectives disappear immediately on closer scrutiny: either because they are essentially complementary positions (i.e., critical of Israel *and* supportive of Hamas/ Palestinians) or because accounting for the author's 'evaluative perspective' renders them so (i.e., synoptic perspective on a position supportive of Israel *and* critical perspective on a position supportive of Hamas/

Palestinians). These cases are, simply, 'overlaps' in a technical sense as opposed to offering some genuine fusion of perspectives.

Illustration for the first type of 'overlap' in a technical sense:

> Extract 5.1
> So where does the suspicion that he [Barack Obama] is a closet Israel-bashing, Palestinian-supporting peacenik come from? (*The Times*, 212)

Clearly, the overlap occurs between two values: critical of Israel and supportive of Palestinians. Yet is it a genuine overlap we encounter here? Surely not. Those supporting Palestinians may well be expected to be critical of Israel. The overlap exists, then, only in a very narrow technical sense.

Illustration for the second case (featuring very highly in the newspapers):

> Extract 5.2
> Once again, *Washington and Europe have opted to aid and abet the jailer*, occupier and aggressor, and to condemn its victims. We hoped Barack Obama would break with George Bush's disastrous legacy but his start is not encouraging. While he swiftly moved to denounce the Mumbai attacks, he remains tongue-tied after 10 days of slaughter in Gaza. But my people are not alone. *Millions of freedom-loving men and women stand by its struggle for justice and liberation* – witness daily protests against Israeli aggression, not only in the Arab and Islamic region, but worldwide. (*Guardian*, 523 – emphasis added)

The overlap between perspectives here is once again technical and clearly not genuine. It is just that there are two sets of agents: Washington, Europe and 'millions of freedom-loving men and women'. The latter are simply right (in being pro-Palestinian) whilst the former just wrong (in being pro-Israeli).[3]

There are, of course, somewhat more promising instances, if the aim is to find genuine overlap. Interestingly, in this respect, an exchange occurred in the *Guardian* where both authors exhibited a perspective that, on appearance at least, promised a genuine overlap and the potential for dialogue between political positions.

In a comment piece, writer and academic Colin Shindler disparaged the president of the *University College Union*, Sally Hunt, for what he perceived as bias in Hunt's response to the armed conflict:

Extract 5.3
We were shocked at the images coming out of Gaza, but outrage through Hunt's eyes is selective. Yet this negates any pretence at serious examination of a problem – the core of our educational raison d'etre.

As our statement concluded: 'As teachers of Israeli and Jewish studies to Israelis and Palestinians, Jews and Muslims at Soas, we cannot bury our heads in the sand in the belief that this issue is one-sided. We are a small minority at Soas, but our academic training tells us to look at narratives beyond our own opinions. This is why we have chosen to speak out and not to remain silent.' (*Guardian*, 603 – emphasis added)

Indeed, a genuine overlap of perspectives appears to emerge from Shindler's passage. Not only is the position on display that of an apparent overlap, the writer expresses 'selective outrage' (i.e., lack of overlap between political positions) as the negation of the mission of education. The passage in the article preceding Extract 5.3 may, however, be taken to alter this state of affairs:

Extract 5.4
While the Palestinians interpret disproportionality in terms of the powerful Israeli military machine pitted against the highly trained, 15,000-strong Hamas militias, the Israelis understand disproportionality in terms of the potential threat to their unarmed civilians from bigger missiles. Will proportionality only be achieved if a rocket hits an Israeli university building filled with students? (*Guardian*, 603)

Whilst these lines contain no explicit orientation to criticism, they are clearly phrased as counterarguments against the idea (critical of Israel) of 'disproportionality'. The overlap of positions is not visible in them as the interpretation of 'disproportionality' the author chooses to argue against is clearly risible. Whatever the correction to 'disproportionality' may mean, it certainly does not mean a wish for Hamas rockets to hit an Israeli university building. As such, Shindler's argument is not presented against a genuine opponent, and does not exhibit a genuine engagement with the 'other'. Rather, the reconstructed 'other' is either idiotic or downright malicious. Either way, space for reason and morality to 'overlap' with them is nigh on impossible. And if so, one may actually wonder what it was that induced Shindler's shock at 'the images coming out of Gaza'. Whilst human death and suffering, wherever and whenever they happen, is indeed shocking, the context Shindler depicts for those physical images certainly prevents one from being shocked in any political or moral sense.

What then, does Sally Hunt make of this criticism as to her perceived bias?

> Extract 5.5
> I have watched in horror as the violence, death and destruction have unfolded in Gaza over the last three weeks. I have also read and listened to the *accusations, counter-accusations and attempts by people on both sides to justify their actions or those of others*. (*Guardian*, 655 – emphasis added)

Once again, at face value, this passage conveys the impression of a genuine overlap between positions and a perspective where dialogue of different political-moral values may coexist. The last part of this passage expresses clear and general unease with the state of the debate otherwise. The UCU president expresses clear dissatisfaction with those taking part in the debate. Indeed, what we have here are not exactly reasonable attempts at debating important issues but either *ad hominem* arguments (i.e., accusations and counter-accusations) or interested rather than neutral positions (i.e., 'attempts by people ... to justify').

So what would the author herself offer in the place of this partisan debate? What alternative is conjured up out of the critical attitude towards the malicious and partisan form the 'debate' has taken and the ostensible 'opinions' or 'arguments' this 'debate' has on offer?

> Extract 5.6
> My personal view on the current situation is that rocket attacks on Israel have helped no one; and that the full-blown, targeted and continuous attacks on Gaza are killing any chance of dialogue with the death of every innocent man, woman and child. I strongly believe that education will be central to any chance of finding a lasting and just peace in the Middle East, and I fear that what is happening now is destroying that possibility, along with the educational infrastructure. (*Guardian*, 665)

This is how the author concludes her article, aiming to serve up the paragon of genuine 'overlap' with both sides being equally criticized here. A closer look, however, may punctuate this analytic assessment. First, whilst Israeli 'attacks' are described in some vivid detail ('full-blown, targeted and continuous'), Hamas rocket attacks are not conveyed with such intensity. Second, whilst the consequence of Israeli attacks is again detailed both in moral (i.e., they result in deaths of innocents) and political (i.e., killing any chance of dialogue) terms, Hamas rocket attacks are only described and disparaged in a vague term without clear reference (i.e., they have helped no one). Third and most crucially, whilst the outcomes of Israeli actions are clearly terrible in that they kill people and politics, the problem with Hamas actions simply is that they are *not helping*. This may still imply less than savoury, rather than neutral, consequences. But certainly not the intensity that incessantly threatening a civilian population does.

Thus, whilst both Hunt and Shindler attempted to position themselves as somewhere middle-of-the-road, neither of them quite succeeds. Though obviously less transparently than in the previous extracts cited, their contributions may still not be termed as genuine overlaps of positions or fusions of different yet equally reasonable political-moral perspectives. The actual arguments offered make subtle suggestions as to which 'side' they actually were on. As such, for all their efforts to suggest the contrary, their arguments remained little more than the rhetorical management of identity positions – and not the contemplation of genuine overlap of perspectives.

Moving on from occasions where overlap of positions is either downright technical/non-genuine or its ingenuousness may indeed be questioned when considering the overall stream of arguments on offer, let us now consider instances where *genuine* overlap of perspectives, and a balanced political-moral position, appears to occur.

> Extract 5.7
> To make sense of a conflict in which both sides claim to be victims requires more than an emotional response to gory pictures. *I support the Palestinian right to self-determination.*
>
> But *I am disturbed by the rise of anti-Israeli sentiments in Britain and the West*, as when my old friends on the Left declared: 'We are all Hezbollah now.' There is a tendency to reduce the Middle East to a simplistic morality play where Good battles Evil, projecting our own victim politics on to other people's complex conflicts. (*The Times*, 180 – emphasis added)

The writer of this passage follows up an apparently pro-Palestinian utterance with one that counters 'sentiments' critical of Israel. Thus, she offers the possibility of dialogue between different political-moral positions. The two statements professed, however, are not on the same level and not of the same significance. Not simply because a statement of principle is followed by an assertion on actual practice. More so, because the principle stated is a most mundane, most uncontroversial one. One consideration that united *all* the British newspapers was their uniform advocacy for a two-state solution. In this context, asserting that one indeed 'support[s] the Palestinian right to self-determination' amounts to little more than a banality.[4] Whilst the overlap may be understood to be genuine here, it is very difficult to argue that it occurs between *genuine* positions of moral/political gravitas: those who would not own up to the 'pro-Palestinian' position endorsed would be, again, either lunatic or malicious. Most certainly, they would be outcasts in newspapers that explicitly endorse the two-state solution.[5]

A somewhat similar instance occurred in the *Guardian*:

> Extract 5.8
> All those involved, and most of those following the bloodshed in Gaza from afar, are sure who is in the right and who is in the wrong. They know who the innocent victims are and who are the wicked perpetrators. These certainties are held equally firmly by those who will be demonstrating in solidarity with the Palestinians in London today and those who plan to stage similar shows of support for Israel later this month.
>
> Both sides see the conflict in moral terms. For supporters of the Palestinians, it could not be clearer. Israel is committing a war crime, killing people in their hundreds, hammering a besieged population from the sky (and soon perhaps on the ground too), claiming to aim only at Hamas but inevitably striking those civilians who get in the way.
>
> Israel's cheerleaders are just as clear. Israel is the victim, hitting out now only belatedly and in self-defence. Its southern citizens have sat terrorised in bomb shelters, fearing the random rockets of Hamas, since 2005, longer than any society could tolerate without fighting back. (*Guardian*, 482)

Regular *Guardian* columnist Jonathan Freedland's position is formed *in opposition* to precisely those who would subscribe to the either-or logic. By distancing himself both from 'Israel's cheerleaders' and 'supporters of Palestinians', he claims the middle ground as the position he himself represents. That middle ground, however, is a rather wide one. It is not achieved via a real overlap between political positions but via keeping an equal distance from them. Whilst it is clear that 'cheerleaders' or 'supporters' should have no role in reasoned discussion, no positive statement is encountered in the article as to what positions, indeed, should.[6]

Thus, in-depth examination of sequences promising a genuine overlap of politically, morally or even empirically genuine positions proved to be a rather curious exercise. The vast majority of the sequences turned out to exhibit an overlap only in a very narrow and technical sense (cf. Extracts 5.1 and 5.2). Yet even the handful of instances where genuine fusion of different political perspectives was seemingly on offer fell short of our expectations. In arguing for their position to be crossing over boundaries of partisanship and manifesting therefore a perspective of dialogue, they inevitably resorted to arguments which either, ultimately, supported one side or the other (Extracts 5.3 and 5.6) or were meaningless/too extreme to characterize any genuinely dialogical perspective where different yet reasonable positions can coexist (Extracts 5.7 and 5.8).

In fact, only one instance may be found in the entire sample of comment pieces where a genuine overlap appears to have occurred between two genuine positions. The column by former peace envoy Alvaro de Soto reads:

> Extract 5.9
> In September 2005 *the international community gave its tacit blessing to the participation of Hamas in the elections*. It is much more than simply a terrorist organisation; it is a grievance-based resistance movement that thrives on the continuation of Israeli occupation, and it has a wide and plural following. Hamas has become a formidable political player and it cannot be ignored in the search for peace.
>
> And yet *the international community has ignored it, undermined it and sidestepped it since its election to a majority in the Palestinian legislature.* Instead of seizing a rare opportunity to bring a militant movement into the mainstream, the international community disregarded their steps towards democratic rule and peaceful negotiations, punished the population in the hopes that they would oust their elected leaders and condoned Israeli policies of collective punishment. It should not surprise us that many in Hamas see no other recourse but continued armed struggle.
>
> ...
>
> *The methods that some Palestinian militants use, indiscriminate rocket attacks at civilians, however ineffective, are condemnable.* But as long as the plight of Palestinians in Gaza, who are refugees from what is now

> Israel, is not addressed convincingly, it is just not realistic to expect them to sit quietly while their neighbours in Israel lead normal lives. (*Independent*, 972 – emphasis added)

Three utterances engaging with criticism may be detected in this passage. The first two either endorse a position supportive of Hamas or distances itself from one that is critical. The third one critiques Hamas. Indicative of the state of affairs at our hands, of course, the ingenuousness of even this piece may be questioned. Whilst the author phrases the rocket attacks as indiscriminate (i.e., making no distinction between civilians and combatants) and condemns them as such, the alternative course of action envisaged for Hamas/Palestinians cannot be taken as a serious proposal of action: sitting quietly. That the options of a non-sovereign entity with no control of its borders and its development of military capacity are restrained in dealing with disputed questions with its neighbour is without a doubt. That the only alternative would be that of indiscriminate attacks against civilians which subsequently will be condemned by any reasonable person – is either highly questionable or at any rate would require further expanding.

Yet de Soto, whilst condemning the policies of the international community, condemns Hamas for what is a true crime against humanity. And, for the sake of humanity, his contribution will therefore feature here as an example of a (somewhat) genuine overlap between perspectives of political-moral ingenuity.

Discussion

Findings of previous chapters represented certain convergences and divergences in the way British quality newspapers reported on fatalities, action and historical context of the armed conflict in Gaza. Even where differences were found, these were mostly non-systematic, haphazard or downright counter-intuitive. And where differences of some tendency did appear to emerge (i.e., the broadsheets' coverage of historical context), they were still differences of degree rather than kind. The findings of this chapter, in turn, appear to suggest a growing polarization where issues of evaluation and criticism are concerned: not only did the daily newspapers systematically differ; they started to form rigid and incompatible ideological poles when covering explicit criticism and evaluation.

Not that their content appeared absolutely dichotomous at first sight. In each newspaper, agents adopting some position towards major actors in the conflict were overwhelmingly neutral. Issues of criticism and support were not simply an outcome of 'identity politics'. Those who spoke, spoke their *mind*. However, subsequent findings in themselves seemed to negate the somewhat naive assumption of the very possibility of treating anyone and anything with some stake in the conflict as *neutral* on some rather narrow, empirical ground.

For what happened as agents started to display a critical attitude towards Israel and supportive of Hamas/Palestinians *versus* those supportive of Israel and critical of Hamas/Palestinians; or as evaluations of such positions were engaged with? A progressively widening gap between the left-liberal and the conservative pole of newspapers became conspicuous. The conservative and the left-liberal newspapers (the *Independent* and *The Times* in the main, with the *Guardian* and the *Telegraph* somewhat less so) progressively appeared to converge towards two distinct and incommensurable poles, a dichotomy, where anything anathematic to their evaluative perspective became expressed with distance indicated from it.

Furthermore, the next to complete neglect of the value that by its nature would engage different arguments rather than set them even further apart – the value of 'overlap', that is, where the potential of dialogue is discernible between different political-moral perspectives – also contributed to this state of affairs. And when close reading examined instances that appeared to offer a genuine dialogue between different political-moral perspectives, it was found that such a promise simply disappeared in all but a minuscule part of the sub-sample. There was almost no place for presenting different, though more or less reasonable, perspectives as equally valid – let alone engaging one with the other. As far as criticism explicitly was concerned, someone almost always had to be plainly, simply, unequivocally right/wrong. Dialogue in such circumstances is obviously a non-possibility.

Such a conclusion may be catchy enough. Yet, as at the end of each of the preceding chapters, certain powerful caveats are in place here, too. First of all, numbers by their nature are relative creatures. What we can say on the basis of frequencies is that the *Independent* and *The Times* became more polarized in this sample than the *Guardian* and the *Telegraph*. What we cannot say is that any of these publications became polarized in some absolute sense. Further comparisons should be conducted with the newspapers engaging with other issues. Without this, we know neither whether this polarization is actually radical, nor whether this is specific to the question of Israel/Palestine.

Second, it is a valid counterargument that the very fashion in which the question of criticism was posed (i.e., *explicit* criticism), the way it was operationalized (i.e., breaking down articles in small units of meaning) may have heavily influenced the findings reported here. Indeed, a more implicit as well as holistic approach may detect genuine overlaps of genuine positions across the articles.[7]

Whilst both of these caveats are important and valid, their force may be discounted by the findings presented in the second half of the chapter. The purely qualitative investigation suggests two things. First, in terms of polarization, not a great deal of difference would be found with a more holistic approach either. Second, polarization is indeed a theoretically interesting issue, in that even in cases where overlap of perspectives was apparently present, closer scrutiny revealed that it was not quite genuine. The jury is out, nonetheless, and we shall see in the coming chapters whether the newspapers' engagements with war (where criticism will of course feature, though in a more implicit fashion) present us with a less polarized picture.

One more dilemma needs to be discussed, though, before such a venture starts. The reader may by now be disconcerted by this book's rather cavalier attitude to the question which, surely, is of the most importance: *truth*. Whatever their rights or wrongs, the arguments presented in the newspapers at least addressed this question. And whatever the rights or wrongs of the analysis presented in this book so far, it must appear cynical that it is this very question that has so far been completely sidestepped. For, by qualities of reason and morality, who the hell cares whether an 'overlap' is presented in arguments if, in any given question, someone is simply right? More generally, if Israel/Hamas is basically wrong, why should we engage with their arguments at all?

The dilemma of truth will be addressed in later chapters. Here, another manoeuvre of sidestepping will have to suffice.

For truth to be found, meaning has to exist. Human sentences, which may be evaluated for their truth or morality, must, first and foremost, mean something. The most frequently recurring content of the critical/supportive utterances occasioned by the authors analysed in this chapter concerned the idea of 'disproportionality' (cf. Extracts 5.4 and 5.5). Articles in conservative newspapers debated and ironized the idea, at least up to a certain point in time, during the war; liberal contributions powerfully asserted it. *Disproportionally,* of course.

Yet, one finds not a single instance in the *entire sample* where the meaning of 'disproportionality' is expressed with any kind of exactness. What, exactly, is 'disproportionate'? The force Israel uses? The number of people it kills? The combatants it kills? The civilians it kills? The ratio of the two? The ratio of how many Hamas kills versus how many Israel kills? The relationship between Israel's military objectives and the number of people it kills? Or those objectives and the number of civilians it kills? Or the disparity between Israeli humanitarian rhetoric and the consequences of its actions? Or, *horribile dictu*, the disparity between the intentions of Hamas and those of Israel?

These questions, the very questions that would make a claim for or against 'disproportionality' a *meaningful claim*, were virtually never engaged with during the discussions of the Gaza war. And whilst one may suggest that it might be due to the fact that the idea of 'disproportionality' is a consensual one (i.e., everyone knows what it means), the few occasions where it *did* actually get extrapolated quickly rejects this suggestion.

Let us remember the argument of Extract 5.4 from the *Guardian* where the author asked, 'Will proportionality only be achieved if a rocket hits an Israeli university building filled with students?' Or let us read the following treatise of 'disproportionality': 'Now, as with the Lebanon war, Israel's critics charge that its action in Gaza has been "disproportionate" – "proportionate", presumably, being a few home-made rockets fired into civilian areas of Gaza as and when' (*Independent*, 850).[8] 'Disproportionality' may, indeed, actually mean something and be used as a concept to evaluate events of political-moral purport (cf. Walzer, 2009a, 2009b). But it certainly cannot mean anything that is proposed above and cannot be used towards those ends. Thus, inasmuch as the reason for the lack of examination of the idea in the debates is that there is a consensus about it, empirical evidence appears to suggest that this consensus pertains to something that, here and now, means virtually nothing.

What this state of affairs indicates is that pure identity politics may take over arguments. The position of this book is, of course, not that identity as such should be eradicated from political-moral deliberations. Nor is it that whatever identity is drawn upon must somehow be stripped of emotions and material relations causing possible bias. The claim here is merely that when identity politics as such take over, and when ostensible arguments turn out to be not much more than reinforcements of one's identity and community, then we cannot really talk about politics or morality (Gutmann, 2003; Kymlicka, 1989).

At best, we can talk of a game. At worst, we can talk of war. Winning can still be important, but it has no genuine political-moral implications whatsoever.[9]

6
Engagements with Antisemitism

Introduction

As reviewed in Chapter 1, the meta-discourses of 'new antisemitism' and the 'anti-new antisemitism' have a very heavy investment in the status of the British broadsheets in disputes over Israel/Palestine. The arguments usually propose two distinct poles where conservative newspapers would support Israel whilst liberals would criticize Israel and support Palestinians (if not necessarily Hamas). In terms of such polarization, previous chapters offered some interesting insight. Namely, no extraordinary, black-and-white difference could be ascertained as concerned the coverage of fatalities and action in war in the British broadsheet. In terms of historical context, some pronounced divergences appeared to surface, yet they could still not be attributed to straightforward and categorical differences. Resemblance to the theoretical-ideological lines drawn between conservative and liberal newspapers was only detectable when examining explicit engagements with criticism. This concerned not simply the divergence towards poles where (advocates of) *either* Israelis *or* Palestinians/Hamas were right/wrong but the virtual impossibility of constructing acceptable positions in-between these black-and-white opposites.

It is against this background that this chapter will examine the question of how antisemitism was explicitly engaged with in the broadsheets. As such, utterances across the newspapers where reference was made to terms such as 'antisemit-', 'anti-Semit-' and 'anti-Jew-' will be scrutinized. Just as with criticism, then, the chapter promises not so much an engagement with antisemitism as such, only with instances where the issue becomes explicit. As with criticism, it is Chapters 7 and 8 that offer insights in the way of antisemitism 'between the lines'.

The fact of antisemitic incidents

Very few in number, the utterances explicitly engaging with antisemitism were rather divergent and addressed a variety of issues, from the antisemitism of Hamas to the shenanigans of the Vatican; from contemporary antisemitism to the act of judging something as antisemitic. It is the latter two aspects that will be analysed here.

Inasmuch as antisemitism was an explicit issue for the newspapers, the most significant part of their treatise, numerically, concerned the rise in Britain and Europe of antisemitic incidents during the conflict. Indeed, all articles *devoted in full* to antisemitism were written on this issue. At this level, no important difference can be found between the newspapers' coverage. They equally agreed that inasmuch as antisemitism was an issue at all, it was the rise in the number of actual antisemitic incidents in Britain/Europe that was worthy of attention.

Probing deeper into the data, however, reveals important variations. First of all, the *Independent on Sunday*'s coverage of the issue may be taken to stand out from the rest. In an article devoted in full to antisemitism, we read:

> Extract 6.1
> Israel's assault on Gaza has prompted a rise in anti-Semitic attacks in Britain, with more than 150 incidents reported by the Community Security Trust (CST), an organisation for the protection of Jews. But the past two weeks have also seen aggression by Jews towards those sympathetic to the plight of Gaza. (*Independent on Sunday*, 981)

The first sentence of this extract could have featured in any other publication. Nothing like the second ever did. It is unique that when talking about antisemitism (and its rise) as a matter of fact, the newspaper finds it important to mention that, when it comes to Israel/Palestine and Zionism, aggression against Jews is also perpetrated *by Jews*. Indeed, the headline of the article was 'British Jews attacked for pro-Gaza solidarity', with nearly half of the short item devoted exactly to this topic:

> Extract 6.2
> British Jews have been attacked for expressing support for Palestinians. Police confirmed yesterday that they have provided protection to a number of people believed to be victims of UK-based Zionist extremists. (*Independent on Sunday*, 981)

It is difficult to decipher the exact message that the *Independent on Sunday* wishes to convey. The two issues (antisemitic acts and *anti-Jewish* acts by 'Zionist extremists') are implicitly treated as being of equal significance since the newspaper devotes the same space to each. Yet this equivalence is never explicated: the specific number of general antisemitic incidents is cited, with no comparable numbers highlighted regarding the Jewish victims of 'Zionist extremists'. Therefore what is implied on the one hand is made irrelevant by the lack of explicit details on the other hand. This makes the coverage inconsistent and questionable as regards the actions of 'Zionist extremists'.

At the same time, it might be claimed that the article's intention is to convey the fragmented nature of the Jewish community. This is an important topic and seems worthy of coverage. It is indicative, though, that this fragmentation is also mentioned on one occasion in the *Guardian* – without any recourse to the aggression of 'Zionist extremists':

> Extract 6.3
> Opinions in the 250,000-strong Jewish community vary, from strong solidarity with Israel to vehement backing for the Palestinians, and many shades in between. This can be difficult for rabbis; some struggle to keep their congregations united. The Chief Rabbi, Sir Jonathan Sacks, has commented only briefly on the situation – by lending his support to a pro-Israel rally. (*Guardian*, 576)

All in all, then, the *Independent on Sunday*'s idiosyncratic divergence from the consensus on what exactly matters when talking about antisemitic incidents remains puzzling. It is doubtful whether the prevalence of Jewish anti-Jewish violence is a significant empirical issue. It is equally doubtful whether it is fortunate to report on important political-moral divisions within the Jewish community in the extreme terms of violence, as that violence is probably a rather marginal phenomenon. It is not just that the *Independent on Sunday* diverges from the newspapers' consensus; it is that it does so for no apparent reason other than sensationalism.

Yet the consensus between newspapers appears fragmented in other respects as well. To report, as they uniformly did, on the *fact* of the rise in antisemitic incidents does not mean that there is agreement as to *why* this fact occurred. In line with current debates on the 'new antisemitism', two distinct causes may be offered. Antisemitic incidents may occur simply because there is a latent antisemitism in British and European societies, with the armed conflict being merely an excuse to outpour existing animosities (Rosenfeld, 2006). Alternatively, incidents may occur precisely because of the armed conflict and with no significant component of underlying social prejudice (Finkelstein, 2005, p. 66; Lerman, 2003). European Jews here are merely the unfortunate victims of a vehemence directed in fact towards the State of Israel. To assess the newspapers' coverage of the topic, it is important to analyse where they stand on this continuum of explanations.

There is no explicit perspective of evaluation of the issues offered by any of the newspapers. Nonetheless, the way these events were reported reveals a range of implicit orientations.

One way to address this important issue is to sidestep it altogether. This occurred in the *Financial Times*: '[French Jewish groups] have recorded 60 anti-Semitic attacks or incidents of abuse in the three weeks since Israeli forces launched their offensive, almost three times the normal rate' (*Financial Times*, 1194). Here the connection is depicted simply as temporal. This thing happens, and then that thing happens, and we cannot really ascertain the causal connection 'this' has with 'that'.

Most often, however, the newspapers did imply some kind of causal connection when reporting the rise of incidents. One pole of the conceptual spectrum could be found occasioned in two surprising sources:

> Extract 6.4
> The Israeli offensive in Gaza has provoked a surge in anti-Semitic violence in Europe with attacks on Jewish sites in France, Belgium and Britain. (*Daily Telegraph*, 54)

> Extract 6.5
> Jewish groups said yesterday that the invasion of Gaza had provoked a surge in anti-Semitic intimidation and violence in London and Manchester. [...] Police said that the incident was believed to be a direct result of events in the Middle East. (*The Times*, 254)

It was some rather *unusual* suspects conveying the notion that 'anti-Semitic violence' may actually stem from distinctly a-Semitic, international political causes; it was the two conservative newspapers that aired this idea. Regarding its provenance, they made direct references to the objective authority of the 'police' and the subjective authority of 'Jewish groups'. Crucially, while the fact of violence and its 'anti-Semitic' nature was never put in question, the idea that it was a response to 'provocation' puts that violence into a curious perspective. While it certainly does not justify violent acts, it unequivocally puts the onus on the events in the Middle East as the main, or even exclusive, cause for them.

An even more striking formulation of the idea could also be found in *The Times*, again invoking the authority of the 'police':

Extract 6.6
As the Gaza death toll rises, police are increasingly concerned about the possibility of 'reprisal' attacks on Jewish people and buildings. (*The Times*, 268)

The violence here is constructed as '"reprisal" attacks' against Israeli action, and while the use of quotation marks indicates the perspective of the police rather than an undisputable fact, the suggestion nonetheless is that what are, objectively, anti-Jewish attacks actually derive from grievances against the State of Israel and not (necessarily) against Jews. The picture offered in the extracts of *The Times* and the *Daily Telegraph* puts the emphasis on the responsibility of Israeli action in bringing about anti-Jewish acts.

Granted, conceptual distinctions are certainly not this clear-cut. In fact, the occurrences of attacks against individual Jews when the assailant supposedly intends to attack representatives of the State of Israel demonstrate the empirically fragile nature of the conceptual distinction. The question is what mediates between motives against the policies of a state and actual acts against people officially unrelated to that state (i.e., non-citizens). Conceptually, a variety of factors may do so, and a variety of commitments may be responsible for being attuned to those factors. One can be an antisemite and implicate the Jews collectively for the perceived wrongs the Israeli state perpetrates. One can subscribe to some version of Zionism and identify the Jews collectively with Israel and conceive of them as quasi-citizens. One can, then, assume that while no official connection exists, European Jews predominantly endorse the relevant Israeli actions.[1] Yet inasmuch as newspapers engaged with the problem at all, accounts were offered from a different, and ultimately inconsequential, direction:

Extract 6.7
Jewish leaders and security services across Europe are worried that emotion over the Gaza conflict could cause anti-Semitic acts or attacks. (*The Times*, 254)

The simple idea here is that the 'emotion' over Gaza is intensive and it therefore causes people to do unreasonable things. Yet the question is why, precisely, sentiments of one kind would 'spill over' (cf. *Guardian*,

576; *Daily Telegraph*, 84; *The Times*, 286; *Independent on Sunday*, 981) to sentiments of a completely different kind.[2] Treating human beings as malfunctioning organisms will never answer what is at its heart a conceptual dilemma. The question is not about the mere intensity of the actions against European Jews but the supposed category mistake in conflating European Jews with the policymakers or (Jewish) constituents or prevailing ideology of the Israeli state.

Conceptually speaking, it was only in the *Guardian* that a broader horizon appeared to account for the dilemma as to why anti-Israeli sentiments transform into anti-Jewish acts in Europe in relevant conceptual terms. The left-liberal newspaper (alongside its sister publication, the *Observer*) gave voice to a line of argument that did not surface elsewhere in the sub-sample. Even though it occurred only in the form of quotations, as well as in a comment piece, it therefore represented an important opening up of the conceptual debate:

Extract 6.8
There is also concern that the wave of hostility is symptomatic of underlying antisemitism. Rabbi Herschel Gluck, from Hackney, believes people are looking for an excuse to attack Jewish people. 'These are not from people who care about Gaza, they want to vent their feelings,' he said. (*Guardian*, 576)

Extract 6.9
Others found the protest upsetting. Rabbi Dr Sidney Brichto of Liberal Judaism, a federation of liberal synagogues, said the march had been easy to organise 'because most of the demonstrators want more than a ceasefire. Most of these people want the end of Israel. Hamas are able to plug into latent anti-semitism in the West. It breaks my heart.' (*Observer*, 506)

Extract 6.10
I am resolutely, irreducibly British. I love Marmite and Labradors and Sunday lunch. If you step on my foot, I will reflexively apologise. New York, where I will go if I have to leave the UK, does not feel like home for me nor, I suspect, could it ever. But as the British establishment sides with the appeasing of Islamism at home and abroad and as the word Zionism is increasingly bastardised, hijacked by a new definition comprising traditional antisemitic libels and demonising conspiracy theories, and as the liberal media and campaigning groups single out Israel disproportionately among all other countries for

> criticism, perpetuating the myth that Israel is responsible for mushrooming anti-western sentiment, I feel increasingly that I cannot stay. (*Observer*, 584)

With these extracts, we have firmly arrived at the other pole of the spectrum of possible explanations of antisemitic incidents in Europe during the armed conflict. They represent the idea that alleged grievances over Gaza are but excuses. The real issue is antisemitism, only seeking some (any) alibi. *Why* there would be antisemitism in British or European society is an important question, of course, and is never addressed in these utterances. Yet the (near-exclusive) tendency to treat antisemitism as some purely irrational state of mind and thus without the need to explain its occurrence in terms other than personal pathology makes this question easy to ignore in practice. As such, the 'theory' of latent antisemitism is manifest in the discussions as the only fully-fledged political-moral *framework*. That is, the only framework of explanation which may be accepted (if, of course, one accepts it) with no practical need for further conceptual clarification.

To sum up, then, a number of conceptually important issues have been revealed regarding the newspapers' utilization/description of 'contemporary antisemitism'. First of all, we have seen that insofar as antisemitism was an explicit concern for newspapers, it was actual antisemitic incidents in Europe that were reported with the most significance, both concerning the total occurrences of explicit antisemitism and the full articles devoted to it.

Second, however, a partial exception to this 'rule' has been identified. Although the *Independent on Sunday* did publish an article, half of which concerned the rise in antisemitic incidents, its other half as well as the article's title occasioned a quite different and somewhat idiosyncratic form of anti-Jewish action: 'extreme Zionists' abusing Jews harbouring 'pro-Gaza' sentiments. Whilst the article successfully conveyed a conceptually important point worthy of debate – namely, that the Jewish community is far from united in its political-moral outlook – two problematic issues have been raised above about its coverage. The political-moral divisions within the Jewish community could certainly have been recorded without recourse to people committing violence against others. This may be considered a problem (not, of course, of antisemitism but of journalistic practice) in that, by awarding half the space in the article to 'Zionist extremists', the *Independent on Sunday* implies that the problem of this violence is roughly on the same level as the problem of violent attacks on Jews by non-Jews. This, however, was not explicitly warranted by the article, as the number of incidents was only cited in the case of general antisemitic incidents, and left blank in that of violence committed by 'Zionist extremists'. Whatever the reason for this, it makes the allocation of space and, crucially, the choice of the title, highly problematic journalistic practice in its portrayal of antisemitism and the Jewish community.

Third, a question was raised regarding the newspapers' orientation towards what might account for the rise in antisemitic incidents. As has been demonstrated, together with uniformly reporting on the fact of the rise in incidents (and treating them *as facts*), there was an equally uniform lack of explicit concern about its causes. It was virtually never treated as something that calls for reasoned explanation or reflection. Not surprisingly, then, what could be gathered from the newspapers regarding their implicit position on the issue varied considerably.

Beyond the variety of the accounts given, however, some important conceptual issues arose. Namely, it has hopefully become clear that the arguments that the antisemitic incidents are mainly a result of the Israeli state's 'provocation', or 'spill-overs' of animosity originally directed against the State of Israel and its actions, *never* in themselves suffice as explanations. They do not answer what is, at its core, a conceptual dilemma and a confusion of categories: why exactly would intentions against a state translate into actual actions against people with no official connection to that state.

Locating the cause in Israeli action ultimately raises the question as to whether these admittedly anti-Jewish acts are, in fact, acts of *antisemitism*. Indeed, it is on this very ground that some academic commentators associated with the political left explicitly deny that such incidents, directed towards European Jews, can be categorized as antisemitic.

However, *if* these acts were accepted to be antisemitic acts (and not simply acts against people who are Jewish), the only account that sufficed on conceptual terms was the one based on the presumption of some latent societal antisemitism. This is the idea that European societies continue to nurture an antisemitic attitude towards their Jewish population. In time of peace, these emotions are blocked by the shadows of European past. There is nothing, however, to stop them in times of crisis.

Antisemitism as dilemmatic: the social judgment of calling something/someone antisemitic

As mentioned previously, the connection between Hamas and antisemitism was mentioned in a number of paragraphs. Characteristically, the issue was treated as a matter of fact, even if its implications were certainly not glossed over.[3]

There was, however, one notable exception to this, in a comment piece written by *Independent* columnist Robert Fisk.

> Extract 6.11
> But watching the news shows, you'd think that history began yesterday, that a bunch of bearded anti-Semitic Islamist lunatics suddenly popped up in the slums of Gaza – a rubbish dump of destitute people of no origin – and began firing missiles into peace-loving, democratic Israel, only to meet with the righteous vengeance of the Israeli air force. The fact that the five sisters killed in Jabalya camp had grandparents who came from the very land whose more recent owners have now bombed them to death simply does not appear in the story. (*Independent*, 851)

If in the form of a rather over-the-top expression, Hamas's attribute in this extract once again establishes the organization's antisemitic nature. Yet, in the context of the extract, this is not presented as a fact. Rather, a *perspective* is explicitly invoked, that of the 'news shows', and it is this perspective which presents Hamas as 'a bunch of anti-Semitic Islamist lunatics suddenly [having] popped up in the slums of Gaza [...]'. While it is clear that some part of this statement is made relative in this utterance to the perspective of the 'news shows', it is not exactly clear which one. It can be the antisemitism of Hamas, thus implicitly questioning whether the movement is in fact antisemitic. But it can also be the fact that they *as antisemitic Islamist lunatics* have 'suddenly popped up in the slums of Gaza'. In this case, it is not Hamas's antisemitism and Islamism that would be implicitly problematized but the apparent irrationality and out-of-nothingness of these positions: even if they are antisemitic and Islamist and lunatic – this can still be for a historical reason.

The interpretation of the extract is therefore quite difficult and no final word of unquestionable validity can be said of it within the remits of this inquiry.[4] However, the reason this extract has been found to be important does not hinge on this question. Rather, the point is that it uses the rhetorical tool of 'distancing': indicating that the perspective of the article is taking a critical distance from that of the utterance/position reported. That is, it indicates that the position reported is coming from a certain perspective. As such, from a fact the existence of antisemitism at once becomes a dilemma:

Extract 6.12

B'Tselem's workers are threatened constantly. Each week the office switchboard receives insulting phone calls (normally accusations of anti-Semitism) and, about once a year, a credible enough threat of violence against the group that a complaint must be filed with the police. 'There's also the fact that you go to your nephew's bar mitzvah and people just come up to you and get in your face about the things B'Tselem does,' says Montell. 'You get used to it.' (*Sunday Telegraph*, 159)

Clearly, the distance indicated in this paragraph from a social judgment is of an evaluative nature. Antisemitism is explicitly described here as an 'accusation', not a 'report' or even a 'claim' or something formulated from a certain perspective. The newspaper's coverage makes it patently clear that B'Tselem is, of course, *not* antisemitic. Distancing is a rhetorical tool to make this state of affairs transparent for the reader.[5]

But this state of affairs has a further implication. If someone judges something antisemitic and if that judgment is presented as counter-factual, then the question may arise as to *who* those people may be accusing B'Tselem of antisemitism and *why* they may do so. Likewise, *why* do the news shows in Extract 6.11 present Hamas as 'a bunch of bearded anti-Semitic Islamist lunatics [having] suddenly popped up in the slums of Gaza'? The more factuality becomes denied, the more the question becomes relevant: why would anyone present empirical untruths as facts?

Conceptually, people's opinions can be counter-factual for a variety of reasons. They can simply be misguided and lacking information; they can be downright irrational; they can then be malicious and disingenuously advancing suspicious agendas (cf. Hirsh, 2010); but they can also be expressions of genuine differences from alternative but equally arguable political/moral perspectives or, simply, understandable emotions and fears. It is of interest to explore which of these subject positions are attributed to those social agents whose judgment of something as antisemitic is indicated to be dilemmatic.

Extract 6.13

After a week of bombings, Israel launched an invasion. All the while, Israel's protector in chief – the US – looked on silently, swallowing the myth that Israel was just another ordinary country responding to terrorist attacks. Israel is not an ordinary country: it is built by children of Holocaust survivors, forcing themselves on Arab land over Palestinian dead bodies.

Saying the above is not antisemitic. I received emails and phone calls from extreme Zionists, and public attacks from fanatics such as Melanie Phillips, for daring to question Israeli actions. Many urged me to calm Muslim anger, but why should I? If this does not make me and other Muslims angry, then what could? (*Observer*, 583)

When the author of this extract classes his stance as 'not anti-Semitic', he expresses it as fact and not personal opinion. But who are the people implied, here, to claim otherwise? They are 'extreme Zionists' and 'fanatics' who 'attack' the author. The difference of opinions certainly cannot simply stem from lack of information, with the alternative positions' irrationalism already implied by their designation (especially in that of 'fanatic'). What is more, to brand someone antisemitic merely for 'daring to question Israeli actions' is certainly not setting the bar too high. It is a thoughtless and wholly unreasonable practice. Thus, the perspective of judgment can in no way be assessed as genuine or arguable. It is just wrong as regards questions of knowledge and politics, as well as, quite possibly, morality.

Yet it still remains a question whether these people are malicious or just misguided by their flawed irrational ideologies. It is still possible that these people, however irrational they may be, are not simply *bad*. That is, they do not choose a wrong political-moral position from suspicious motives. To use Hannah Arendt's term, they may still be *banal* in opting for evil (Arendt, 1994, 2003, pp. 17–189).

While this matter is not explicitly settled in the extract above, in the majority of articles it is:

Extract 6.14

As so often in the tragic history of Palestine, the victims were blamed for their own misfortunes. Israel's propaganda machine persistently purveyed the notion that the Palestinians are terrorists, that they reject coexistence with the Jewish state, that their nationalism is little more than antisemitism, that Hamas is just a bunch of religious fanatics and that Islam is incompatible with democracy. But the simple truth is that the Palestinian people are a normal people with normal aspirations. They are no better but they are no worse than any other national group. What they aspire to, above all, is a piece of land to call their own on which to live in freedom and dignity. (*Guardian*, 544)

As can be seen, this comment piece once again counters someone's judgment of antisemitism in the noble name of 'truth'. It is simply *not* the case that Palestinians are terrorists, antisemites, and religious fanatics. The established fact that they are not is not just the 'truth' but a 'simple truth': no sophistication or special moral rectitude is required to recognize it. Yet if this is so, the social actor pronouncing that flawed judgment becomes the object of scrutiny. And, indeed, the source of the judgment is explicitly indicated: 'Israel's propaganda machine'. The author does not acquaint the reader with the epistemological, political or moral status of this social agent. We do not really learn how the judgment of the 'propaganda machine' went so radically wrong. But then, of course, the very designation may be taken to contain the account itself. 'Propaganda machines', after all, are not commonly known for being interested in reality for its own sake. All they care about is the political objectives of their masters and the subsequent *misinformation* of the people. It is not by chance that the judgment on antisemitism went wrong, then. It went wrong by design.

This position was pushed to the extreme by the *Independent* columnist Robert Fisk.[6]

> Extract 6.15
> Twelve years earlier, another Israeli helicopter attacked an ambulance carrying civilians from a neighbouring village – again after they were ordered to leave by Israel – and killed three children and two women. The Israelis claimed that a Hizbollah fighter was in the ambulance. It was untrue. I covered all these atrocities, I investigated them all, talked to the survivors. So did a number of my colleagues. Our fate, of course, was that most slanderous of libels: we were accused of being anti-Semitic.
>
> And I write the following without the slightest doubt: we'll hear all these scandalous fabrications again. We'll have the Hamas-to-blame lie – heaven knows, there is enough to blame them for without adding this crime – and we may well have the bodies-from-the-cemetery lie and we'll almost certainly have the Hamas-was-in-the-UN-school lie and we will very definitely have the anti-Semitism lie. (*Independent*, 918; cf. 851, 862, 912)

Arguably, these paragraphs convey the most extreme expression of someone's 'misjudgement' of antisemitism. Not simply is it an opinion or even untrue, but categorized unequivocally as a 'libel' and a 'lie'. The reason that people mistake antisemitism for the lack of it is that they are motivated by ulterior and suspicious motives. The distortion of reality is not a side-effect of the judgment but its very purpose: they misjudge precisely in order to distort reality, accuse other people, and destroy the credentials journalists must retain so that they are believed. The judgment is not simply wrong in factual terms but is *intended to be wrong* for no other purpose than smearing other people.

While reporting antisemitism as a fact is one end of the spectrum where the relationship of facts and opinions is concerned, the extracts in the present section showcased not so much various steps as a sudden and almighty jump towards the other pole of the spectrum. Intriguingly, as the perspective of social judgment and thereby the political-moral position of the other emerged in earnest, from a fact antisemitism immediately became not just an explicit outcome of a judgment and not just a dilemma, but an unambiguously *invalid description of the situation concerned*. And correspondingly, as 'antisemitism' changed from a factual truth to a rhetorical accomplishment, the perspective of its enunciator changed from the locus of neutral observation (a non-person, that is) to that of fanaticism (at *best*) or malice (at worst).

Discussion

Mimicking the overall course of this book and foreshadowing things to come in the final empirical chapters, this chapter covered a journey from consensus to radical dissensus. The British broadsheets', quantitatively speaking, rather limited engagement with antisemitism started with broad agreement as to the factual nature of a growing number of antisemitic incidents during the war. And it finished with cases where the factuality of antisemitism was firmly denied and the perspective of those claiming antisemitism thoroughly undermined.

Inevitably, where many stakeholders pronounce their opinions in a fragmented social space, issues become dilemmatic. As people of many different backgrounds, histories, and political outlooks start to debate it, antisemitism will be such a dilemmatic issue. Much as we would like an issue of such gravitas to be unambiguous, there is no surprise if antisemitism becomes a matter of contestation. Yet columnists here did not simply problematize or interrogate others' judgment as to the antisemitic nature of an event/person. They immediately pronounced a judgment to the contrary. There was no time for debate and no space for argument.

Inevitably, disagreement calls for an account. Differences of opinion not only entail our version of the events to be established, but to explain why others might have come to a faulty conclusion. During this exercise, as mentioned above, a variety of positions could be alluded to: people may mistake antisemitism for the lack of it because they are misinformed/misguided, irrational, intent on distorting reality for some suspicious ulterior reason, or subscribe to their (wrong) opinion for some genuine and understandable reason. Utterances in this chapter made some use of the explanation in terms of 'irrationality'. The overwhelming majority of them, however, attributed differences of opinion to the existence of vicious and *malicious agendas* on the other side (cf. Hirsh, 2010). The counter-factual nature of opinions on antisemitism *never* led to the desire to either enlighten or educate those opinions, let alone to understand them. It was never a question of why others' judgments were faulty, as commentators already knew why faulty judgments were made and the source of those judgments further erased the space where debating or understanding others' positions might occur.

It appears, then, that moving beyond the surface, radical differences between perspectives exist when it comes to the British broadsheets' engagement with the armed conflict of Gaza. In Chapter 5, overlaps and thus possible dialogue between different political viewpoints could never be established. In Chapter 6, the legitimacy and genuine nature of the other's perspective was consistently undermined. A radical schism prevailed in both cases, where something or someone was wrong and had simply to be blamed. And something or someone was just right and had to be completely innocent. There were no shades in-between. This is how the battle becomes a sporting contest between entrenched ideological positions and beliefs. Indeed, this is how it becomes a battle where the opinion of the other is not simply invalid but is not conceivable as an outcome of genuine convictions.

A full analysis needs to account for these perspectives and the phenomena of radical disjuncture between fact and opinion, right and wrong, genuineness and malice. It is these issues that we shall continue to examine in the final two empirical chapters of this book. They will concern narratives and arguments about the most fundamental political, moral and legal aspects of the armed conflict: when to launch war, and how to conduct it?

7
War – Purity of Arms and Souls in the Conservative Press

Introduction

The two empirical chapters to conclude this book will move closer to what may be at the heart of the matter. Chapters 2, 3 and 4 concerned explicit textual occurrences and addressed them at their numerical face value. Though Chapters 5 and 6 offered some interpretative analysis concerning the implications of utterances, it was still explicit textual occurrences that were addressed. The current as well as the following chapter, in turn, will take an exclusively interpretative orientation to the analysis of narratives and arguments the editorials of conservative and liberal newspapers utilized to account for the armed conflict of Gaza. That is, this chapter will aim to understand *political-moral perspectives*.

As we will see, the concepts investigated previously will reappear in this examination. We will thus encounter death, rockets, war crimes, the Israeli occupation, white phosphorous and the likes again. Similarly, we will encounter the activity of criticism. And, who knows, we may even encounter antisemitism. Yet, in distinction from previous chapters, they will make their appearance couched in arguments and narratives. As we shall see, the primacy of the perspectives newspapers offered in tackling dilemmas of the armed conflict will not only be built of the concepts encountered in previous chapters. Rather, it is as much from the light of these perspectives that these supposed 'building blocks' (i.e., fatalities, events, occupation) will ultimately acquire their meaning. As such, this analysis will have the potential to subvert findings of the quantitative analysis on facts and on historical events.

The ultimate result of any war is death. And the ultimate question therefore is whether death could have been evaded or at least minimized. What the newspapers' political-moral perspectives will therefore be concerned with are the two enormous dilemmas of war: *ius ad bellum* (law to war) and *ius in bello* (law in war). As such, the newspapers' perspectives here will address the questions hitherto ignored by this report: they will be concerned with the ultimate issues of rights and wrongs when humans die.[1]

The right to launch the war

War carries with itself a number of political, moral and legal dilemmas that ultimately decide the meaning and interpretation of the war. The foremost question pertains to whether war was a right choice to answer a situation, whether its launching can be justified. What was it that brought war into being? This can be *casus belli* (cause of war) as traditionally understood; that is, the act or sequence of acts that is directly responsible for the war. Equally, however, causes of the war may be understood in a broader sense, pertaining to a variety of factors that contribute to the outbreak of war, without necessarily directly, in themselves, causing it.

In the conservative newspapers' account of the armed conflict, a clear *casus belli* was detectable, suggesting a direct link between certain actions and the fact that war eventually had broken out.

> Extract 7.1
> The first reaction of most commentators was that the air attacks on Gaza were unnecessarily savage. The deaths of nearly 300 Palestinians, including civilians, seems disproportionate to the small number of Israelis killed by rocket attacks. Hamas was not expecting retribution on this scale, but we can be sure that it will extract the maximum possible propaganda advantage from the slaughter. Israel's enemies in the liberal West are already pinning the blame squarely on 'Zionists'. So are most Muslims.
>
> But, before we jump to conclusions, we should pay close attention to the response of Mahmoud Abbas, chairman of the Palestinian National Authority. He blamed Hamas for triggering the Israeli raids by not extending its truce. His Fatah party is engaged in a vicious feud with Hamas, so this is perhaps what one would expect him to say. But he is right, none the less. Hamas did engineer this crisis,

by firing rockets whose range has been increased so they can reach southern Israeli cities. (*Daily Telegraph*, 7)

Extract 7.2
After eight days of rocket attacks from Gaza the Palestinian group Hamas seemed to have left Israel with little choice but to retaliate. On Saturday it did so, launching one of the deadliest series of air assaults in the history of the 60-year-old conflict. As a result, innocent lives are being destroyed. (*The Times*, 187)

As can be seen, in the conservative narrative of the war, it was the Hamas rockets that constituted the *casus belli*. They are the events accountable for war. Indeed, in the *Telegraph*, rockets are constructed as the events without which the war would simply have not taken place (*sine qua non*): not just acts that reasonably justify the launching of the war but acts that causally 'trigger[ed]' the war (Extract 7.1).[2] The sequence between rockets and war is a straightforward stimulus-response relation. Indeed, in this account, Israel did not even make the *right choice* but had in effect no choice at all but to launch the offensive. As such, its conduct is not so much politically or morally justified, but simply beyond political-moral deliberation.[3]

Inasmuch as the rockets are accountable for the war or, indeed, 'triggered' it, our task is then to learn more about them. What are they? Where do they come from? What damage do they cause? And why are they fired in the first place?

In the extracts above, the description of rockets advances in a number of rather interesting ways. On the one hand, we learn of some general qualities of the rockets, Extract 7.1 stating that their 'range has increased' and Extract 7.2 asserting the temporal immediacy of rocket fire. The implication of both extracts is that whatever rockets and in whatever number had in the past been fired, *these* rockets now represent a growing immediate danger. The rocket fire was also occasioned in later editorials, pointing out either their immediate number ('[a]t least 70 such rockets were launched from Gaza into Israel in December ... ' [*The Times*, 278]) or their general prevalence ('8,000 rockets have been fired at their territory in recent years' [*Daily Telegraph*, 17]).

On the other hand, we may wonder what these rockets achieve and what the specific damage is that they cause. Curiously, this issue is, by and large, neglected in the conservative publications. They are somehow of no interest. Indeed the *Telegraph*'s first paragraph on the war explicitly states that only a 'small number of Israelis [were] killed by rocket attacks'. At face value, this state of affairs is most counter-intuitive. If rockets 'triggered' the war nearly automatically, one would expect them to have caused considerable damage. This, in the conservative account, has not happened. But this does not appear to be problematic for the conservative account either. How can this be so?

Another element of the construction of the rockets in Extract 7.1 is 'Hamas… triggering the Israeli raids by not extending its truce'. Thus, whilst we do not learn much from the conservative newspapers about the consequences of the rockets and, indeed, what we do learn about Israeli deaths is explicitly tagged as an apparently 'small number', we are also informed that rockets had not been fired all the time. There is a pattern in which they are (or are not) fired, and this pattern may depend on certain factors unaccounted for. This may open up the relevance of questions such as *why* rockets are fired in the first place – and why is it that they ceased to be fired, if only temporarily?

However, ceasefire or 'truce' for both conservative newspapers is interesting not because it indicates a period of relative peace. In *The Times*, we read of an 'uneasy six-month truce between the two sides' having been 'unravelled' (*The Times*, 187) and a 'nominal ceasefire, which expired on December 19, [that] was always less than scrupulously observed' (*The Times*, 244). The significance of the ceasefire is thereby thoroughly undermined. If it had been 'uneasy' and 'was always less than scrupulously observed', then it may be perceived as a ceasefire in nothing but name. The fact that rockets may not be fired during a period, and people may not be destroyed, loses its significance considerably if rockets are still fired and the danger to humans is still present during that period nonetheless.[4]

Moreover, the only agent accountable for the end of this insignificant ceasefire was Hamas. In the account of the *Telegraph* (see Extract 7.1) as well as *The Sunday Times*[5], it broke down due to unilateral action by Hamas. What is common in both cases is that the State of Israel has no role in the ceasefire coming to an end. The only agent made accountable by the conservative press for the end of the ceasefire – and, thus, for the fact that rockets are fired again by Hamas in huge quantities – is Hamas.[6]

Thus, it is Hamas and only Hamas whose characteristics explain, in the conservative press, why the rockets are fired at Israel, and what the motivation is behind these acts that trigger the war. It will therefore be the conservative construction of Hamas that will shed light on the seemingly puzzling feature of why even a 'small number' of deaths justifiably and inevitably cause war.

In line with this, the *Telegraph* devotes ample space to the question. And, given that the factor of virtually sole direct responsibility for the outbreak of the war is Hamas, such attributes are painted in unexpected colours.

> Extract 7.3
> Only one group of people can have derived any satisfaction from the footage of blood-covered children being pulled from the rubble in Gaza: the fanatics of Hamas. This terrorist organisation has been firing rockets into Israel ever since the breakdown of the ceasefire, in the hope of provoking a furious Israeli response. And that is precisely what materialised. (*Daily Telegraph*, 7)

Though the explicit term used to describe Hamas in the extract above is 'fanatics', the picture arising arguably is one of perverts, relishing in the destruction of their own people. The force behind the rockets thus aims not even, simply, to cause harm to Israel or Israeli citizens. Hamas is not simply a terrorist organization, but one that is downright suicidal to the very Palestinian lives and interests they claim to represent.

Other descriptions of Hamas in the initial account of the *Telegraph* offer a similarly dark picture. As in Extract 7.3, we learn that Hamas 'is not a reasonable political movement. It cannot thrive without crisis; the blood of innocents is its own lifeblood. These are not Palestinian nationalists who happen to be Muslims; they are totalitarian Islamists whose Palestinian identity is of secondary importance. They have nothing but contempt for Arab Muslim states' (*Daily Telegraph*, 7); that it is determined 'to wipe out Israel – and, eventually, every secular Arab state' (ibid., 7); that its leaders are 'anti-Semitic' (ibid., 17) and its members 'religious fanatics' (ibid., 7) who hate not only the Israeli state but 'Jews' as such (ibid., 7).

Thus, rockets are not fired by any political actor but by an essentially unreasonable, immoral and, shall we say, *evil* actor. The attributes above are constructed as belonging to Hamas *per se*. It is not that Hamas *does* fanatical, terrorist, totalitarian acts. They *are* fanatics, terrorists and totalitarian Islamists. Presenting these certainly less than desirable characteristics as characteristics of a people (of Hamas) rather than characteristics of a people's actions suggests, in the absence of any attributes to the contrary, the essential, immutable and homogeneous nature of these features in what constitutes Hamas. Such a depiction of humans evidently makes it impossible to *engage* with them in any other form than destruction/containment. Indeed, any attempt at engagement is implicitly ruled out either as idiotic or immoral. Where there is a complete lack of reason and an overwhelming presence of destruction, there is no one to be argued with or to be convinced.

Such a state of affairs has a number of implications.

First, what makes the specifics of the rockets fired by Hamas virtually irrelevant is that their meaning is defined by the pure intention with which they were fired. The material damage they cause notwithstanding, they carry the message of evil. They carry the *motive* of their source in *intending to kill civilians, and only civilians.*[7]

Second, Hamas, as the source from which the meaning of the rockets derives is not just an entity that does undesirable things. It is, homogeneously and essentially, a destructive and evil entity. If rockets carry the message of pure hate in themselves, it is because Hamas *is* that very hate, directly intending to kill civilians and only civilians. Not as a strategy, but as such.

Third, inasmuch as Hamas embodies an unalterable essence, no other factor than this essence may have a constitutive impact on its identity/acts. Hamas does not have a history, an evolution, or a future that can be engaged with and influenced externally. It does not have internal divisions of any significance. Its actions may not be explained or understood by recourse to external factors either. Any Israeli action simply loses its relevance as to what Hamas is and what it does.

It is this construction, rather than the simple material reality of rockets, that leaves Israel without any other choice than waging a war. Negotiation with an entity that by its nature speaks not the language of humans is impossible, deluded or dangerous. Likewise, the timing of the war may be linked to the proximal cause of increased prevalence/range of rockets. It may look 'better' or more justified in the eyes of the international community when there are more rockets. Yet the prevalence of rockets is not conditional on Hamas's dark intention, only on its actual capability to fire them. There is no such moment in time when Hamas would not want to fire rockets. There are only times when, due to external constraints or internal tactics/strategy, they do not fire them. And by the same token, there is no moment in time when war is not justified against evil. There are only times when, due to external constraints or internal tactics/strategy, it can be better sold to people that do not quite understand the nature of Israel's enemy.

Correspondingly, though the *Telegraph* often alluded to the moral/legal principle of Israel's right to defend its citizens, fighting evil gives a broad mandate in interpreting 'defence' or 'protection'. Indeed, the newspaper wrote that '[t]he Israelis seem to have decided on an all-out offensive against Hamas, because while the Iranian-backed militia holds sway in Gaza there is no hope of progress' (*Daily Telegraph*, 17). As evil is without boundaries, fighting evil too may only happen without boundaries. And as the evil of Hamas is the ultimate cause of this war, Israel is not simply blameless in launching it and conducting it in ways it sees fit – it is *role-less* and beyond the remit of political-moral-legal criticism.

This, then, was the *Telegraph*'s account of why war is happening. It was not, however, that of the conservative press as such. Facing the question of law to war, beyond certain similarities, there also are certain points where the accounts of the *Telegraph* and *The Times* appear to diverge, and, at face value, significantly so. Indeed, an important difference may be spotted even at their point of departure. Whilst the *Telegraph* occasioned the phrase 'triggering the war' (see Extract 7.1) in explaining the rockets' role and supporting its argument as to Israel's lack of choice, *The Times* only mentioned that Israel had 'little choice' (Extract 7.2). 'Little choice', of course, may mean in practice no choice at all. But, seemingly at least, it certainly leaves room for the freedom of choice and, as such, political-moral deliberations regarding how that freedom was exercised.

As has been seen above, we do not learn much of the actual consequences of the rockets. In the *Telegraph*, this was accounted for by their construction of the evil nature of Hamas and how it is the organization's antisemitic and destructive urge that fills the rockets with meaning. Interestingly, however, the first two editorials of *The Times* are completely devoid of the descriptions that the *Telegraph* occasioned in regard to Hamas. In fact, not only is the *Telegraph*'s vivid construction of Hamas absent, but an alternative perspective is presented. Namely, in none of the editorials the *Telegraph* devoted to the war do we find any reference to the Israeli occupation or the blockade. The reason for this is clear, for inasmuch as Hamas constitutes the manifestation of an evil and destructive *essence*, no external factor needs to be accountable for its conduct. *The Times*, however, offers a rather different perspective:

> Extract 7.4
> The latest tragedy is the outcome of a vicious cycle that has gripped Gaza since Hamas seized full control of the territory from the more moderate, secular Palestinian Fatah movement in June 2007. Israel tightened its blockade as a result, and has been demanding that Hamas cease its rocket attacks. Hamas vowed to continue them until Israel opened the border and stopped retaliating. (*The Times*, 187)

A number of points are interesting here. First of all, Hamas, whilst not being the paragon of evil, is certainly not depicted in positive terms here. They seized the control of Gaza off Fatah in what may be described as a 'civil war', and they fired rockets at Israel. Second, however, at least part of their *present* rocket-fire may be accounted for by an external factor: Israel 'tighten[ing] its blockade'. The full meaning of the 'vicious cycle' becomes clear where, for Israelis, the blockade is the indication of their strong expectation of Hamas not stopping the rocket-fire; and, for Hamas, the *very reason for doing so*. Obviously, we do not learn whether Hamas would have really stopped the rockets if 'Israel [had] opened the border'. But as no other account is given for the Hamas rocket-fire than the implied effect of Israel's blockade and its 'tightened...blockade', we cannot exclude this possibility.

Indeed, the next paragraph asserts that following the 'unravelling' of the 'uneasy six-month truce', 'Israel has tightened its control of the border, permitting only the intermittent delivery of humanitarian supplies.' (*The Times*, 187) That is, Israel did something that had already been known to lead to rocket-fire. It may not have been the cause of it, but its conduct most certainly did not help.

The editorial continues in a similar vein:

> Extract 7.5
> Both the Israelis and Palestinians have failed in Gaza. The Israelis had hoped to make life intolerable for Hamas, intending either that it would reform and start to co-operate, or that the people of Gaza would decide that they had had enough of their Government. Neither has happened. On the contrary, the bold words of Hamas leaders suggest that they have found renewed strength through the conflict. In their turn, the Palestinians have claimed to want peace. But they have been only occasional partners in the peace process, and sometimes openly hostile. (*The Times*, 187)

The position constructed for Hamas in this extract is, once again, not a black-and-white one. On the one hand, the editorial asserts that the Palestinians have been 'only occasional partners in the peace process, and sometimes openly hostile'. What the general category ('the Palestinians') may imply is that it is quite possibly Hamas that actually is *the* element that has been 'openly hostile' and not the one that has been 'occasional partner in the peace process'. On the other hand, whatever Hamas is and does now is not simply coming from its veins. We learn that 'Israelis had hoped to make life intolerable for Hamas, intending either that it would reform and start to co-operate, or that the people of Gaza would decide that they had had enough of their Government'; an understandable intention and an arguable political strategy in itself. But not with the consequences Israelis would have hoped for: 'Neither has happened. On the contrary, the bold words of Hamas leaders suggest that they have found renewed strength through the conflict.' For what happened did not just defy Israeli intentions. It actually went against them as it ended up bolstering Hamas's 'bold words' and lead to its 'renewed strength through the conflict'.

Thus, *The Times*'s early engagement with the war is rather different from that of the *Telegraph*. In terms of launching the war, there is some room implicitly constructed for Israeli choice and deliberation rather than a stimulus-response mechanics. Accordingly, Hamas is not depicted in the colours of evil. More importantly, it is not depicted as merely *acting out an essence*. Israeli actions were shown as being, to some extent, constitutive of Hamas's conduct and identity; certainly not creating either of these as such, but still contributing to them.

At face value, these are absolutely crucial differences between the accounts of the *Telegraph* and *The Times*. The former left no room for Israeli deliberations and freedom of action in launching the war, and, consequently, for political-moral criticism of those deliberations and that action; the latter's construction of Israeli action as partly constitutive of Hamas and its rockets suggests that Israelis *did have* a 'little choice'. If blockade means rockets and if the tightening of blockade means even more rockets, then, in the absence of information to the contrary, there is a real possibility that *no blockade* would mean *no rockets*.

Up to this point, *The Times* has not explicitly reached this conclusion, and we still do not know what exactly 'little choice' means as far as the launching of the war is concerned. Likewise, we do not know what the possibilities of practical alternatives were. In fact, we do not even explicitly learn that there *were* alternatives. The conclusion as to the possibility of the lifting of the blockade resulting in the end of rocket-fire is never reached. And the six-month ceasefire that was 'uneasy' certainly does not straightforwardly suggest that an alternative course of action was available for Israel.

In any case, the *Telegraph* has so far excluded free choice and corresponding criticism of choices made on the basis of Hamas's identity. *The Times* suggested some freedom in Israel's act but alternative courses of action were not explicitly pondered; just as it opened room for possible criticism but did not exercise that criticism, or even refer to explicit acts of criticism. These questions will be further engaged with as we enter the arena where the question is not whether Israel had the right to launch the war but whether it was right in doing so.

Being right in launching the war

What needs to be further examined, then, is whether there is substantial difference between the *Telegraph* and *The Times*: between a description of Hamas as acting out an evil essence versus a version where Hamas is acting *partly* in correspondence with Israeli action and *being*; Israel's 'no choice' versus 'little choice'; categorically outlawing criticism of Israel's choice to launch war versus practically allowing it or even implying it. This will be done here by incorporating the question of whether Israel *was right* in launching the war into the question hitherto engaged with: whether Israel *had a right* to launch the war. The two questions are obviously related to each other as a war's likely or potential outcome influences decisions about whether to launch it in the first place.

The question regarding the consequences of war was attended to by the *Telegraph*. As we encountered above, the newspaper's first paragraphs on the war read:

> Extract 7.1 (see above)
> The first reaction of most commentators was that the air attacks on Gaza were unnecessarily savage. The deaths of nearly 300 Palestinians, including civilians, seems disproportionate to the small number of Israelis killed by rocket attacks. Hamas was not expecting retribution on this scale, but we can be sure that it will extract the maximum possible propaganda advantage from the slaughter. Israel's enemies in the liberal West are already pinning the blame squarely on 'Zionists'. So are most Muslims.
>
> But, before we jump to conclusions, we should pay close attention to the response of Mahmoud Abbas, chairman of the Palestinian National Authority. He blamed Hamas for triggering the Israeli raids by not extending its truce. His Fatah party is engaged in a vicious feud with Hamas, so this is perhaps what one would expect him to say. But he is right, none the less. Hamas did engineer this crisis, by firing rockets whose range has been increased so they can reach southern Israeli cities. (*Daily Telegraph*, 7)

The problematic consequence occasioned by the newspaper as a matter of fact is that '[t]he deaths of nearly 300 Palestinians, including civilians, seems disproportionate to the small number of Israelis killed by rocket attacks.' This is then countered by the argument we have already encountered. The 'Israeli raids' are 'triggered' by Hamas rockets. Given that this account comes from the territory of *ius ad bellum*, the implication at this point is, simply: *c'est la guerre*. If war is justified, this, unfortunately, still does not mean that people will not die. Many people, perhaps, if the enemy one is fighting is an evil one and if, accordingly, even narrowly understood defensive measures may actually include an 'all-out attack'.[8]

However, the interesting part of this passage is not so much this. It is the presence of an alternative argument. We read that, through certain eyes, the war may be evaluated rather differently. It may be seen as 'disproportionate' and 'unnecessarily savage'. Whose are those eyes? Are they to be taken seriously?

It is of note here that these judgments of Israeli action are 'first reaction[s]'. What is implied therefore is that they may not stem from reasoned political-moral deliberations and careful assessments of rights or wrongs, but indicate an instinctive response to the scenes. As such, rather than being relied on or argued with as judgments, they may be taken to be indicative of *dispositions* of people.

Who are those people, then, that immediately brand Israel's efforts 'unnecessarily savage' and, possibly, 'disproportionate'? In the first line of the passage, the seemingly neutral category of 'commentators' surfaces. Later on, however, two further categories are introduced. They are not related explicitly to those immediate and instinctive 'response[s]'. But they offer an explanation for the events and as such it may be surmised that they would also agree with the judgments ('disproportionate', 'unnecessarily savage') that the *Telegraph* occasions as belonging to 'commentators'.

It is 'Israel's enemies in the liberal West' as well as 'most Muslims' that propose an account for the events. They pin the blame 'squarely on '"Zionists"'. The *Telegraph* uses scare quotes to display this group of people. No wonder. This war was launched and is conducted by the Israeli Defense Forces, on the instructions of the Israeli government with a democratic mandate as well as the actual support of sizeable segments of Israeli society. Political-moral responsibility may belong to them. And, most certainly, they would consider themselves to be Zionists. But so would millions of people living outside of Israel – with certainly no direct political-moral responsibility for the events. Those on the 'liberal West' as well as the 'many Muslims' could make this distinction clear, but they do not.

As the newspaper offers no further detail on the position of 'Israel's enemies in the liberal West' and 'most Muslims', one can only hypothesize as to why they resort to blaming a far larger category than those with actual and direct political-moral responsibility. It may be that it is a community subscribing to an *idea* that they want to discredit. But even in that case, the upshot of their act is either the implication of many, many Zionists who opposed the war, *or* the wholesale blackening of this idea: it somehow being inherent in the idea of Zionism that it will lead to a 'disproportionate' ratio of killing. And if both of these basically unaccountable explanations are possible, then one should not rule it out either that at the core of putting 'blame squarely on "Zionists"' is a motive to blacken not an idea but an *ethnic-religious community*. It may be this community that 'Israel's enemies in the liberal West' and 'most Muslims' want to collectively and unjustly implicate in the 'disproportionate' death of 300 people.

Thus, the *Telegraph*'s unhesitating support of Israel's right to launch the war extended to the dilemma of whether in fact Israel was right in launching the war. As war was presented as stemming not so much from the right political-moral choice but from a natural necessity beyond the realm of politics and morality, the question of its outcome simply could not be engaged with. As a result, those critics who did engage with it could only be categorically wrong – to the extent that they were not simply misguided or misinformed, but immoral and, quite possibly, antisemitic. Lack of critical engagement, in this construction at least, thus became lack of antisemitism.

Let us turn now to *The Times*, however, and see what the possibilities of criticism were in an account where, in theory, there *was* room for criticism.

Just as the construction of Israel's choice was different in *The Times* than in the *Telegraph*, it also offered what were at face value different arguments in regard to whether war is the right choice of action. The subtitle of the newspaper's first editorial read 'Israel had little choice but to respond to the Hamas attacks. But its deadly action shatters hopes for the already battered Middle East peace plan'. What is foreshadowed here is that the consequence of war, with its inevitable implication of causing death, may not prove to be fruitful, politically and morally speaking. It does not just destroy lives right now – more than that, it carries with it the destruction of lives in the future by destroying chances of peace.[9] Such an argument is further extended, later in the editorial, to Israel *itself*: 'Israeli leaders must consider whether their country's security would really come from more bloodshed' (*The Times*, 187). War, thus, may be impractical and deadly in the longer term not just as regards the geographical area and its inhabitants, but even as regards the interests of the State of Israel itself.

The newspaper's second editorial appears to continue in a similar vein:

> Extract 7.6
> Israel is entitled to defend its civilians against rocket attacks, but its military options are constrained and shrewd diplomacy would serve its interests. (*The Times*, 202)

Alongside the assertion of Israel's moral-legal right to defend its citizens, the subtitle occasions the dilemma[10] of actually following up that course of action. What is the dilemma? And what would the alternative course of action – 'shrewd diplomacy' – entail?

As to the first question, we read the following:

> Extract 7.7
> If Israel persists with an aerial campaign, then the very success of its actions so far will have diminished the number of military targets and increased the risk to civilians. Israel has a right to defend itself but criticism from some European governments that disproportionate force is being used might soon become more persuasive in these circumstances. The use of ground troops would be risky, owing to the inevitable casualties that Israel would suffer. (*The Times*, 202)

We read about two dilemmas here. The 'criticism of European government that disproportionate force is being used' is not an argument about *law in war,* as it may only become persuasive (if it does at all) in the future. The fact that a ground operation may result in Israeli casualties does not concern *law concerning war* at all. It is a practical consideration regarding Israel's interest. The course of argumentation of the first editorial with the shadow of the long-term damage to the peace process being a distinct possibility disappears from *The Times'* argument. In fact, it is something absolutely different that we encounter concerning long-term peace:

> Extract 7.8
> Preventing Hamas's attacks should hasten withdrawal from the West Bank and enhance the prospects for the eventual creation, as justice and equity demand, of a sovereign Palestinian state. (*The Times*, 202)

Whilst in the beginning the war was just but potentially tragic and impractical, as it actually becomes tragic, it now also starts to offer the prospect of very real practical benefits – for Palestinians themselves. The loss of 'innocent lives' (*The Times*, 187), when actualized, does not any more threaten to break down the peace process. It promotes it in fact and, as such, is in the very interest of the Palestinian people currently in danger of dying. As can be seen, then, it is not just that growing concerns do not lead to stronger critical arguments. They actually lead to the *muting* of originally critical arguments and to the *enhanced* expression of support as far as Israeli conduct is concerned.

Correspondingly, it is the following that we read about the 'shrewd diplomacy', mentioned in the subtitle of the editorial:

> Extract 7.9
> There are two ways in which politics might be brought to bear on this conflict. Pressure by an intermediary – possibly Egypt, or Tony Blair in his capacity as Middle East envoy – on Hamas to announce a ceasefire, and Israel to respond, is necessary. But it will be a temporary palliative, even if successful, while Hamas's rejectionist aims are unchanged. An armed conspiracy must be confronted. But – as the remarkable turn in the fortunes of Iraq this year suggests – it can also be undermined by shrewd diplomacy. Israel should reiterate willingness to move speedily to a territorial accommodation, even with a Hamas led government, conditional on a permanent abandonment of violence. (*The Times*, 202)

There are two crucial points to be made here. First, though Hamas is obviously still not depicted in terms witnessed in the *Telegraph* (e.g., 'rejectionist aims'; 'armed conspiracy'), 'shrewd diplomacy', practically speaking, does not involve negotiations. In fact, the spectre of negotiations is useful only in that they may *'undermine'* Hamas. Whether this is because of the 'rejectionist aim' that Hamas stands for and the ideas that may lead to those 'rejectionist aims', or because of the group as such, is not clear. But, in any case, Hamas at this stage is not an agent to engage with but, in one way or another, to be eliminated. The points of *contact* made relevant in the first editorial disappear by the time of the second.[11]

Second, the proposed 'shrewd diplomacy' of Extract 7.9 refers to the time *after the war*. The juxtaposition in the article's subtitle and starting sentence between the principle of Israel's right to defend itself and the practical suggestion of exercising 'shrewd diplomacy' thereby turns out not to refer to alternative courses of action.

This way, the potential for criticism of Israel's decision to launch the war is never followed up. *The Times* does occasion problems arising from the war: threat to long-term peace, and 'disproportional' conduct. But given that the first outcome refers to the distant future and the second to *law in war*, neither of these challenges the principle that Israel has a right to defend itself. For it is only a present and realistic alternative course of action that could do so, and it is only from the perspective of an existing reasonable alternative that the act of starting a war could be the subject of political-moral deliberation. As no such thing is presented, criticism becomes, practically speaking, impossible. And the concept of 'little choice' equally becomes, to all intents and purposes, the equivalent of no choice at all.

From the perspective of *law to war*, then, the apparently substantial differences between the two conservative newspapers ultimately disappear. Israel's 'choice' of starting a war remain not so much justified as uncontested.

This is theoretically so in the *Telegraph*, where the construction of Hamas meant that Israel was acting like an object of nature. To subject it to criticism is, therefore, either an act of lunacy (for who would criticize Newton's apple for falling down?) or an act of malice bordering on racism (for it is not an apple that is an object of criticism but a people). And it is practically so in *The Times*, where the possibility of acts of criticism residing in the notion of 'little choice' and the set of allusions that launching the war may not have been the right course of action to pursue never eventually got followed up, examining the possibility of Israel's pursuing alternative courses of reasonable action.

As a result, the decision of launching the war, regardless of its deadly consequences being either taken for granted (*Telegraph*) or posed as a problem (*The Times*), remained uncontested in the conservative press without subjecting it to political-moral deliberation. Israel thereby became not just right in making the choice, but even without responsibility in the proceedings.

The right conduct of war

Challenges to any piece of discourse may arise from inside or outside, with the boundary itself between the two being sometimes fuzzy and ever (wo) men-made. As we saw in the previous section, in the case of conservative newspapers challenges to the conception of a war (basically induced by the intentions of Hamas, where Israel was left with no choice) rarely surfaced from the inside, especially in the case of the *Daily Telegraph*. As Israel acted as an object of nature, all other issues of potential relevance could be sidestepped or presented as being of no direct relevance.

Indeed, even potential or actual consequences of the war were initially attended to from such a framework. The *Telegraph*, whilst obviously not cheering on the death of civilians, adopted the implied shrug of the shoulder in the position of *c'est la guerre*[12], coupled with the presentation of a counterargument as stemming from immoral sources. *The Times*, whilst expressing strong doubts about the future outcome of a predicted course of destruction of 'innocent civilians', did not find these concerns important enough to undermine its ultimate argument about the inevitability of war.

As war soldiers on, however, arguments about *law to war* may become less pertinent and simply must be replaced by proper consideration of *law in war*. The question of why so many (civilian) people die may not possibly be countered by events that happened *before* the war. If problems arise *during* the war, new arguments may have to be marshalled.

This is exactly what happened in the case of conservative newspapers. In fact, both the *Daily Telegraph* and *The Times* seemed to have reached a turning point in their support of the war. To examine how this was reached and what sort of arguments it brought forward is to understand how they faced a challenge to their discourse, one that did not simply emerge in encountering arguments of rival newspapers or unreasonable 'others', but in witnessing what they understood as facts on the ground and as gravely problematic aspects of the (previously not so much blameless but role-less[13]) Israel's conduct of war.

Thus, in its final two editorials, the *Daily Telegraph* announced:

> Extract 7.10
> At this sombre juncture, there is no point glossing over the mounting concern felt by Israel's friends. Eight days of ceaseless air strikes have taken a fearful toll on Gaza's Palestinian population. At least 485 have died, with the United Nations suggesting that about a quarter were innocent civilians. Meanwhile, four Israelis have been killed by rockets fired from inside Gaza. These missile attacks on the harmless inhabitants of southern Israel are reprehensible, but the fact remains that the response is beginning to appear disproportionate.... That means minimising the ordeal of ordinary Palestinians. Above all, it means finishing the defensive job and leaving Gaza quickly. (*Daily Telegraph*, 43)

> Extract 7.11
> When Israel began its assault on Gaza a fortnight ago, we made the point that much of the responsibility lay with Hamas. It has fired thousands of rockets into Israeli territory in recent years, apparently with the intention of provoking the very response that has reduced buildings and villages in Gaza to rubble. In reaction, Israel has exercised its legitimate right to self-defence and to destroy the military power of Hamas. But there comes a point beyond which an operation of this sort becomes counter-productive and morally unjustifiable. And now we have reached that point. (*Daily Telegraph*, 76)

As the *Telegraph* explicitly asserts in these extracts, while arguments about *law to war* are still pertinent and should not be forgotten, a situation developing *in a war* requires novel considerations. The first extract states that the response is 'beginning to appear disproportionate' and the second duly concludes that the operation became 'counter-productive and moral unjustifiable'. In short, Israel's mandate for the war has expired due to the 'fearful toll' its attack took on the Palestinians and the ratio of 'innocent civilians'. A course of action that the newspaper has been supporting and justifying must come to end, and an agent previously beyond the realm of political-moral deliberations and criticism must now be scrutinized.

Given that, in broad terms, the newspaper turns from a supportive position to a critical one as far as Israel is concerned, it is interesting to see just how this turn is accomplished. Whereas there is no need to account for action that is justified, acts seen as 'morally unjustifiable' clearly need to be explained, especially as the newspaper has, up until that point, supported the agent responsible. What went wrong? Why did an initially just enterprise become immoral? And what does this unsavoury state of affairs reveal about the previously blame/role-less agent of Israel?

The passages above exhibit some rather remarkable characteristics. It is of interest, of course, that precisely at the point when Israel's conduct first becomes questionable and then downright 'morally unjustifiable', the *Telegraph* announces itself to be a 'friend of Israel'. The relationship between the writer and its object of writing becomes an *affiliation*. Not that this relationship may be based completely on irrational motives of attachment. Common accounts for a special relationship with Israel usually feature reason and/or morality: Israel is often constructed to be the outpost of the democratic West in the Middle East; its existence and practices are often praised as morally just enterprises. Besides, the newspaper explicitly announces that Israel 'cannot assume its friends' support indefinitely' (*Daily Telegraph*, 43), implying that this support is not a simple emotional one but is predicated on the actual conduct of the state.

Yet, the consequence of the *Telegraph*'s declaration of support *when* the activities of its object of support become problematic is that *what matters* is still Israel. Let us note that the first term the newspaper uses to classify the development of the war is 'counter-productive'. Inasmuch as the focus is on this concept, what matters in the first place is not simply that innocent civilians are dying or why they are dying but that this may be a bad outcome *for Israel*. From the perspective of 'counter-productivity', if the death of innocent civilians was good for Israel, it would not be an issue. Thus, the conventional discourse of morality where innocent civilians' dying is wrong in principle[14] is complemented by a pragmatic discourse where it is only wrong *inasmuch* as it is not in Israel's interest. Indeed, as expressed elsewhere in the editorial, '[i]f Israel appears to ignore the suffering of ordinary Palestinians, its enemies benefit' (*Daily Telegraph*, 76).[15]

The function of this juxtaposition may become clear from a paragraph in the *Telegraph*'s final editorial:

> Extract 7.12
> The humanitarian crisis in Gaza is so severe that a ceasefire is essential, irrespective of whether Israel feels it has achieved its military objectives. It goes without saying that there will always be civilian casualties in urban warfare; but the deaths of hundreds of people, including scores of children, cannot be countenanced. Israeli army commanders have clear-cut obligations under international law to ensure that civilian casualties are kept to a minimum; and those obligations are binding even if civilians are being used as human shields by unscrupulous Hamas fighters. It cannot be right to seek to protect the innocent victims of southern Israel by the killing of the innocents of Gaza. (*Daily Telegraph*, 76)

The situation in Gaza is categorized as a 'humanitarian crisis' and, as such, it calls for an account. This account looks, within the terms of the *Telegraph*, extraordinary: though it features an extension of the paper's argument for the war in pointing out Hamas's suicidal acts, it quickly turns to Israel's responsibility. Doing this, it occasions the universal, 'clear-cut' and 'binding' obligations of international law. Yet it is the following sentence that presents the conclusion about the application or the possible non-application of these principles: 'It cannot be right to seek to protect the innocent victims of southern Israel by the killing of the innocents of Gaza.'

At face value, 'killing of the innocents' is, of course, the exact transgression of the universal proscription. At face value, those who kill the innocents may commit war crimes. Yet, counter-intuitively perhaps, this is precisely what the sentence *does not* mean. For if established and acknowledged universal principles are transgressed, then this moral/legal transgression (or the possibility of thereof) is not a possibility but a fact. Thus, to say that killing innocents 'cannot be right' *cannot be right*. What must be said, if universal principles are invoked, is that 'protecting the innocent victims of southern Israel by the killing innocents *is not right*'. In fact, wrong.

So, in contradiction to what it appeared to communicate at face value, the reference point of the sentence is not moral or legal, but practical. It means that in protecting our 'innocents' it is not useful to kill theirs.

How is this conclusion about the *Telegraph*'s constant juxtaposition between morality and practicality/self-interest relevant to the question of Israel's responsibility? And to the dilemma of why an originally morally right act went wrong?

The paragraphs of the *Telegraph* quoted above provide no explicit answer. But inasmuch as whatever is going on is 'counter-productive' and, actually, harms Israel's very own interests, it can be concluded that all Israelis are doing is making *mistakes*. No one, after all, would knowingly harm their own interests. If the enterprise had gone wrong, it must have gone wrong accidentally. The focus on Israel's interest therefore does not so much rule out any accounts for Israel's questionable conduct of war other than mistakes (say, potential misconduct). It makes them *psychologically impossible*.[16]

The very idea of political-moral deliberations regarding Israel's conduct is ignored, if not, again, impossible. What the Israeli army is doing in Gaza is bad, but, somehow, without the possibility of some implication that *that* army, on this occasion, may be bad or even politically-morally accountable. This way, the *Telegraph* still sustains its basic perspective where the conduct of the State of Israel is beyond the realm of political-moral criticism. Of sole accountability for war is either Hamas or pure human mistakes.

Let us now turn to the coverage of *The Times* and its account of the 'turning point'. As has been noted at the end of the previous section, the conservative newspapers' construction of the war showed substantial similarities as concerned Israel's basic right to launch the war and its lack of choice in doing so. Yet it also showed apparently substantial divergences as regarded the practical consequences of the war that Israel had launched and the *theoretical possibility* of critiquing Israel for launching it. In short, beyond the basic consensus, whilst the early coverage of the *Telegraph* was characterized by complete and unconditional support of Israel's conduct, the same could not be said of *The Times'*. *The Times'* coverage already expressed doubts as well as featured elements of a broader historical-political context as constitutive in part of Hamas's actions and identity. As that perspective was, relatively speaking, more critical, it will certainly be interesting to see how this vein of criticism developed in *The Times'* later coverage of the war: in a phase which even the *Telegraph* found problematic.

Indeed, *The Times* appears to continue its subsequent coverage in a similarly critical fashion. As could be seen in Extract 7.7, the argument that something might be going wrong with Israel's conduct had already surfaced in their second editorial. Yet that ('criticism from some European governments that disproportionate force is being used might soon become more persuasive') was nothing in comparison to the grave problems pinpointed in the newspaper's third and fourth editorials:

> Extract 7.13
> The pictures do not lie. Laser-guided but blind to the distinction between fighter and civilian, Israeli bombs have reduced schools, apartment blocks and police parade grounds to visions of hell. Aid workers and relatives have removed bodies and pieces of bodies, and survivors too traumatised to talk. On Boxing Day: at least 50 cadets killed at Gaza City's main police station alone. On Monday: reports, not denied by Israel, of phosphorus shells used over civilian neighbourhoods. On Tuesday: 40 children and teachers found dead in the wreckage of a school. And yesterday: reports of up to 30 more children killed in a house to which Israeli troops had moved them for their own safety.
>
> For all Israel's claims to have launched only targeted strikes on Hamas targets, it has shown scant concern for civilians caught in Gaza's crossfire in the past two weeks. (*The Times*, 278)

> Extract 7.14
> Eleven days ago *The Times* reported that Israel appeared to be using white phosphorus shells over built-up areas of Gaza. Since then, Israeli spokesmen and women have issued a series of increasingly forlorn denials as the number of Palestinian deaths in Gaza has passed 1,000

> and many of the injured have been treated for burns caused, apparently, by white phosphorus.
>
> It is time to clear the air. (*The Times*, 331)

These are, without a doubt, enormously strong words. They do not simply describe a tragic scene or 'disproportionate' action. They also imply some account for it. Extract 7.13 finishes with the assertion that Israel 'has shown scant concern for civilians'; Extract 7.14 raises the possibility that white phosphorous is being used in 'built-up areas'. White phosphorous not only featured in subsequent inquiries into the war as a possible war crime (cf. Amnesty International, 2009, pp. 27–36; Goldstone Report, 2011, pp. 140–143; Human Rights Watch, 2009; Operation in Gaza, 2009, pp. 145–151), but is characterized in the next paragraph of *The Times* itself as 'illegal'. Thus, what is raised is not simply concerns about facts on the ground, as in the *Telegraph*, but also the *intentions* that may be responsible for those facts. This is a potentially explosive topic, given *The Times*' reluctant (if ultimately unconditional) early support of Israel's war.

So how does the newspaper continue tackling the issue that an agent that it supported in terms of *ius ad bellum* shows 'scant concern for civilians' and uses a weapon forbidden to be used in 'built-up areas' in terms of *ius in bello*? How does the newspaper deal with the implications of morality (i.e., that the Israeli conduct of war may be unjust) as well as the spectre of legal accountability (i.e., that there may be war crimes committed)? In short, how does *The Times* attend to the prospect that what went wrong may not entirely be against the intentions of the Israeli state?

> Extract 7.13 continues
>
> Yet this is as nothing next to the contempt shown by Hamas.
>
> Unlike the IDF, they deliberately target civilians with their own rockets. At least 70 such rockets were launched from Gaza into Israel in December. This was the criminal act that *triggered* the current crisis; every time that bewildered Gazans are corralled by Hamas fighters into a human shield, it is compounded by rank cowardice. (*The Times*, 278 – emphasis added)

> Extract 7.14 continues
>
> It is time to clear the air. Israel has a right to defend itself, and the nature of its enemy makes that task extraordinarily hard. Hamas, like Hezbollah in southern Lebanon, regards the use of civilians as human

> shields as a central plank of its strategy for tormenting Israel. Like its principal state sponsor, Iran, Hamas's rallying cry is not the creation of a Palestinian state but the destruction of the Jewish one. This is why, when a ceasefire ended last month with an onslaught of Hamas rockets aimed at civilian Israeli targets, Israel had no choice but to prosecute this war. But the need to strike back does not excuse the mistakes that Israel has made in doing so. (*The Times*, 331)

As we see, the possibility of Israel's moral/legal responsibility is directly followed up in both cases by arguments about *ius ad bellum*. Not, however, by the arguments the newspaper presented in its earlier editorials. The Israeli conduct is juxtaposed by that of Hamas's evil nature and the organization's ensuing *triggering* of the war in the first place.[17] This shift of argument is predicated on the same factor as it was in the *Telegraph*: Hamas's evil nature. From *The Times'* extracts emerge not only the kind of vivid descriptions that were absent in the newspaper's first editorials, but we also start to read that Hamas 'promote[s] a nihilistic doctrine of self-defence through terror, and to foster a delusional pan-Islamism with no tolerance for unbelievers, let alone a Jewish state' (*The Times*, 278); that its 'rallying cry is not the creation of a Palestinian state but the destruction of the Jewish one' (*The Times*, 331); and that it is *'defined'* by its *'dread of peace'* (*The Times*, 331 – emphasis added). Just as in the *Telegraph*, portraying an entity as essentially evil leaves no room for a perspective from which what Hamas does or is may partly be constituted by Israeli action.

This means that the perspective *The Times* initially presented has completely disappeared. Israel's 'little choice' turns out to be no choice at all. As a consequence, the possibility of being wrong in launching the war, even if having the right to launch it, disappears, too. Retrospectively, criticism of the action Israel took in launching the war is now also outlawed in *theory*, not simply ignored in practice.

That the essentially evil nature of Hamas and the resulting absolute justification of Israel's starting of the war appears, and that criticism of Israel regarding *law in war* becomes illegitimate in *The Times'* argument precisely at the point when very grave doubts about Israel's particular conduct of this war are aired, is a remarkable thing indeed. However, it is not just that *The Times* retroactively presents war and Israel's decision to launch it as justified or even beyond the need of justification. The characteristics of Hamas that had directly led to war become extended so that they influence considerations of law in war as well. As we read, some or many or most 'bewildered Gazans are corralled by Hamas fighters into a human shield' and Hamas 'regards the use of civilians as human shields as a central plank of its strategy for tormenting Israel'. Interestingly, then, not only does Hamas *retroactively* become solely responsible for the war, but it is also responsible for the tragedies arising from the war. And this, to repeat, at the precise point when *The Times* started to query Israel's conduct of the war.

However, what is of even more interest here is that learning how inhuman Hamas is even towards its own population does not in itself explain why *Israelis* show 'scant concern for civilians' or use weapons in precisely those physical surroundings where their use is 'illegal'.

To be sure, *The Times* does offer an explanation following one of the extracts above. What was implied by the *Telegraph* is made explicit here: Israelis are guilty of 'mistakes', with the notion further explicated by the newspaper:

> Extract 7.15
> The dreadful death toll from 20 days of fighting points to three possible conclusions about Israel's methods and intentions: first, that the Israel Defense Forces (IDF) are guilty of woeful failures of execution, not least the shelling of a UN aid distribution centre in Gaza City; second, that despite years of meticulous intelligence gathering on the Hamas threat, the IDF have committed needless tactical errors in fighting it; or, third, that Israel actually intends to send a message that it is willing to incur international opprobrium for the bloodshed in Gaza if that is the price of breaking the will of Hamas and the Palestinians of Gaza who suffer under its rule.
>
> The first two conclusions are broadly accurate.
>
> The third is not. (*The Times*, 331)

'Mistakes', then, include 'woeful failures of execution' and 'needless tactical errors'. But not intentional wrongs. Essentially, whilst *The Times*' logic in questions of war was ultimately characterized by the juxtaposition of an intentional moral wrong (Hamas launching rockets and being evil) versus an intentional moral right (Israel's right to defend itself), it now becomes a question of an intentional moral wrong (Hamas being evil as well using civilians as human shields) versus an accidental wrong (Israel makes mistakes).

Yet the problem is, once again, that whilst such an account would have fitted the coverage of the *Telegraph* and its concerns with the death toll, it simply cannot do for *The Times*' argument. For what *The Times* originally topicalized (see Extracts 7.13, 7.14 and 7.15) was not simply facts and events but *accounts for them implying Israeli intentions*. 'Showing scant concern' for civilian lives is not an accident and not a mistake. And the pervasive use of white phosphorous in built-up areas is, arguably, not a 'failure of execution' or a 'tactical error'. In contrast to the account of the *Telegraph*, what needs to be explained here is not the simple fact that many people die, but the specific (lack of) *circumspection* with which Israel conducts the war and the specific methods it uses – both of which in itself *imply that many civilians may die.*

Either for this or for any other reason, *The Times* does engage with these questions as we read on:

> Extract 7.15 continues
> The first two conclusions are broadly accurate.
>
> The third is not. Israelis grieve as all humans do for the children cut down in Gaza's maelstrom, and their leaders know full well the damage that this conflict is doing to the country's reputation, especially where images of Palestinian suffering are broadcast more as propaganda than news. (*The Times*, 331)

As can be seen, the question of Israeli *intention* in causing or at least contributing significantly to the 'dreadful death toll' is explicitly raised here. And flatly denied. The argument offered is twofold.

The first is moral-existential: 'Israelis grieve as all humans do for the children cut down in Gaza's maelstrom'. Being human, Israelis' intention is not to kill children (and, presumably, civilians). Other than making a noble assumption about what constitutes human beings, the utterance has another implication. Namely, if all humans grieve as children die, then adherents of Hamas (who, to remember, fire rockets indiscriminately towards Israeli civilians and use their own people as human shields) are *not* human. This much has, of course, been implied in previous depictions of the organization. To find it in a passage explicitly tackling the dilemma of Israeli intention is, nonetheless, rather remarkable.

The second argument to dismiss possible inferences about malevolent Israeli intentions is pragmatic: 'Their leaders know full well the damage that this conflict is doing to the country's reputation, especially where images of Palestinian suffering are broadcast more as propaganda than news.' Just as in the *Telegraph*, the counterargument is that killing civilians does not serve Israeli self-interest and that the leaders of the country are aware of this. Why does it not serve Israeli self-interest? Presumably, because the Western world supports it *inasmuch as* it confirms the

Western world's political-moral standards. Whether this exhausts the full arsenal of reasons that may motivate Israeli leaders in making decisions about how and whom to kill is left unexplored. What is attended to is, instead, what aggravates the world's negative reception as it witnesses the 'dreadful death-toll': 'Palestinian suffering [broadcasted] more as propaganda than news.' That is, Palestinian suffering or the 'dreadful death toll' is simply a tool in unworthy hands. Those that bang on about them use them more as propaganda than news. This undefined 'broadcast' cares therefore not so much about Palestinians. Some other evil motives may lurk behind some of the coverage of the conflict. Thus, just as the moral-existential answer, the pragmatic answer to the interrogation of the responsibility of Israeli intention concludes not simply in the defence of Israeli intentions but in the implication of other dark forces. Hamas there; 'broadcast' of some suspicious motivation here.

This, then, is the argument of *The Times* as to how an agent showing 'scant concern for civilian lives' somehow still remains without substantial moral or legal responsibility as far as civilian deaths are concerned. Like the *Telegraph, The Times* too reaches a conclusion where malevolent Israeli intentions are, simply, an impossibility. As they are human (and humans recoil from killing civilians) and as it is in their self-interest (and humans recoil from harming their interests), Israelis *cannot possibly intend to kill civilians or take less than reasonable precautions to prevent doing so.* Facts on the ground or inferences made on the basis of facts on the ground *cannot possibly* contradict these basic truths about humanity.

There is, however, one particular fact on the ground that *The Times* has to contend with. Namely, if Israelis are guided by noble human intentions as well as actual practical interests, both of which exclude the possibility to either cause intentional harm to civilians or to lack in circumspection or restraint in minimizing civilian casualties – why then do they use a weapon that, in 'built-up' areas, causes indiscriminate harm, thereby committing possible war crimes? Extract 7.15 continues with attending precisely to this issue:

> The IDF's continued obfuscation on white phosphorus only compounds that damage.
>
> White phosphorus is illegal under international law when used in built-up areas, but a legitimate weapon of war when used to provide cover for troops in open country. There is scant evidence of the IDF using it deliberately against civilians, but northern Gaza, where the fighting is concentrated, is one of the most densely populated places in the world. Civilian casualties were inevitable, and the deep

> burns that white phosphorus can cause are virtually untreatable. The longer that the IDF equivocate about its use, the more ammunition they hand to those who would accuse them of war crimes. (*The Times*, 331)

In line with the argument analysed previously, the newspaper asserts that there is 'scant evidence that the IDF is using' white phosphorous 'deliberately against civilians'. The illegal use of a weapon in 'built-up areas' does not therefore imply malevolent intentions. Yet the newspaper also states that 'northern Gaza, where the fighting is concentrated, is one of the most densely populated places in the world'. That is to say, without the intention to kill civilians though, the IDF is using white phosphorous precisely in areas where its use is 'illegal'.

Such a construction begs a profoundly grave question. Namely, is it at all possible to use weapons 'illegally' whilst not being responsible for causing indiscriminate damage with them? (In fact, what would ever constitute morally and legally accountable killing of civilian population if not using a potentially criminal weapon *precisely* in the environment where it is illegitimate *precisely* for the reason that it is bound to cause harm to civilians indiscriminately?)

The answer from Extract 7.15 above is that it is only possible if the political-moral-legal responsibility is exclusively reduced to the agent's subjective 'deliberat[ion]' and intention: the definition of an act and of responsibility is nowhere to be found but in the agent's pure *will* to do precisely what came about. It is from this perspective that it is possible for white phosphorous shells on the ground to become irrelevant.

Yet if this is so, such a state of affairs has obvious consequences for political-moral inquiry as such. A concept of agency and responsibility that exclusively depends on the concept of pure subjective *will* logically entails that critical enquiry of the conduct must likewise be exclusively located in the subjective account of the person possibly harbouring that will. Political, moral and legal enquiry then becomes an exercise in introspection, with the sole authority of the meaning of the agent's conduct being: that very agent themselves. And it is exactly in this vein that *The Times* concludes its line of argument in Extract 7.15: 'The longer that the IDF equivocate about its use, the more ammunition they hand to those who would accuse them of war crimes' (*The Times*, 331). Thus, to counter possible claims of war crimes or *actual claims* by *The Times* of weapons used in such a way that is illegal, mere lack of equivocation is called for. The newspaper simply wants the IDF to counter the evidence on the ground and disclaim/confess the possible inferences arising as to

Israel's moral conduct with some unequivocal statement. Israel, in this construction, appears duly to become the sole authority to interpret its own conduct and an omnipotent author that fully and exclusively owns the meaning of its deeds.

The problems with such a reductionist conception of bare intention must be obvious: only the most upfront or most insipid of war criminals could be convicted on these grounds. *But not necessarily the most evil ones*; for example, leaders of Hamas featuring in the conservative newspapers' account. For in court, Hamas leaders would surely testify to their own innocence and lack of malevolent intentions. And then a comparison would have to be made between their present statements and their past statements/behaviour. And *then* it would become obvious that not even agents firing rockets indiscriminately at civilians and only civilians accompanied by a rhetoric which makes these aims clear can be convicted on the assumptions with which *The Times* constructs the concept of intention.

For this reason, there are of course alternative conceptions of morality, and it is not simply through acts of pure will that one's moral conduct can be assessed.[18] Needless to say, the conceptual space between Evil and Good, pure will and pure mistake, is *ample*. Indeed, *The Times'* phrase of 'scant regard concerning civilians' implied something considerably more nuanced in terms of responsibility and critical judgment: not pure intention to kill civilians but relative lack of intention *not* to kill civilians. So why is it that, apparently unarguably and unnecessarily, Israel has to be the sole authority as regards the interpretation of its political-moral-legal conduct – to the extent that *The Times* does not logically follow up the claims *it* makes in terms of moral-legal accountability. What is it that appears to defy logic and ultimately *outlaw political-moral-legal criticism*?

To answer these questions, let us investigate what happens when, defying the newspaper's conclusion, some agents do indeed attempt to claim some authorship of and autonomy in assessing Israel's moral conduct.

Indeed, there were people who exercised critical judgment of Israeli acts. The spectre of war crimes as the conclusion to the argument of white phosphorous being or having been used in an illegal way is raised in Extract 7.15. Not by *The Times*, of course, but by some unspecified mass of people referred to as 'those'. Just as the straightforward examination of Israeli 'intentions' concluded in the implication of the evil that is Hamas; just as the considerations of Israel's practical interests concluded in the implication of suspiciously propagandist 'broadcasts':

it is once again a position outside the remit or responsibility of the State of Israel that *The Times*' rhetoric ultimately occasions. It is some other people that follow up the critical perspectives evaded by the newspaper. Who are they? And what do those perspectives ultimately amount to?

They may include those rather sinister segments of the media referred to earlier in this section, for whom Palestinian suffering is to be used as a tool for 'propaganda'. Other than this, however, no explicit answer may be found in the editorial under discussion. It is therefore previous editorials that we have to examine to gain a better understanding of possible subject positions that are critical of Israel and that may also entertain the perspective of claims of war crimes.

> Extract 7.16
>
> [...] Israel has a powerful ally in the United States.
>
> Its critics are wont to condemn this alliance as a Jewish axis blind to heart-rending realities in Gaza and to the sacrifices necessary for peace.
>
> No one can be unmoved by the suffering witnessed by the Norwegian surgeon who texted friends to tell them 'we're wading in death, blood [and] amputees'. But the way to end it is not to abandon Israel. It is to defeat Hamas. As Washington contemplates an opening to Iran, its reluctance to condemn Israel is not ideological but rational. The alternative would be to open talks with Tehran while its proxy in Gaza still threatened much of Israel with Iranian-built rockets. (*The Times*, 278)

Here we find a rather radical and unequivocal description of 'Israel's critics'. Certainly, the category of 'critics' excludes *The Times*. The newspaper may express criticism towards Israeli practice (as has been seen above), but is not a critic. To be a critic, then, involves either a characteristic identity or, at any rate, some sort of extended act of criticism. But what kind of identity? Extended criticism or an inclination to be critical along what lines?

The passage above presents a conundrum. It refers to 'suffering' and, of course, explicitly describes this suffering as something that needs to be ended. So how would 'critics' end it? They would end it with the most radical and potentially destructive way possible: by 'abandon[ing] Israel'. The problem of law in war, thus, leads once again to a far wider consideration. This time, though, not even to one concerning law to war, but the downright existential question of the very *being* of Israel. The position that the newspaper is arguing against is the most extreme viewpoint on the conflict possible. For if we still entertain some doubts about what 'abandon[ing] Israel' would mean, these doubts will have quickly dispersed as we read another claim of these 'critics' of Israel. Dubbing the relationship between Israel and the United States simply a 'Jewish axis' is a blatant manifestation of antisemitism, invoking one of the oldest antisemitic tropes: a worldwide conspiracy of the Jewish people.

What is important here, then, is that the subject position of 'those', of the other that is a 'critic' of Israel, is constructed in the most extremely immoral terms possible. Just like, incidentally, the sole critical positions on Israel's right to defend its citizens, which were engaged with by the *Telegraph*, implied an antisemitic stance (see Extract 7.1 above). 'Critics' are beyond the boundary of reasonable and morally just discourse. And inasmuch as these 'critics' comprise 'those who would accuse Israel of war crimes', or, in any case, comprise the majority of 'those' – then the whole possibility of accusing Israel of war crimes becomes a very suspicious enterprise, tainted by the very motivations of evil of 'those' who would make such accusations.

Thus, the simple act of raising the serious question of Israeli moral-legal accountability becomes a dangerous act. Doing so, one may find oneself in the midst of antisemites. One may even have become one if such thoughts occur. No wonder that these acts and these companies must be avoided.

Of course, it is perfectly understandable that one does not wish to find oneself in the midst of antisemites, let alone become one. However, this still does not answer the question of why on Earth it is that to begin substantial political-moral-legal criticism of the State of Israel somehow implies an antisemitic position? Even if, practically speaking, people who accused Israel of 'war crimes' were antisemites, this does not explain why, theoretically speaking, anyone should become an antisemite by virtue of concluding that if weapons appear to be used illegally, then some substantial investigation should follow.

There is only one explanation to be found, in the extracts quoted, for what defies logic and the mere possibility of independent critical examinations regarding Israel's conduct. Namely, if the moral meaning of one's act is solely defined and reduced to that of pure will, if killing of civilians can only happen with moral accountability on the condition that it is caused *by pure will*, and if killing civilians happens only for the purpose of killing civilians – then we are indeed staring in the face of something very frightening. Then killing civilians *by definition* means nothing less than doing evil. If it is the pure will of Israel that defines its gravely serious acts, then raising the moral responsibility of that pure will cannot but amount to the attribution of an evil essence to Israel. No wonder this implies being an antisemite.

What is of wonder, though, is that this conclusion only follows from *The Times'* far from consensual account of Israeli action that effectively prevented the newspaper from offering a far less categorical account. It is *The Times itself* that occasions a conception of political-moral-legal responsibility which is exclusively defined by the agent's *pure will* to achieve precisely what was achieved. It is therefore *only The Times's reductionist conception of agency and responsibility* that makes it forbidden for anyone to criticize Israel (for what *The Times* constructs as seriously problematic acts) and that creates the reason for this prohibition. And, as a consequence, that equates criticism with racist inhumanity. So why keep to that concept of the pure destructive will and the protective shield of Israeli authority over interpretation, if it is *exactly* the concept of that pure destructive will that creates the spectre of antisemitism of critical judgment in the first place? Why not follow up the viable concept of 'scant concern' instead, and attend to the vast realm of moral alternatives between the pure will of evil and pure mistakes?

The answer may not be found in *The Times,* but in a paragraph from the *Telegraph*:

> Extract 7.17
> Sadly, Mr Olmert has allowed a degree of confusion about his country's war aims to emerge. Fighting talk from his defence minister, Ehud Barak, of a 'war to the bitter end' has given the impression that Israel seeks to destroy Hamas or, at the very least, overthrow its administration in Gaza. In reality, Israel's war aims are almost certainly confined to halting the rocket attacks which have sown such misery in its southern cities. Mr Olmert should make clear that this defensive measure is the only objective. (*Daily Telegraph*, 43)

Intriguingly, taken at face value, this paragraph contradicts what has been found in the latter parts of this chapter so far. As we can see, the tension here is precisely the contradiction between what, according to a senior Israeli leader, Israel's intention and pure will *is* with the war and what, according to the *Telegraph,* that intention *must be*. We have the lack of equivocation *The Times* called for. We have one of the most important authors' interpretation of Israel's conduct. Yet the editorial calls for Ehud Barak to be corrected. How so? Where does the interpretation come from that he *must be* incorrect in saying what he says?

What this may indicate is that, in fact, it is the *necessity of Israel's intention rather than the actual intention professed* that is of valid status for the newspaper. What this means, in turn, is that the *necessity* is not of objective (i.e., white phosphorous shells on the ground) or even subjective (i.e., a declaration by Israel), but of a more categorical nature. Israel's intention must be pure not because of the laws of subjective/objective empirical facts, but by definition. As a consequence, the purity of Israel is not a simple descriptive fact, but, in conflict even superseding empirical elements of objective or subjective nature, an *injunction*. And if this injunction actually supersedes both objective facts on the ground and subjective confessions, we may conclude that it is because the realm and the agent it concerns are, indeed, 'in Heaven' (cf. Deuteronomy, 30:12).[19] It is the existence of such an injunction that induces in one fear and trembling about finding something impure in the midst of 'Heaven' – an act only antisemites would wish to do.

Discussion

In the beginning, conservative newspapers' arguments about law to war and law in war concerned the question of morality: of arms and of souls.

Apparent differences in earlier arguments notwithstanding, Hamas ultimately did not present much of a problem in these terms. It was constructed as an essentially evil entity: Nihilistic, antisemitic, totalitarian, whose defining feature is its 'dread of peace'. Hamas's conduct of war, accordingly, was defined and tainted by these characteristics, in terms of either intending to kill Israeli civilians and exclusively civilians (argument for law to war), or in terms of allowing their 'own' civilians to be killed (argument for law in war). As Hamas was exclusively defined by this essence, the group had no history, evolution or future influenced by any other factor than this essence. As such, no consideration posed any challenge to the conservative newspapers' description of this pole of war.[20] And no consideration helped us to understand what Hamas is, other than its essence.

Nor did, in the beginning, Israel's conduct pose much of a challenge to the conservative account. Inasmuch as the war was ultimately presented as having been 'triggered' by Hamas rockets carrying the message of evil destruction (cf. Extracts 7.1 and 7.13), Israel was presented as having no choice but to launch war. As a consequence, Israel's arm(y) and soul were not even good. They were *pure*, they were *invisible*, simply beyond the realm of political-moral deliberations.

Yet the actuality of war presented the world with a 'fearful death toll' of Palestinians, many civilians amongst them, and as the conservative newspapers duly reflected on this development, they could not but reflect on the fact that something had gone deeply wrong and was going even worse. This, then, could not but pose a challenge for their starting point: the morality of Israel's arms and soul. Thus, they could not but engage with dilemmas of *law in war.*

This was achieved, first, by the extension of arguments about Hamas's evil character from law to war to law in war. Second, Israel's own interests were invoked, suggesting that whatever Israel is doing on the ground it *must be* accidental, as it is bound to harm its practical interests. There are mistakes, to be sure, perhaps too many of them. Yet political-moral deliberations into motives are still essentially a different matter.

The *Daily Telegraph* could duly stop at this point, preserving the essential purity of Israel whilst still acknowledging the scene of death. Indeed, not even 'collateral damage' or 'mistakes' were mentioned. Deeds and deaths were juxtaposed by the *psychological impossibility* of Israel acting against its own interests and character. Deeds and deaths were not negated. But, as far as its responsibility was concerned, Israel remained not just morally right, but pure and invisible.

However, it was in *The Times* that the greatest possible challenge to the morality of Israeli arms and souls was encountered. For *The Times* did not simply mention so many Palestinian (civilian) deaths. It also offered an account for them by occasioning the possibility of Israel's 'illegal' use of white phosphorous in built-up areas and explicitly disparaging Israel for its 'scant concern' for civilian life. And – whatever Hamas is, however Hamas behaves in the war, and whatever the character/interests of the Israeli state are – the distinct possibility therefore remained for *The Times* that the Israeli army did something which is not just horrendous in its consequences but must *warrant an inquiry into Israel's responsibility in bringing it about*. Some deed and some death remained which, simply, could not be explained with recourse either to Hamas or to mistakes.

Yet what may have been taken as the logical conclusion of *The Times'* assertions was never followed up. This was possible on the condition that the concept of political/moral/legal responsibility was stripped down to pure subjective will/intention of destruction and the investigation thereof. As a consequence, political-moral criticism became an exercise in introspection, with the exclusive authority becoming the agent itself. In this case: the State of Israel.

Of course, reducing meanings of acts of political-moral-legal import to subjective will does not comply with any reasonable standard according to which critical inquiry may be carried out. But there is more to it: it fills us with dread. For this precise act, basically appearing to immunize Israel from outside criticism, has a potentially terrible consequence. If the meaning of an act of killing civilians becomes exclusively dependent on pure subjective ill will, then this implies that this will *willed* to kill civilians. This pure will is categorically impure. In other words, evil. The alternative to non-criticism therefore could not be but the attribution of an evil motive to Israel. An act of antisemitism, that is. And if this is so, then reasonable and morally just people must not simply refrain from critiquing Israel but exist in a state of *fear* that they may do so. Giving Israel full mandate over its moral meaning, making any attempt to recover such meaning independently of that mandate, means to exist in fear.

So why was it still maintained, against what appeared to be logically, legally, morally right? Why would fear of antisemitism overwrite logic, law and morality?

The answer appeared to be that the investigations conservative newspapers offered were, ultimately, not of a moral nature. They did not concern morality/politics/legality where responsibility and critical judgment comes in degrees. Rather, they ultimately concerned a realm where things are far more categorical and where transgression cannot be but fundamental. Not the morality of arms and souls but their *purity*. And criticism of purity induces fear because the distinction between what is pure and what is impure comes not in degrees but in kind. An entity is either pure or impure. One cannot make a pure entity a little bit impure, just as *one cannot kill a human being a little bit.*

Criticism induces fear and trembling if keeping essences from contaminating each other is at stake. What must be kept, lest we become evil, is the pure from the impure. The victim from the perpetrator. The innocent dead from the living. Indeed, the pure, the victim, and those innocent dead, must not be dragged down into human affairs – they are 'in Heaven'.

> Extract 7.18
> Israel holds itself to higher standards than its enemies. So does the world. That is why, as the world waits for Hamas to accept Israel and renounce violence, it also expects Israel to prosecute this war with greater respect for civilian life. (*The Times*, 331)

Such is *The Times*' concluding paragraph on the war; and an ostensibly very odd one at that. Theoretically, it asserts with confidence and pride the existence of selective 'double standards' in assessing Israel's political-moral(-legal?) conduct. Practically, it stands in flat contradiction with the newspaper's enormous rhetorical efforts ultimately *not to assess Israel's conduct* regarding 'respect for civilian life'.

The contradictions are deceptive, however. For the 'higher standards' the paragraph mentions are not standards of politics, morality, let alone legality. They are 'in Heaven'. As such, they will routinely not be applied to political-moral affairs of humans.

This state of affairs is not without very serious consequences though. For, to all intents and purposes, the State of Israel is *not in Heaven*. It is a group of humans: with sometimes noble and other times less than noble aspirations, with principles and emotional baggage, with success as well as failure of arms and souls. It may be more just than the rest of the world. It may be less so. It is just that it is not (as it cannot be) *pure*. As a result, it can never ever live up to heavenly expectations. And if those expectations are in place nonetheless, then it will mean that the door behind which the inescapable human reality of Israel's actual arms and actual soul is must be guarded very, very heavily indeed. For *if that door defined by heavenly expectations* is opened, only hell knows what frightening and absolutely monstrous reality will stare at us from behind it.

8
War – Purity of Arms and Souls in the Liberal Press

Introduction

Our attention will now turn to the liberal press's account of war and its engagement with issues of law to war and law in war.

If the major discursive challenge for conservative newspapers was the(ir) growing unease with Israel's *conduct* of the war, we may expect the liberal spectrum's area of dilemma to start right at the beginning of the war. Not that *ius in bello* would be some plain question where the attribution of subject positions and the allocation of responsibility could be left unattended, but, inasmuch as these newspapers adopt a broadly critical stance towards Israel (cf. Chapter 5), a major dilemma may lie right at the beginning of the war.

Namely, it is not only the conservative media's straightforward and predominantly black-and-white picture that needs to be addressed. As quantitative analysis showed in Chapter 4, the issue of rockets fired into Israeli civilian territory before the war featured relatively highly on the agenda of the *Financial Times*, the *Guardian* and the *Independent* (as well as of their sister publications). As rockets were often invoked by Israeli spokespeople as *casus belli*, and as the newspapers duly reported on them, the question of how these newspapers approached the question of *law to war* may be particularly interesting. Or, in other words, in what sense and to what extent can the outbreak of war be explained with recourse to the *casus belli* on display?[1]

War or negotiations

To begin with, aspects of the conservative press's standard argument were taken up by the liberal spectrum as well:

Extract 8.1

> There are, in any case, problems with the notion of proportionality in situations such as these. No state can be expected to tolerate rockets being launched at its civilians. No leader of such a state can be expected to shrug and say that it is not worth trying to stop small mobile rockets being fired from high-density residential areas. On the other hand, the persuasive argument against too heavy a military response is that it is counter-productive. (*Independent on Sunday*, 838)

Israeli leaders are constructed behaving responsibly and reasonably here, as implied by the imagined counter-position where leaders 'shrug' at a phenomenon of vital importance to their population. Again, the idea of 'no choice' is important. The fact that Israeli leaders had no choice carries the implication that war is inevitable, and the cause for it is rockets fired by Hamas. Just as it carries the implication that Israel is morally/legally right or, indeed, is even beyond the realm of such deliberations.

At the same time, whilst the passage essentially represents a position not dissimilar to that of the *Telegraph* and the earlier editions of *The Times*, it also displays clear misgivings about the enterprise. First, it airs the notion (completely unattended to in the conservative press as regarded law to war) that the battlefield Israel has to engage with is located at 'high-density residential areas'. What the territory is like, what its characteristics are, thus, become relevant considerations to the dilemma of starting the war. Second (and completely unattended to by the *Telegraph*), the *Independent on Sunday* points out that while launching a war may be justified or reasonable or inevitable, it nonetheless has the capacity to lead towards something undesirable. What 'counter-productive' may mean is not clear at this point, and it does not appear to jeopardize the essential judgment regarding the launching of war (it is 'too heavy a military response' that is problematic, rather than military response as such). Yet, even in adopting a stance whereby Israel's basic position is supported through the idea of 'no choice' and where additional criticism is not aimed *at* Israel but is displayed in a form of *engagement*, considerations partly (*The Times*) or completely (*Telegraph*) neglected in the conservative press are occasioned. Whilst rockets are an essential part of the story of Israel going to war and the concept of 'no choice' is acknowledged, the newspaper's horizon remains relatively broad.

The phenomenon of rockets rarely featured in the liberal press in such a (relatively) uncompromised manner as regards law to war. In fact, the paragraph above is just about the only one that bears any resemblance to those in the conservative press.[2] And this state of affairs, of course, had consequences in scrutinizing the idea of (no) choice – as well as, ultimately, Israel's responsibility.[3]

> Extract 8.2
> Covering just 365 square kilometres and home to 1.5 million people, Gaza is one of the most densely populated regions in the world. So it is unlikely that Israel would be able to launch a military offensive against Hamas militants, who have fired hundreds of rockets across the border in recent days, without inflicting terrible casualties on the civilian Palestinian population. But, say Israel's leaders, the threat to their own civilians leaves them no choice. (*Observer*, 424)

As can be seen, the *Observer*'s opening paragraph on the war features some of the explicit or implicit arguments of Extract 8.1. Yet it does this with an altogether different rhetoric. The main thrust of the argument is that, given the territorial features of the battlefield, *even* an operation of defensive nature ('against Hamas militants') will lead to terrible consequences. Strictly speaking, such an argument would concern law *in* rather than *to* war. However, these are reflections made on the very first day of the war. And by foreshadowing 'terrible casualties' on this very first day, they imply that, in this case at least, some dilemmas of *ius ad bellum* and *ius in bello* cannot actually be separated.[4]

The position displayed in Extract 8.1 was, of course, less than favourable to the war. But war was depicted as inevitable. The idea of Israel having 'no choice' equally emerges from Extract 8.2. It does so, however, with a rather different rhetoric. Israel having 'no choice' is not a statement of fact, but that of an opinion – Israel's leaders'. Whilst neither the legitimacy of such an opinion nor the 'threat to their own civilians' is questioned (indeed, 'hundreds of rockets' fired in recent days is stated as a fact), a statement of opinion by an obviously interested party may carry less rhetorical weight than that of a fact.

Yet, due to the fact that it displays (but does not counter) Israel's choice as an opinion, the *Observer*'s becomes a rather peculiar construction. One may indeed question the legality/morality/wisdom of *launching* a war, if solely by virtue of it having been launched it is likely to lead to an untenable *conduct* of war. This is one version of the argument of disproportionality or counter-productivity. Yet leaving the question of choice ultimately open, the argument itself becomes less than conclusive. For if Israel *really* did not have a choice, in that the actuality of 'hundreds of rockets' fired at its civilians left it with no other option than starting a war (as in fact the leader of the *Independent on Sunday* claims), then the foreseen consequences are simply unfortunate at this point. In themselves, they constitute no argument against launching the war.

Attempts at forming an argument may be gathered from the following extract:

> Extract 8.3
> It is why, however great the provocation from Hamas and other fighters, and however urgent a political issue security on the southern flank had become in the run-up to Israel's election, this was a conflict that always cried out for a negotiated solution. And the outlines of a settlement were clear, almost before the first Israeli bombs fell. The Hamas authorities had to guarantee a stop to the rockets fired into Israel. Israel had to open the crossing points that had kept Gazans effectively imprisoned. (*Independent*, 987)

As in previous extracts, the severity of the issue is not denied here. Rockets constitute a 'great...provocation'. Yet the idea of choice is introduced to the equation with the novel argumentative element that 'this was a conflict that always cried out for a negotiated solution'. What is more, 'the outlines of that settlement were clear'; that is, the solution to be negotiated was there to be seen for all. This way, the *Independent*'s editorial does not simply negate the argument of 'no choice', but makes the alternative choice the exclusive, eminently reasonable and evident choice. In a similar fashion, the alternative solution is presented in two short sentences. War did not come out of necessity; it came out of the non-realization of obvious and peaceful alternatives.

If the alternative solution as well as the counter to the argument of 'no choice' is that simple – why, then, is there war? Why did Israel not go down the route of negotiations? And why is Hamas firing rockets? And would the fact that these rockets, in line with the conservative argument, constitute a 'great provocation' not influence the very idea of a relatively simple negotiated solution? Or, likewise, the fact that 'crossing points' are still closed? Whilst the idea of an alternative choice opens up new possibilities, it also begs these questions that must ultimately be answered, especially since the projected peaceful alternative solution never materialized.

For a 'negotiated solution', there must be people willing to enter and be capable of negotiation. What we have learned so far from the liberal editorials certainly does not make it obvious that Hamas is capable of negotiations, nor why Israel was unwilling to enter negotiations, launching a war instead. At the very least, as we have seen in the previous chapter, Israel's choice is conditional on what Hamas is/does. Just as in the conservative press, then, the question of law to war ultimately revolves around two issues: the meaning of Hamas rockets and Israel's options in responding to them. It is this dynamic that needs to be unpacked.

Hamas and rockets

The first element of the liberal press's alternative to war that will be examined is Hamas. For negotiations to be possible, Hamas and its rockets must carry a meaning radically different from those constructed by the conservative press. What, then, is Hamas in the liberal account? The *Independent* takes up the point in explicit relation to the idea of negotiations.

> Extract 8.4
> Talking to Hamas does not mean supporting the group's fanatical creed, condoning its terrorist methods, or accepting its territorial demands. Nor does it mean asking Israel to sit idle while Hamas fires rockets into Israeli territory or smuggles arms across the Egyptian border. Some form of dialogue – with European and Arab involvement – would be a practical move to build trust and open the way for concessions and peacemaking from both sides. It is in the best interests of the Israeli and Palestinian people. (*Independent*, 939)

In line with Extract 8.3 above, the newspaper's stance is a relatively straightforward one. The possibility of dialogue is presented as a fact, and as a desirable fact (being 'in the best interest' of the people concerned).

However, one may again wonder *whether* or *how* anyone can possibly talk to people with 'fanatical creeds', firing rockets towards civilians. Inasmuch as Hamas is depicted in terms implying its gravely problematic nature, it poses a challenge to the proposed solution of negotiations. Can those with 'fanatical creed' and 'terrorist methods' enter reasonable dialogue at all?

The dilemma is never attended to in the *Independent*. One way of solving the conundrum appeared in the *Guardian*, though:

> Extract 8.5
> The Palestinians have always had a rejectionist wing, which for so long was represented by Fatah. Israel, too, has those who reject a Palestinian

> state, including many settlers. To think a solution can be found by killing rejectionists is to deny the entire course of the history of the Middle East. There is no military solution to Hamas's rockets, which continued to rain down on Israel yesterday. Nor is a ground invasion likely to stop the rockets. It could displace them, perhaps. But if that happened, Hamas's next tactic could be to use the Palestinians of East Jerusalem to wield the launch tubes. (*Guardian*, 441)

The *Guardian* repeats the *Independent*'s statement of an alternative to war: 'There is no military solution to Hamas' rockets.' The war as such is constructed as futile, with dreadful consequences either foreseen or already actualized. Whilst not put explicitly, the implicit alternative solution to rockets 'which continued to rain down on Israel yesterday' is negotiation.

So how to negotiate with Hamas? The passage does not seem to put any great problems in the way of negotiations, in the way that the *Independent*'s formulation did: Hamas is branded 'rejectionist', a considerably more mitigated version of the group's identity than anything encountered hitherto in the press. What is more, Israel, too, is described as having 'rejectionists', implying that whilst Hamas is not an ideal candidate to pursue alternative solutions with, it is certainly not unique in its stance of 'rejection'. It is normal to have rejectionists, at least in the context of Palestine/Israel, and their existence should not lead to any special measures.

What we see here, then, is a reorganization of political-moral poles accountable for the lack of negotiations and the ensuing war. Hamas ceases to be an absolute evil ruling out the possibility of compromise. Elsewhere in the *Guardian,* we read of the group being 'more than just a guerrilla army': a 'political movement as well', where, of course, even the identity denied or superseded by the newspaper's account ('guerrilla army') is once again a far more charitable one than anything encountered so far in the British press. Likewise, we learn that '[t]heir tactic and their strategy is no more and no less than resistance' (*Guardian*, 441), where the alternative ascriptions countered might include nearly anything we have read so far, whether in the conservative or the liberal press.

What exactly the newspaper bases its rather optimistic judgment of the group upon is never explicated, just as the alternative ascriptions offered by the conservative (as well as, we shall see, the rest of the liberal) newspapers is never showcased, let alone argued against. Yet the clear upshot is that, whilst Hamas is of course not depicted in positive terms, the *Guardian*'s rendering does not raise any doubts whatsoever as to their ability to compromise and work towards mutually satisfying political solutions.

However, the passage is comprised of even more than this. As one crucial agent of the conflict is repositioned, the repositioning of other elements follows it. Indeed, there is something of real concern for the *Guardian* here. Not rejectionists, as such, but Israel's belief that the solution to the problem is 'killing [those] rejectionists'. Not only is Hamas presented as far less of a problem than in the account of any other newspaper, but the problem explicitly engaged with stems from Israel's attitude. An attitude, incidentally, which is not a simple failure of judgment but a wildly unreasonable one: it 'denies the *entire* course of the history of the Middle East' (emphasis added).

At this point, we do not quite know why Israel would deny the entire course of this history and why it does not act in what may be supposed to be in its self-interest. The newspaper's account for this will be analysed in the next section. What we may suspect, however, is that such a realignment of moral poles has clear implications for the supposed *casus belli*: the rockets themselves. If Hamas is a 'mere' rejectionist, guerilla-political movement whose tactic is 'no more and no less than resistance'; furthermore, if what contributes to the war is Israel's as yet inexplicable lunacy of 'killing rejectionists', then we may reasonably expect the status of the rockets to be changed.

And the newspaper certainly lives up to these expectations. Its first paragraph on the war concludes:

> Extract 8.6
> The death toll by last night had climbed to nearly 290, with more than 700 wounded. This in reply to hundreds of rockets from Hamas militants which killed one Israeli in six months. But the equation is always like this. (*Guardian*, 441)

Let us note first that the utterance asserts the disparity between the number of people killed by those rockets ('one Israeli') and the responding Israeli operation in less than two days ('nearly 290, with more than 700 wounded'). What to make of these pieces of information is left to the reader, especially as the editorial offers only a somewhat cryptic aside to account for this. What '[b]ut the equation is always like this' suggests is some stereotypical pattern, a 'script' (Edwards, 1995; Schank, 1999) of these events and the pinpointed disparity between casualties. Patterns, however, beg some deeper explanation, which most certainly does not come *explicitly* here, either in the concluding expression or in the next paragraph. Just as we were left wondering why Israel's chosen solution is the unreasonable killing of the other side's rejectionists, we have no clue at the moment as to why this constantly recurring pattern of disparity in casualties may be the case. To this point, again, we shall return in the next section where the topic is the newspapers' construction of Israel.

At the same time, we may remember that this disparity in numbers was also acknowledged by the *Daily Telegraph*. In the conservative newspaper, however, this was not much of a problem. How might this be the case? The conservative paper's construction of the rockets depended on Hamas and its evil motivations. Rockets carried the message not simply of indiscriminate death but *intended death of civilians and only civilians*. As Hamas loses its evil character, the *Guardian* focuses more on the *consequences* of rockets in concrete material terms. The distinguishing feature of the rockets thereby becomes not the fact that they embody evil intention but the relative lack of damage they cause (*relative*, that is to the Israeli response).

There are two huge political-moral dilemmas here. First, what counts as material damage and to what extent does that material damage justify counter-operation? Certainly, one death is a death too many. Besides, it is reasonable to count damage to infrastructure or to psychological well-being (i.e., trauma) as well. The *Guardian* does not engage with this problem, which is, to repeat, 'accounted' for by that mere aside at the end of the paragraph. This suggests the irrelevance of the question and the operation of other factors that provide a solution to this dilemma.

Of course, neither of the conservative newspapers reflected on this state of affairs. This actually leads to the second political-moral dilemma. The reason that the material damage caused by the rockets was of relative irrelevance stemmed from the fact that in their construction the *meaning* of those rockets was located firmly and exclusively in Hamas's homogenous and evil *intention*. The meaning of the rockets was the intended death to civilians, and civilians only.

To its credit, the *Guardian* at least ventures into this most crucial of moral dilemmas, if only in the last of its editorials on the war. We read there that 'Hamas and other militant groups…continu[e] to fire rockets at the civilian population in southern Israel' (*Guardian*, 661). The context of the assertion is, however, the futility of Israel's devastating campaign and, as such, the dilemma opened up is never reflected on.[5] The dominant tone of the newspaper remains that with which it began its coverage: implying the insignificant consequences of the rockets *relative* to Israel's response.

As such, the *Guardian*'s depiction of the rockets (if not exactly of Hamas) becomes a mirror image of those of the conservative papers. As inhuman intention is the sole arbiter there, relatively immaterial consequences rule the day here. The implication is not only a sustained black-and-white picture but one where no connection whatsoever exists between the two poles: intention and consequences. Whether this state of affairs will also persist regarding Hamas and Israel (the two agents that, once again, were depicted as categorically different and incommensurable by the conservative newspapers), we shall see. What is for sure is that the *Guardian*'s preferred alternative to war (i.e., negotiations) was established via simply *brushing aside* both the attributes/acts of Hamas and those of the rockets that could well pose vexing problems for such negotiations.

The *Guardian*'s approach to Hamas stands virtually alone on the liberal spectrum, however. Elsewhere in the liberal press, we read about 'Hamas crav[ing] confrontation' (*Observer*, 424), pursuing 'terrorism' (*Independent on Sunday*, 838), being a 'terrorist organization' (*Observer*, 424), calling 'for the complete annihilation of Israel' (*Observer*, 424) and 'the destruction of the state of Israel' (*Independent on Sunday*, 838). It is also designated as 'Islamist' (*Financial Times*, 1039) and having 'delusional belief[s]' (*Financial Times*, 1226). The most powerful expressions came from the *Independent*:

> Extract 8.7
> With its fundamentalist tunnel vision, this Islamist movement appears to have an interest in the virtual destruction of what is left of society in Gaza, perhaps believing that such a dreadful social upheaval can only tighten its theocratic control over a frightened and shattered population. (*Independent*, 858)

As opposed to what we have read in the *Guardian*, these are very strong words implying the gravely problematic nature of Hamas. Yet of importance is not so much how uncompromisingly *bad* Hamas is, but that it is constructed in such manner as to make negotiations, *proposed elsewhere by the Independent*, seem nothing but wishful thinking, or worse. If the destruction of the population is in the interest of Hamas, negotiations are clearly not possible, for two reasons: first, Hamas simply does not want negotiations, full stop; second, Hamas, its main aim being destruction, cannot be negotiated with, full stop. If there is a middle ground between the conservative argument and that of liberal papers, it is not found in simply putting together one element from the right (i.e., Hamas is evil) and another from the left (i.e., let them negotiate).

It is from this perspective that the following passage from the *Observer* is of crucial importance:

> Extract 8.8
> Even those Israeli and Palestinian politicians who are minded to negotiate are boxed into uncompromising stances, and for both the main reason is Hamas. But attempting to remove the problem with military power will not work. Hamas craves confrontation because its support increases when ordinary Palestinians are collectively punished, as has happened under the blockade. There are compelling reasons why Israeli politicians do not try to talk Hamas out of its militancy. But the near certainty of failure is also a more compelling reason not to try force instead. (*Observer*, 424)

If an unmovable object is at the same time an unstoppable force, how is dialogue possible at all? Simply pronouncing that talks should take place might express noble ideas about the power of dialogue or the essential qualities of all human beings. It may not, however, be a political or indeed moral *argument*. Extract 8.8 from the *Observer* addresses some of these points.

Repeating their earlier position that 'military power will not work', the newspaper comes to the conclusion that the 'near certainty of failure' should be a reason 'not to try force'. As we have seen in Extract 8.4, however, merely denying one choice (i.e., that of launching war) does not in itself realistically open up another one (i.e., peaceful negotiations). Yet the *Observer*'s argument here contains another element. It mentions that Hamas 'craves confrontation because its support increases when ordinary Palestinians are collectively punished, as has happened under the blockade'. This is most interesting as this argument starts to open up for understanding what is apparently an unreasonable organization, 'craving confrontation'. The reason that Hamas in this account does not dread, does not accept, does not tolerate, but *craves* confrontation may in part derive from an essentially democratic impulse: 'its support increases as ordinary Palestinians are collectively punished.' Hamas therefore is not a stand-alone agent, simply imposing itself on Israel/Gaza, or standing in the way of negotiations. It also is a *choice* of a population. And whatever else that choice is informed by (hope, despair, human wickedness, religious conviction, etc.) it also is informed *by unreasonable Israeli actions*.

As opposed to the conservative account of an inhuman monstrosity, Hamas becomes a human agent, in relation to and partly constituted by its surroundings. As opposed to the *Guardian*'s account, the monstrous political-moral character of its deeds is not simply explained away. The game is not a zero-sum one, where one agent's contribution by definition lessens that of the other. Rather, it begins to be a game of human relations – if thoroughly terrible ones.

The call for Israeli restraint is therefore not simply supported by some *magic solution:* talking with no regard to anything else. Reasonable Israeli restraint may contribute to the very possibility of talking by altering the preferences of a population on which Hamas's existence/ success hinges. Such an argument is of paramount importance as it introduces an element into the discourse that has hitherto been unaddressed. Namely, Israeli actions are *constitutive* of what Hamas is or what it does.

Thus, just as with the conservative account, the construction of what Israel and what Hamas is alters the *meaning* of the rockets fired towards Israeli civilians. They are not simple if devastating objects, facts of the matter. They become suffused with the meaning of the context from which they arose. And whilst that context in the conservative press was Hamas's timeless, essential and homogenously dark inhumanity, and in the *Guardian* explained away by the organization's *relatively* unproblematic 'resistance', the passage in the *Observer* brings history and the role Israel plays into this context as well. As a result, Israel does not simply acquire a new array of choices (other than shooting back) to *address* the danger of the rockets. Rather, those choices contribute to the very existence of the rockets and obtain political-moral responsibility.

Such a perspective becomes visible in Extract 8.8 of the *Observer,* above, but never quite so in the accounts so far from the *Independent* and the *Guardian.* Indeed, concerning Hamas, of all the newspapers analysed, it may only be found systematically and with coherence in the *Financial Times*:

> Extract 8.9
>
> Yet Israel, backed by the US and the mute assent of Europe, has sought to isolate Hamas. After Hamas fought it out with Fatah and ejected it from Gaza 18 months ago, the 1.5m Gazans have suffered a blockade rationing food, fuel and medicine entering the enclave.
>
> This policy makes Palestinians dependent on Hamas for basic needs. It makes violence an attractive alternative both when (Hamas) truces fail to lift the blockade and (Fatah) peace talks fail to deliver

> peace. It is in any case delusional for Israel to imagine it can make peace with half the Palestinians while waging war on the other half. (*Financial Times*, 1039)

What these paragraphs from the *Financial Times* communicate is that the Israeli economic blockade on Gaza operates on three levels as regards Hamas. First, it helps the organization to solidify its monopoly and tighten its hold on the population of Gaza. Thus, it produces a situation where Palestinians *cannot* help but 'support' Hamas: it is their lifeline. The popularity of Hamas does not derive from a choice of the people but of a necessity, as their 'basic needs' are addressed by Hamas and only by Hamas.

Second, the passage also presents the six-month truce between Hamas and Israel in a different light from other newspapers' account. A *purpose* becomes visible, as having driven Hamas to agree to the truce, the subsequent lack of realization of its hopes becomes an account as to why Hamas did not renew the truce. Its resort to the ultimate kind of violence may be thoroughly inhuman, but is, nonetheless, presented here as a *tactic* (however deplorable), rather than an *essence* (which followed the breakdown of the promise of a more peaceful alternative). In line with this, the argument presents Hamas as a relatively reasonable political-moral agent, as far as its constituency is concerned. Though the economic blockade would make its monopoly incontestable, it nonetheless aspires to make Israel revoke it.

Third, we also learn that the blockade of Gaza makes 'violence an attractive alternative'. This utterance has several implications. While it certainly does not imply that Israel would somehow *create* that violence out of nothing, it does mean that Israeli policies have a role in what Hamas chooses. At the same time, it also means that there are alternative courses of actions at Hamas's disposal, and that Hamas is capable of pursuing them. Violence is therefore not something that unstoppably and exclusively flows from Hamas due to its nature. Neither is it, of course, the causal effect of Israeli actions. Rather, it is something emerging from a set of relations between what Israel does and what Hamas is/does. It is only inevitable while this set of relations persists.

Besides the blockade (and international isolation in a wider sense), another element of historical context was evoked in the liberal press to help understanding of the outbreak of the war as well as Hamas. Significantly, other than a short reference in the *Guardian*, it, too, emerged systematically only in the *Financial Times*' account of the war.[6]

Extract 8.10
Israel's refusal to treat with Hamas is understandable, if futile. The destructive fury of its assault on Gaza was not only intended to get over the relative failure of its 2006 war on Hizbollah in Lebanon. Israel was also determined not to repeat the outcome to its 1996 Lebanon war, which ended with codified and internationally underwritten rules of engagement with Hizbollah.

But Israeli unilateralism is a blind alley. Its unilateral withdrawal from Gaza in 2005 has resolved nothing. The existence of organisations such as Hamas and Hizbollah – which both arose as responses to Israeli occupation – cannot simply be wished away. (*Financial Times*, 1256)

In part, the passage from the *Financial Times* once again repeats arguments previously seen. It brands 'Israel's refusal to treat with Hamas' as both 'understandable' (presumably due to the nature of Hamas) and 'futile'. Partially repeating the argument of the *Independent* and the *Observer* above, it concludes with the necessity of talks nonetheless: given that Hamas is not a product of fantasy but a fact, it cannot be 'wished away'.

Yet, again, there also resurfaces another element of argumentation, concerning not simply the visible present characteristics of Hamas but their *origin*. Namely, Hamas did not simply spring out of nothing, of some dark urge. It is partly a result of Israel's conduct and its occupation of Palestinian territories. Israel once again is not simply responding to an (undesirable) given. It also constitutes and shapes this present given.[7]

What is more, the perspective of the *Financial Times* adds a historical dimension to these questions as well. It is not just this particular war that is deemed problematic from the point of view that it will further contribute to those precise characteristics in Hamas that make lack of engagement either impossible or at least 'understandable'. Israel's policies in a wider sense, such as the blockade of Gaza or the ongoing occupation, contribute to what Hamas is at present. It is therefore not (or not simply) that Israel responds to rockets fired at its civilian territories. It also is that the origin of those rockets in itself is, amongst other things, a response to Israeli military actions and policies.

Indeed, though *all* of the British newspapers' favoured political position is the two-state solution, the *Financial Times* was unique amongst them in consistently linking the events and, in particular, Hamas's conduct and *raison d'etre* to the ongoing Israeli occupation:

Extract 8.11
The Islamists are not blamed enough by Palestinians, not just for their sectarianism but for the vainglorious delusion they can emulate the deterrent power Hizbollah established by creating a balance of terror across the Israeli-Lebanese border. Palestinians elected Hamas three years ago because Fatah, their traditional vehicle of national aspiration, was sunk in corruption and had failed to end Israel's occupation and create an independent state. Nevertheless, a majority of Palestinians still believes in a negotiated solution, not Hamas' violent tactics. (*Financial Times*, 1039)

Again, what is important here is that Hamas's conduct is far from being praised. Their tactics are branded as 'vainglorious delusion', 'violence' and 'terror'. Their mandate, however, is constructed as coming from their political opponent's 'failure to end Israel's occupation' (as well as corruption). Elsewhere, its appeal is depicted to come from its 'resistance to occupation' (*Financial Times*, 1226).[8] And it is within such consistent and coherent argumentation that one may reasonably claim to have reached the 'root' of the problem:

Extract 8.12
It must be remembered that the root cause of the Israeli-Palestinian conflict is the Israeli occupation – which Israel's 2005 withdrawal from Gaza was meant to consolidate, through its subsequent expansion of Jewish settlements in the West Bank and Arab east Jerusalem. (*Financial Times*, 1039)

Now, as quantitative analysis has shown, liberal newspapers mentioned the issues of the blockade and occupation in their coverage – and in their editorial coverage – far more than conservative ones. However, the question of context does not stop at the quantity of information. It is the way newspapers construct that information, and how they connect them to each other so as to form an argument, that matters.

With the sole exception of the *Financial Times*, the newspapers' editorials that mentioned the blockade and the occupation contextualized those terms simply in terms of Israel's identity.[9] They were depicted as politically counter-productive, or even morally bad policies. But this did not mean that they would have constituted a *perspective* from where Hamas and its rockets became understandable (not good, but possible to be understood through a set of relations with Israel).

Context, therefore, matters not just in providing more information. The Israeli blockade and, especially, the IDF's deployment of white phosphorous featured in *The Times* without ultimately altering the essential equation. Just as talking of Israeli violence did not do so in the case of the *Guardian*. Context also matters because and when it is constitutive. Putting any human agents and their actions in context has the potential to make those actions and identities understandable. Not pardonable or acceptable, but being more than the consequence of some fixed essence residing in the agent's heart and mind: an outcome of (gravely problematic) *human relationships*. And it is only by invoking human relationships, and not simply the matter of who is to blame, that the prospect of negotiations becomes different from a doctrine or wishful thinking; it becomes a horizon.[10]

In this sense, even though other liberal newspapers also mentioned the blockade as the 'core of this conflict' (*Guardian*, 661; cf. *Independent*, 1005) towards the end of the war, it constituted little more than a 'rhetorical bubble'. This is especially true of the *Independent*, where the idea that it was the economic blockade that 'sewed the seeds of this conflict in the first place' (*Independent*, 1005) came virtually out of nothing. An argumentative perspective that leads to analysis such as this, by relating these historical events to Hamas and its propensity to fire rockets, occurred only and consistently in the *Financial Times*.[11]

As a result, the apparently huge differences between the conservative and the liberal newspapers regarding their stance on *law to war* suddenly vanish. Yes, the liberal papers uniformly presented negotiations as a real and viable alternative to war deriving from necessity/lack of choice. Yes, they wrote (more extensively) about contextual factors such as the blockade and occupation. But no, with the important exception of the *Financial Times*, they did not connect these two argumentative points systematically together and, consequently, they did not provide any substantial political argument to justify their position by giving an alternative account of Hamas and the meaning of its rockets.

Either in line (as in the *Independent* or the *Independent on Sunday*) with or in opposition (as in the *Guardian*) to the conservative newspapers, Hamas was simply bad or not-so-bad. The theoretical problem with the former account is that it makes the idea of negotiations risible. The practical problem with the latter account was that it aspired to give no justification whatsoever for its clearly counter-intuitive descriptions.[12] In both cases, we got no further away from the conservative account, in that Hamas did not became understandable in terms of human relations. Such an understanding was only consistently achieved by the *Financial Times* through relating context and Israeli agency to Hamas. Thereby, Hamas did not become less bad, it only started to have historical-political-moral meaning instead of a timeless essence. Thus, negotiations did not become virtually impossible or inevitable (depending on this essence) either. They became a possibility where humans have the chance to sit down and discuss their differences – and without denying that realizing this possibility may be incredibly difficult.

Israel and power

As we saw in the previous chapter, the practical possibility of Israel's accountability was only raised in the conservative press when its conduct of war started to become problematic. The phenomenon of Israel *acting* and not simply automatically *reacting* out of necessity only became relevant as war soldiered on. In contrast, for the liberal account Israeli agency was already relevant at the start of the war. In fact, the war is implicitly or explicitly constructed as a disproportionate response at its very beginning, and this equation only changes in degree, not in kind, as the death toll approaches the final count. Thus, in contradistinction to the conservative account, the question of power is raised in the liberal press from the very beginning of the war. It is only a different aspect of it that *also* becomes relevant as war proceeds.

> Extract 8.13
> All the signs are that the Obama administration is not going to be sympathetic to a future of failed blockades or the intransigent refusal to talk to Israel's enemies. (*Guardian*, 618)

Though not explicitly considering the lack of negotiations, the *Guardian*'s utterance clearly accounts for them. Israel's refusal to sit at the table is expanded by the adjective 'intransigent', implying some ingrained disposition that made it impossible for dialogue to take place/come to fruition. Whilst we know nothing about Hamas's readiness to talk, we do not really need to know anything about it, either. Even though the partner in the would-be negotiation is designated as 'Israel's enemies', being an enemy in itself does not seem to pose problems to negotiations in this extract. What we are left with is a mysterious disposition, Israeli 'intransigence', standing in the way of talking to each other.

What might this intransigence derive from? The *Guardian* nowhere explicitly asks this question or attends to the issue of negotiations. Just like the newspaper's aside '[b]ut the equation is always like this' (Extract 8.6) or its cryptic account of Israel's unreasonable position of killing 'rejectionists' when they too have 'rejectionists' (whom they would presumably not wish to kill) and when this 'den[ies] the entire course of the history of the Middle East' (Extract 8.5), the account of 'intransigence' does not in itself explain anything. However, in the newspaper's account of the unfolding course of the war, and of events that even the conservative press found challenging, we may gather some understanding of what Israel's disposition is.

Indeed, shortly after quipping 'the equation is always like this', we do encounter something like an account.

> Extract 8.14
> A hammer blow is intended to terrorise and that is exactly what Israel did yesterday. Dr Haidar Eid, a Gazan academic who saw the bodies and children with amputated limbs, told Haaretz journalist Amira Hass: 'To pick a time like this, 11:30 (AM), to bomb in the hearts of cities, this is terrible. This choice was intended to cause as large a massacre as possible.' The targets were not the training camps of Hamas's military wing, which were empty when the jets struck, but rather police stations. The raids were intended to destroy the infrastructure on which Hamas builds its administrative as much as its military hold over Gaza. But that means killing policemen, not just the militants who assemble and fire the rockets. Presumably it also means targeting judges, officials, and doctors too. (*Guardian*, 441)

In this passage, a crucial argument starts to develop as the *Guardian* raises the question of Israeli responsibility and intentions. As we saw previously, this was anathema to conservative newspapers, so much so that even when it was made blatantly visible, it could not be anything but flatly refuted. But as the timing of the attack (11:30 am) is made relevant by the *Guardian,* the question appears both valid and inescapable: what is Israel's role or motive regarding the quantity and quality of the death toll?

The way the newspaper relates to the question of responsibility is rather curious. Just as previously, there are many implicit orientations to it. The first two uses of 'intended' are put without caveats, and their object is 'to cause as large a massacre as possible' and 'to terrorize'.[13] What Israelis intend thereby is not simply to kill, not simply to kill civilians, but to kill the maximum number of civilians possible. Arguably, and given the state's international standing, Israel could not possibly be more evil in doing so. No wonder, then, that the word 'terrorize' is utilized by the paper, just as a couple of lines before the extract (and again in conjunction with the timing of the attack) we read that Israel shows 'the same indifference to human life that Israel charges its enemies with' (*Guardian*, 441). The intricate thing about this characterization is that the newspaper does not simply locate Israel *on par* with an organization that pursues terrorism, but with the *accusations* Israel levels on that organization. Whatever those accusations might be, we can be sure that (these being accusations) they will be far more severe than actual reality.

Thus, the question of intention is not so much raised in this extract as already answered in the affirmative and pushed to the absolute extreme. Israel's intentions did not simply become relevant to the terrible events in the war. Arguably, they became monstrous enough to fully explain the monstrosities, especially as no other factor contributing to the deaths is mentioned. In fact, in the *Guardian* Israel starts to look very much like Hamas did in the conservative accounts.

Of course, choosing the time of midday to attack does seem to raise strong doubts about the picture depicted by the conservative press. But to justify that of the *Guardian*, more information is needed. Presumably, this is why we do indeed duly learn about the targets of the Israeli raids (i.e. 'police stations'). However, we never learn why Israel would strike exactly 'police stations' if it wanted to cause 'as large a massacre as possible'. The newspaper shifts its argumentation. What becomes relevant immediately after the quotation is not timing anymore, but the target. A separation is drawn, in line with just war theory (Margalit & Walzer, 2009; Walzer, 2000), between combatants ('camps of Hamas's military wing) and civilians ('judges, officials, and doctors'), and it is explicitly stated that Israel did not target the former, but the latter. It is not clear whether the argument is that Israel blithely kills civilians on top of militants or that Israel actually aims to kill civilians in the first place (just like Hamas in the conservative account). What is clear is the straight separation between combatants and Israel's main targets: policemen. And as a number of other occupations (judges, officials and doctors) are added to this latter category as hypothetical targets, the implication is clearly that Israel's midday targets all happened to be civilians.[14]

There is some divergence between the two strands of the newspaper's argument, possibly even a contradiction. For if the timing of the attack is 'intended' to cause maximal possible damage, then why target police stations and police stations only/mainly?[15] Nonetheless, in itself, both strands of arguments point towards the same conclusion. And that conclusion is not so much that what was intended was a 'massacre', but that it was one of the gravest possible of war crimes: intending to kill civilians and civilians only/mainly. Again, much like Hamas in the conservative account.[16]

Intriguingly enough, though, this strongly worded and uncompromising account looks in a rather different light when reading a paragraph from a later editorial in the *Guardian*:

> Extract 8.15
> The last time the tanks rolled into Gaza in February and March last year, more than half the Palestinian casualties were civilian, according to Human Rights Watch. That pattern is now set to be repeated. After a week's aerial bombardment, the death toll already stands at nearly 500, of which approximately 70 are children and 27 women, according to independent Palestinian sources. Of the 2,650 Gazans injured, more than 270 are women and 650 children. So much for Israel's claim that their targets are Hamas militants. Even if you stretch the term to include policemen, this is a 'surgical' operation in which civilians will die in their hundreds. (*Guardian*, 520)

There are many familiar elements in this extract. Having pointed out not only the overall Palestinian death toll, but also the proportion of women and children, the argumentation concludes with an aside: 'So much for Israel's claim that their targets are Hamas militants'. As we do not read here about the exact civilian death toll and learn nothing more specific about the operation or Hamas's tactics, it is not immediately clear what may be accountable for the grim figures. What is clearly implied, though, is that Israel's claim is either deluded or deceitful. And if this is so, then some other claim, radically different from the one that Israel's 'targets are Hamas militants' must be true.

Yet the main reason to cite this passage is not so much to point out, again, how issues of utmost importance are attended to in the *Guardian* by using rhetorical forms of semi-cryptic 'asides'. Rather, it is to consider the last sentence. There the *possibility* is entertained that the term 'militant' may be extended 'to include policemen'.

It may not be apparent why anyone with a sound mind would extend the category 'militant' to include 'policemen': though they are, of course, carrying weapons, policemen are only in charge of keeping civil order. However, as explained in Chapter 1, there is a reason for the expansion of the category. It is that in the case of Gaza, some/many of them were actually also members of organizations belonging to the military wing of Hamas.[17] Though policemen, *as a group*, were clearly not implicated in military activities (and the IDF's attack on the police stations was subsequently subjected to heavy legal investigations), nor was it true that a blanket exemption could have been issued for them, *as a group*. It is probably this blurry state of affairs that informs the *Guardian*'s argument.

Yet if there is some *tendency* amongst policemen of Gaza to belong to military organizations as well, then their immediate equation with 'judges, officials and doctors', as witnessed formerly in Extract 8.14, becomes rather problematic. For the construction commits precisely that sin which it charges Israel with: *blurring the boundary between combatants and civilians*. As a result, Extract 8.14 of the *Guardian* both 'whitewashes' some sub-category of combatants and taints the entire category of civilians. To keep civilians separate from combatants, of course, is (or, going by the declarations of its political-moral position, should be) the position of the *Guardian*. And, rhetorically speaking, it is exactly this position that gets lost in the pursuit of some straightforwardly despicable and indiscriminately lethal Israeli intention.[18]

Be that as it may, the *Guardian* repeatedly accounted for the terrible events happening in Gaza in terms of a direct Israeli intention to cause precisely what was happening. Our last engagement with the newspaper's construction will concern why Israel might have such devious motives:

> Extract 8.16
> 'We are very violent,' Lieutenant Colonel Amir, commander of an Israeli combat engineers unit, admitted as he explained that he will use any method to prevent casualties among his troops. Meysa a-Samuni would not disagree. She is the 19-year-old survivor of the shelling of a house in the Zeitoun district of Gaza in which 30 people died, six of them members of her family. The UN Office for the Coordination of Humanitarian Affairs would not disagree either. It told us how Israeli soldiers had rounded up 100 Palestinian evacuees and put them in the house, which then was shelled, although the UN stopped short of saying the shelling was deliberate. But it did accuse soldiers of preventing the Red Cross from evacuating the wounded for three days. A few doors away, four children were found cowering next to the body of their dead mother.
>
> None of this is new. Those who remember the details of past military campaigns waged by Israel, a country which claims higher moral

> standards than its neighbours, will experience an overpowering sense of deja vu. (*Guardian*, 577)

Extract 8.16 offers an account of Israeli actions as well as, arguably, an account for Israeli intentions. Although it stops short of explicitly stating it, the recurring motive occasioned in a synoptic fashion is that Israelis are, simply, *'violent'*. It is an *Israeli* 'lieutenant colonel' admitting it, with a Palestinian survivor, whose family members had been murdered, and the UN Office for the Coordination of Humanitarian Affairs 'not disagree[ing]' with it. The *Guardian*'s ultimate answer to the catastrophe of Gaza arrives, therefore, in this passage. Israelis kill civilians, and they intend to kill civilians or, at the very least, they do not mind killing as many civilians as possible. Why? Because, plainly and simply, they are violent.[19] The newspaper never reflects on where this violence might come from. What is for sure, though, is that the picture of Israel thereby becomes a virtual mirror image of the conservative newspaper's picture of Hamas. Not only violent in deeds but violent in being, and inasmuch as it never quite becomes clear why a tendency to be aggressive is directed at civilians, perhaps even evil. In any case, any account referring to the realm of human affairs thereby becomes perfectly ignorable.

Just as was the case with constructions of Hamas and their rockets, however, the *Guardian*'s account for war stands in complete isolation amongst liberal papers (including its 'sister' publication). In fact, the *Independent*'s position was developed to explicitly counter an explanation that closely resembles that of the *Guardian*:

> Extract 8.17
> [...] the idea being pushed by some propagandists in the West that the Israeli state is deliberately setting out to kill innocent Palestinians is just as offensive and wrong. The Israel administration's priority in this operation is to defend its citizens from rocket attacks by Hamas. But while the Israeli state might have succeeded in degrading Hamas' military capabilities in the past two weeks, it cannot plausibly argue that Operation Cast Lead has helped to bring a two-state solution for Israelis and Palestinians any closer. And such a settlement is, ultimately, the only way to deliver the true and lasting security that both peoples deserve. (*Independent*, 939)

This extract flatly denies the attribution of the death toll to the will of the Israeli state. What is more, it is construed to be 'offensive'; that is, morally wrong. In opposition to it, a dichotomy is created where the state's aspiration is 'to defend its citizens from rocket attacks'. It is important to see, however, that the position countered is a most extreme one. Even if, having read the *Guardian*'s coverage, its practical relevance is doubtless, it does not make it any more reasonable. Conceptually, those who 'set out to kill innocent' people are, quite simply, evil. Arguing that Israelis are not evil is not just a rather facile point but leaves a whole range of moral/legal positions unaddressed. These possibilities, moreover, may well be capable of co-existing with an operation the explicit purpose of which is defensive.

Thus, whilst clarifying its position on the fundamental attitude of Israel towards the conflict, the extract does not offer any account for the casualties. It is elsewhere in the newspaper that we have to look:

> Extract 8.18
> However anyone looks at it, this was an unequal war. Israel insists that the high number of civilian deaths in Gaza resulted from Hamas tactics that deliberately put civilians in harm's way. It is also true, however, that the population density in Gaza and the lack of emergency provision made a high casualty toll inevitable, once military hostilities had begun. (*Independent*, 987)

Indeed, this passage sets out the *Independent's* account of the consequences of what it dubs an 'unequal war', and one with 'high number of civilian deaths'. Though explicitly framed as the position of Israelis, the claim that it is 'Hamas tactics that deliberately put civilians in harm's way', which would explain the civilian death toll, is clearly accepted by the newspaper: this is what is suggested by the start of the next sentence, '[i]t is *also* true' (emphasis added). Hamas, then, is to be blamed in part. Other than this, we read about the 'population density' and 'the lack of emergency provision' producing the 'high casualty toll'.

The interesting thing is, of course, that neither of these two other factors are human agents, and as such, they cannot be held accountable. As far as human agents go, it is only Hamas that is found responsible. Just as in Extract 8.17, moral or legal dilemmas are not even discussed in relation to the actions of the State of Israel. The only thing we learn about their conduct remains what came from Extract 8.17, where the most radical of assertions was countered. The only thing we learned about Israel's moral stance was that they are not evil. Just as was the case with the conservative press and the *Guardian,* the *Independent*'s reductionist construction of the concept of responsibility left it ultimately with two possible choices: either to absolve Israel completely or to convict it completely. That the newspaper, along with conservative ones and in opposition to the *Guardian,* opted for the former should not distract us from the more fundamental consequence of the narrowest possible construction of intention: it covers in a conceptual blind spot all the possibilities ranging between acts of pure will of evil and acts of pure mistake/oversight.

To find accounts addressing this spectrum, we need to turn to other newspapers:

> Extract 8.19
> Meanwhile, any increased consideration of Iranian or Syrian sponsorship of terrorism will pale against global outrage at the extraordinary disregard shown by Israeli forces for the lives of Palestinian civilians. It is quite possible, as the Observer today reports, that an Israeli withdrawal will reveal evidence of actions deserving indictment as war crimes. Those allegations must be independently investigated.
>
> Israel's allies in the west, chiefly the US, have traditionally defended the country on the grounds that it is a democracy besieged by despotic regimes and terrorists. But while Israeli citizens do enjoy immense political and social freedom, those values do not automatically prevent the state from committing atrocities. (*Observer*, 641)

These paragraphs from the *Observer* are of crucial importance. For one thing, loss of the lives of Palestinian civilians is accounted for by 'extraordinary disregard shown by Israeli forces'. Importantly, no attribution is made as to the pure will of the Israeli forces. It is not claimed that Israelis *intend* to kill civilians for the sake of killing civilians. What is claimed rather is that they do not *intend* enough *not* to kill civilians. They should try far harder. Even if they kill civilians without the direct intention to do so, they may still be accountable for that accident happening, and why it was not foreseen and was not evaded.

For another thing, such a broad-enough conception of responsibility still implies for the newspaper the possibility of moral and legal deliberations. It is in this context that the acts reported by the *Observer* suggest the possibility of 'war crimes' and the corresponding necessity of independent investigations thereof. The facts, of course, were equally reported or alluded to by all the other newspapers. Without the broad enough conception of responsibility showcased by the *Observer,* however, a conclusion as to the necessity of an independent investigation into possible war crimes could only be reached if one already thought that an agent was violent *as such* or, indeed, evil.

As for the *Observer* itself, attention then turns to what explains the fact that Israel's army did not simply happen to have killed a lot of civilians, but may have political, moral or, indeed, legal responsibility in doing so (i.e., it did not exercise the precautions necessary to distinguish between civilians and combatants).

> Extract 8.20
> That fact alone explains why the operation represents a defeat for Israel, as was always likely to be the outcome. The notion that the country's security problems can be resolved by the unilateral use of extreme force is a persistent delusion among Israeli politicians. In this case, the problem was perceived to be Hamas rocket fire into southern Israel; the solution was judged to be a war against Hamas. That analysis did not allow for the vital, humane recognition that, in densely populated Gaza, an all-out war against Hamas is, by necessity, an attack on the civilian population. (*Observer*, 641)

This passage features an account for Israeli misconduct. At its core is 'unilateral use of extreme force'. This is not dissimilar to the *Guardian*'s explanation. In distinction to its 'sister' publication, however, it is not simply the 'violent' nature of Israelis that is pinpointed as the origin of the predilection to resort unilaterally to extreme force. It derives from a 'persistent delusion'. It is therefore not due to a violent essence that Israel does what it does, but through some psychological distortion.

Not that such an interpretation inevitably leads to a more charitable view of Israeli responsibility. In fact, what may be gathered from this passage of the *Observer* is rather significantly different from that of Extract 8.19. The delusion does not simply explain Israel's acts in the war, but those before. The lack of negotiations may be attributed to resorting to unilateral and extreme force. This use of force, then, is not simply accountable for acts in war but for the very act of war. And as the newspaper describes the scene of war not simply taking place in 'densely populated Gaza' but being, for reasons of geography, 'by necessity, an attack on the civilian population', this act of war itself becomes a crime. Why the newspaper imagines that a densely populated area presents not simply very intricate questions and huge dilemmas of how to conduct a war but *'by necessity'* must result in war crimes is not clear.[20] Inasmuch as it is taken seriously, though, the 'independent investigations' called for in Extract 8.19 have been certainly rendered immaterial. Any act of war as such in Gaza has already been judged to be a war crime.

This is where the *Observer*'s account stops, and just as we never learn why an attack that takes place in a densely populated area would *in itself* be a war crime (and as such would rule out any kind of attempts made to distinguish between combatants and civilians in the actual course of war), we never learn either why Israelis are 'persistently delu[ded]' about the use of unilateral extreme force.

The *Financial Times*' ultimate account for war resembled in important respects that of the *Observer.*

> Extract 8.21
> The disproportionate scale of Israeli air strikes, in response to the pinprick provocations of the home-made rockets fired from Gaza at southern Israeli towns, is less surprising. It fits the Israeli doctrine of overwhelming force, which on Saturday claimed the highest number of Palestinian lives in a single day since Israel occupied the West Bank and Gaza in the 1967 Six Day War. (*Financial Times*, 1039)

Disproportionate conduct is explained with recourse to the 'Israeli doctrine of overwhelming force'; the similarity to the *Observer*'s notion of 'extreme force' is apparent. As should be the difference: it is not a 'delusion' but a 'doctrine'. It refers to a set of ideas, with some intellectual foundation. Indeed, it is possible that it refers to the concept of early right-wing Zionist Ze'ev Jabotinsky's idea of the 'iron wall', which it was crucial, in his writings, to have metaphorically erected so that Israel gained the acceptance of its neighbours.[21] Academic arguments have recently been put forward that his idea subtly but powerfully influenced the orientation of later generations of (left- as well as right-wing) Israeli politicians on questions of foreign policy and power (Shlaim, 2004).

The point here is not that, by virtue of having intellectual foundations, the idea of 'overwhelming force' is a very practical or just one. Clearly it is neither, in the *Financial Times*' construction. Being a 'doctrine', it may not be a very flexible or open position. But it is certainly not simply the manifestation of madness either. Arguments may at least have a chance of altering it.

To understand an argument or a position of intellectual import (indeed, to change it), we need to know the experiences that helped their coming to existence. It is particularly instructive, therefore, that the experience to which 'overwhelming force' was a response is categorized as 'pinprick provocations of the home-made rockets'. A non-event, that is. And if the experience that was interpreted and subsequently acted upon by the 'doctrine' was a non-event, then, in fact, even the *Financial Times*' description of Israel starts to resemble that of a lunatic. Of course, it may yet be the case that the 'doctrine' originally came to light in response to experiences that made it a more understandable framework for interpretation and action. This perspective of possible argumentation, however, is not present in the newspaper's editorials.

In fact, it is almost palpable in its invisibility:

> Extract 8.22
> But if Israel needs to reflect on how its militarist tactics and continuing occupation strengthen its most militant enemies, Hamas should recognise how its attacks on Israeli civilians have enabled Israel to change the subject: from the occupation to threats to its existence. (*Financial Times*, 1256)

The passage displays two crucial features. Its depiction of Hamas is in line with the newspaper's overall coverage, analysed in the previous section. Israeli actions are depicted as *constituting* Hamas's stance and actions. At the same time, whilst rhetorically juxtaposing what Israel needs to do and what Hamas needs to do (i.e., 'Israel needs to reflect on how...Hamas should recognize how'), the juxtaposition is thoroughly asymmetrical. The effects of Hamas action on Israel merely influence (and are used as ammunition by) *Israeli rhetoric*. Hamas's 'attacks on Israeli civilians' do not contribute to the identity and self-conception of Israelis. Not even to the evolution of their 'doctrines'. The fact that rockets are fired indiscriminately on Israeli civilians simply *helps* them to 'change the subject' from facts that would embarrass them.

In Extract 8.21, the *Financial Times*' perspective on Israeli action and identity appeared to show the exact characteristics that emerged from its accounts for that of Hamas. The idea of the 'doctrine of overwhelming force' suggested an account given in terms of some genuine intellectual content arising out of real world experiences, and not in those of violence or evil or lunacy. However, the promise of this perspective may subsequently have been lost. An exercise in understanding Hamas ultimately lead to the flat mitigation of Hamas's actions and, correspondingly, to the implicit denial of the genuine and serious nature of the 'doctrine of overwhelming force'. This resulted in the newspaper's inability to offer the same kind of perspective of *understanding* Israel as it did, consistently and coherently, with Hamas.

Thus, in the end, we are in danger of being left with what characterized all the other newspapers' accounts: little more than the black-and-white allocations of blame. Hamas rockets are constructed as *either* relatively ineffectual in their material consequences (i.e., 'pinprick provocation'), *or* carrying the hateful message of inhumanity (i.e., 'attacks on Israeli civilians'). Correspondingly, Israel is *either* responding violently, madly or cynically instead of pursuing negotiations, *or* has no choice but to launch a war. The fact that the *Financial Times* at least managed to tolerate these polar opposites does not alter the fact that even this newspaper could not begin to address the vital tension between them: the rockets may be of little material consequence but do carry the message of hate, and they may carry the message of hate but are ultimately of little material consequence.[22]

Discussion

Ostensibly, categorical differences could be detected between the conservative and the liberal newspaper's account of the deepest dilemmas of war: law to war and law in war. Whilst conservatives, ultimately, unequivocally justified Israel's right to launch war in response to Hamas rockets aimed at its civilians and, in fact, positioned Israel's 'decision' beyond the remit of political-moral deliberations, liberal newspapers all expressed that a viable alternative – negotiations – could and should have been pursued. Likewise, whilst conservative newspapers ultimately refrained from subjecting Israel to substantial criticism regarding its conduct of the war, where the issue surfaced, the liberal press (i.e., the *Observer* and the *Guardian*) called for independent investigations into what emerged as possible war crimes.

Looking deeper into these issues, however, an altogether different picture became visible. Inasmuch as it remained one of categorically polar, black-and-white opposites, it still showcased remarkable similarities.

The *Independent*'s and the *Independent on Sunday*'s accounts did not overly differ from the conservative press. Their unhesitant and repeated call for 'negotiations' was not grounded in a significantly different account of the events and the participants. As Hamas was still depicted in terms reminiscent to those of the conservative press, the proposed solution of negotiations did not become a realistic alternative to war, only an exercise in wishful thinking. As for the two newspapers' account of law in war, their somewhat more vivid description of the consequences of Israel's offensive did not lead to political-moral criticism of any substance. In fact, much like in the conservative press, Israel's accountability did not even feature in the equation. Without these argumentative/narrative elements, any overt differences in conclusions became immaterial.[23]

Another way of attending to the possibility of negotiations appeared in the *Guardian*. In this newspaper, all the profoundly problematic characteristics of Hamas disappeared. Not that Hamas, absolutely speaking, became anywhere near the image of purity that Israel was in the conservative press (and to some extent in the *Independent*). How could it have been? But the organization was consistently depicted in terms that appeared to pose no substantial challenge to negotiations whatsoever. This, however, was a 'solution' to finding an alternative to war in nothing but name. First, because characteristics of Hamas were simply *asserted*, essentially without any kind of argument addressing the grave concerns of *all* the other newspapers. To statements about Hamas *being* bad, merely the counter-statement of Hamas *not being* that bad was made. Second, in parallel with Hamas becoming 'better' in a way absolutely lacking in argumentative or narrative context, Israel became 'worse' and 'worse'. If Hamas, as such and in its being, did not pose any substantial problem to negotiations, then something else had to. Thus, there still was a subject position basically blocking negotiations. Only that in the place that used to be occupied in other newspapers by Hamas, the State of Israel appeared.

Thus, there were no real differences between the conservative account of war and lack of negotiations and that of the *Guardian*, either. It was simply that the position of *bad* switched occupant, and different essences began to be created to the participants. However, it must be seen that the question of who is good and bad is immaterial to negotiations taking place. The present author has a wife: she is a very nice person. The present author also has a mother: a very nice lady indeed. Yet this altogether nice state of affairs does not alter the fact that, left on their own, wife and mother will not immediately be able to talk. They will need to share a language or have a mediator who shares a language with them. There must be a way for them to *understand* each other.

The question as to the viability of negotiations as an alternative to war is therefore the equivalent of the question as to whether the participants are of categorically different kinds, or there are sets of relations that make one's conduct (partly) constitutive of the other. Likewise, the question is not whom *really* it is to blame. The question, rather, is whether the relevant agents' conduct/identity is understandable *in the light* of the conduct/identity of the other. Or, they are simply isolated, organic, homogeneous essences.[24]

It was only in one publication that an attempt was made to *understand* Hamas in this sense, and therefore present negotiations as a viable alternative to violence. The *Financial Times* consistently occasioned context and Israeli action as factors contributing to Hamas's conduct and (self)identity. And as such, in the place of essences, a set of relations started to emerge. Obviously, the existence of these relations did not in itself solve the problem. It did not simply make Hamas better. Or Israel worse. It was only that it opened a window and a perspective from where words as alternatives to violence became possible at all.

That this window, ultimately, closed once again is, from the perspective of this report, the tragedy of the British broadsheets' coverage of the armed conflict.

Not where it was never opened in the first place. The *Independent*'s optimism persisted without changing the picture seen in the conservative press. As the *Guardian* moved the allocation of blame from Hamas, it simply replaced it on Israel. Yet, accounting for Israel's resort to violence, even the *Financial Times* dismissed the perspective of understanding – the only perspective that makes talk and non-violent engagement *a possibility and not a miracle*. Israel's interpretation of the situation and response to it were, ultimately, not presented as emerging from relations between the state and the Arab world (historically) or the state and Hamas (more recently). They became self-contained and *essential* reactions. And, as a corollary, the exercise in understanding Hamas also became one of absolution as we read about their rockets being but 'pinprick provocations'.

In a deep sense, then, the apparent differences between the conservative press and the liberal one were not differences at all. In varying degrees, the newspapers all in the end became absorbed in the question of whom it is to *blame*. Who is the Good and who is the Bad? They all gave account of the proceedings with recourse to some sort of essence, where the respective agent's conduct and identity is not understandable as emerging from a set of relations with the other agent (or past agents in history) but, simply, from some source or core categorically in the inside. As such, any understanding of the conflict other than the absolutely (conservative press) or relatively (liberal press) straightforward allocation of blame became impossible, as did any peaceful solution other than a miracle.

Why was it the case? Could it not have been otherwise?

What is clear is that the fundamental moral and legal conceptual dilemma behind the accounts concerns the dilemma of responsibility: of subjective *intention* versus objective *consequences*.

As we witnessed in the conservative account, the rockets of Hamas were exclusively defined in terms of the pure evil subjective intention to kill civilians and nothing but civilians: this is why Hamas became the paragon of evil and could not be engaged with. And Israel's actions *too* became characterized with recourse to pure subjective intention; this is why Israel could not be criticized (lest it becomes evil) and became the paragon of purity.

As we have witnessed in the present chapter, where the issue was considered with some seriousness in the liberal press, at significant points the rockets of Hamas were exclusively defined in terms of pure immaterial consequences. As a result, Israel's response to them became characterized with recourse to either some mental deformity (*Observer*, *Financial Times*) or the outcome of a simple violent, subjective intention to kill civilians and nothing but civilians (*Guardian*): this is why Israel became the paragon of violence (if not evil) and could not be engaged with.

So Hamas actions were either defined by evil intention – or were of no significance. And correspondingly, Israeli actions were either defined as pure with no choice – or were the outcome of some deluded/violent essence. What was missing was the perspective where rockets are *both* evil in aspiring to kill civilians *and* of limited material consequences. And where Israeli action does *both* not deviously aspire to kill civilians *and* lead nonetheless to material consequences of enormous gravity. What was therefore missing was a broader conception of the political-moral-legal meaning of human action where it is not exclusively located either in pure will or in pure consequence. One may not simply dread death – one must dread hate.[25] And one may not simply judge direct subjective intentions – one must judge lack of reasonable circumspection.

To account for this 'pathologically' split state of affairs and its ultimate consequences, the clear-cut allocation of blame and the impossibility of peaceful alternatives to violence, it was proposed in the conclusion of the previous chapter that such a state of affairs may stem not from a political, moral or legal perspective but from an essentially metaphysical one. Indeed, it may stem from the memory of an event where evil and innocence, death and life, the activity of perpetrators and the passivity of victims[26] became manifest in their (im)purity. Inasmuch as the memory of this event is transposed to the conflict between Israel and Hamas/Palestinians, these poles cannot be but re-enacted.

The door hiding Israel and its acts could not be opened by the conservative press, for fear and trembling of what a supposedly pure entity would look like once it is. And inasmuch as the liberal press, and the *Guardian* in particular, looked behind that door, their fear and trembling became anger. *Being human,* the agent 'disguising' itself or 'disguised by' purity cannot become simply problematic when exposed in its reality. Just as one cannot kill a human being a little, that agent will become impure. And the impure being disguised as pure will certainly shock the conscience of mankind.

9
Conclusion: Beyond Good and Evil

Overview and summary

Examining the British broadsheets' engagement with the armed conflict of Gaza, this book narrated a story of the war.

By and large, it started with consensus. As the coverage of 'building blocks' with which the narrative of the war was constructed was examined, whatever differences we found were coloured by grey and not categorical black and white. Regardless of political affiliation, newspapers agreed on which conceptual areas and which topics within conceptual areas to prioritize. Any divergence occurred only in the shadow of these broad similarities and may therefore be judged relative rather than categorical.

As for these relative differences or shades of greys, they occasionally appeared in unexpected patterns. Regarding the general importance attributed to fatalities, no left-right axis was discernible, as it was the conservative *Telegraph* and the left-liberal *Independent* that referred to fatalities most frequently. And if this preference was not for the same reason, no ideological divide could be detected regarding specific categories of fatalities either: whilst the *Telegraph* and the *Guardian* displayed an interest in the nationality of the victims (focusing on Israelis or Palestinians, respectively), *The Times* and the *Independent* focused more on humanitarian status (focusing on combatants or civilians, respectively). What is more, even though conservative newspapers attributed more importance to topics representing action and events in war than their (left)-liberal counterparts, all general differences disappeared when specific categories of action were consulted. Indeed, it was the magnitude of the *Telegraph*'s coverage of the Zeytoun incident and that of *The*

Times regarding the Israeli deployment of the chemical substance white phosphorous that stood out amongst individual topics.

Whilst still coloured by the shades of grey, important divergences started to emerge in Chapter 4, where historical context and the critical perspective it implied was examined. The chapter reported that *each* of the liberal newspapers attributed more importance to historical context than *either* of the two conservative ones, and that conservatives devoted far more attention than liberals to the issue of Hamas rockets fired into Israel when compared to the Israeli economic blockade of Gaza. A conservative pole of historical coverage emerged, characterized by the neglect of historical issues; indeed, even Hamas rockets were reported less often than what would have been expected on the basis of *Telegraph's* and *The Times'* general presence in the database. As for the liberal newspapers, it was less than clear as to what qualitative difference their pronounced focus on historical issues derived from. In the case of the *Independent*, no meaningful pattern emerged regarding the target of their criticism; and whilst the *Financial Times* appeared to direct a consistent critical perspective to both participants of the conflict, of the newspapers, they neglected most the seminal issue of Hamas rockets. It was only the *Guardian* where the magnitude of coverage appeared to have been translated into a systematic qualitative difference. The left-liberal newspaper was the only one consistently deploying a critical perspective as it wrote a considerable amount not just about the Israeli economic blockade and occupation, but also about Hamas rockets fired into Israeli civilian territory.

In line with this, as the perspective of the book has been broadening and as analysis turned from facts towards the context of criticism, a recognizable and systematic gap has been opened between the conservative and (left)-liberal coverage of the war.

This tendency characterized Chapter 5 where the subject of analysis became how the *act* of criticism was constructed in the broadsheets' comment pieces. First, as the first half of the chapter demonstrated, when the ratio of positions indicating a broadly 'pro-Israeli' or 'anti-Hamas/Palestinian' stance versus positions suggesting a broadly 'anti-Israeli' or 'pro-Hamas/Palestinian' stance was calculated, a contrastive picture appeared between conservative and (left)-liberal newspapers – one ever more pronounced in the case of *The Times* and the *Independent*. Second, there was virtually no occasion where an *overlap* of these positions would have been showcased across the spectrum of the broadsheets. What is more, qualitative analysis was capable of looking into those articles where the possibility of precisely such overlap or *fusion of perspectives* was seemingly on offer. And, astonishingly, not even those articles that attempted, or at any rate explicitly claimed, to showcase such genuine overlap between perspectives actually managed to achieve that. To find a common ground, to genuinely acknowledge rights and wrongs of both sides, somehow seemed to be practically impossible in the context of the armed conflict.

In Chapter 6, analysing explicit engagements with antisemitism, more of the same was to follow. Mapping the structure of this book, there was a consensus regarding the fact of the increase in antisemitic incidents in Britain and Europe during the war. Yet as soon as the concern was not a fact but a judgment of antisemitism – that is, when newspapers engaged with the judgments that pronounced something as antisemitic – not one instance was found in the newspapers where this judgment would have been genuine. Factually wrong, perhaps, but still genuine. Instead, those judgments were acts of fanaticism or political cynicism. The realm of facts (i.e., antisemitic incidents) and that of humans (i.e., where people judge something to be antisemitic) were radically separated. Antisemitism was either simply, plainly, factually there, or simply, plainly, factually not there. In either case, this construction meant that a claim to the contrary inevitably implied fanaticism, idiocy or malice: certainly not positions that can be engaged with from any reasonable political-moral perspective.

The relative consensus of the early chapter(s) therefore started radically to dissipate. In particular, whenever issues of judgment (as opposed to facts) were occasioned, a separate and rigid dichotomy between right and wrong emerged. And as 'right' became so absolutely straightforward and unambiguous an entity, 'wrong' in turn appeared not simply an error of political-moral judgment but the emanation of suspicious or rather horrendous practices and motives.

The pinnacle of this dynamic was reached in the last two chapters, where the general narrative/argumentative perspectives of the broadsheets' editorials were examined.

As we witnessed, newspapers like the conservative *Daily Telegraph* and the left-liberal *Guardian* became virtual mirror-images of each other, especially as far as the State of Israel and the Israeli Defense Forces were concerned. In the *Telegraph*, both in terms of law to war and law in war, Israel was not so much right in the choices it made but beyond the possibility of criticism. In the *Guardian*, it did not simply carry out action that raised the possibility or indeed the necessity of serious political-moral or legal criticism, but was immediately condemned wholesale. An entity of purity faced that of inherent aggression and violence in the respective accounts of the two newspapers.[1]

The force of the dichotomy between polar and incommensurable opposites and the political-moral-legal consequences of a zero-sum game could also be witnessed in the way these newspapers engaged with what could potentially have subverted, challenged, or at least nuanced their constructions. Even when explicitly raising the grave issue of the Palestinian death toll, and by implication Israel's conduct of war, the *Telegraph* maintained the State's status as being, ultimately, beyond the possibility of substantial criticism. Even when considering Hamas's characteristics, the *Guardian* never seriously engaged with the possibility that its action or overall outlook could have a significant impact on the events. Challenges to the respective discourses were therefore brushed aside brusquely and without any real reflection.

Yet these challenges arising from the *Telegraph*'s and the *Guardian*'s *own* accounts were nothing in comparison to those emerging from *The Times*. The conservative newspaper reported, and then in its editorials duly reflected, on the investigative finding that Israel appeared to have used weapons containing certain chemical substances in what the newspaper itself dubbed 'illegal' ways. Given that, in early editorials, *The Times* expressed only guarded support of Israel's choice to launch a war and as such retained space for criticism, one would have expected such revelations to lead to a genuine exercise of critical judgment of Israel's conduct in the war.

As we saw, *exactly the opposite happened.* It was precisely as the possibility of Israel's 'illegal' conduct of war was raised that its choice of war retroactively became not even an unreservedly good choice, but almost a natural necessity. It was as Israel's conduct was explicitly stated to show 'scant regard' for the life of Palestinian civilians that Hamas started to acquire the essentially evil characteristics that the *Telegraph* exhibited from the outset. Most staggeringly, it was as the gravest questions about its action and responsibility emerged that Israel was positioned as being beyond the possibility of substantial criticism.

It is no exaggeration to assert that such a state of affairs beggared belief. What it showcased, however, was not simply a tortuous rhetoric or some logical inconsistency. Rather, it indicated the power of the un-subvertible and rigid dichotomy and that of the investment in the straightforward allocation of *blame* in the relevant political, moral or legal dilemmas. There *had to be* someone who was not just right but innocent. And there *had to be* someone who was not just wrong but almost the Devil himself.

In the editorials, there was only one serious intellectual attempt to systematically counter this tendency.[2] The radical novelty in the *Financial Times'* account as far as Hamas was concerned was not that the organization somehow appeared to be 'better' than in the conservative press. It was that, in contradistinction to *all the other newspapers*, it was constructed to be not simply something that *is*, in and of itself, but something that *comes to be* what it is and *to do* what it does through encounters with the other relevant agent (i.e., the State of Israel). This construction, therefore, moved beyond the simple allocation of rights and wrongs, of essential innocence and blame, and opened up a way for engagement and understanding. As such, it opened a vista for *politics*.

Likewise, initially analyzing the newspaper's account of Israel appeared to suggest that the *Financial Times* remained consistent with its offer of approaching agents not as, to all intents and purposes, immutable essences but emanating off encounters and engagements. Of course, it did not depict Israel as innocent, as the conservative press did. But neither did it depict it as having some violent substance (*Guardian*) or 'deluded' mentality (*Observer*) at its core. Rather, it was an Israeli 'doctrine' that the newspaper utilized in understanding Israel's conduct. Doctrines, of course, can be problematic, and this particular doctrine was certainly implied to be highly counter-productive. Also, doctrines may be ill at ease with arguments aiming to challenge them. Yet inasmuch as they are, essentially, intellectual positions derived from encounters in the past, they can, in theory, be engaged with and transformed.

The perspective of the *Financial Times*, unique amongst the newspapers, was therefore that of the promise of understanding interrelated and mutually constitutive nature of human political-moral relations. Instead of black and white dichotomies where words hold no power and what matters is the mere allocation of blame and innocence, it promised a vision that makes politics possible at all.

Yet this promise in the end remained unfulfilled. As far as Israel was concerned, the newspaper ultimately reverted to the position where the 'doctrine of overwhelming force' motivating Israel's conduct became nothing but a lunacy (if not the manifestation of some violent essence). It ultimately became unserious in intellectual and dismissed in emotional content. What is more, whilst Israel's destructive actions were constructed as constituting Hamas and its choices, Hamas's conduct started to be depicted as merely an excuse for Israel and petrol for its rhetoric, and not something with a constitutive effect on Israel's conduct and identity.

Thus, in the end, all British newspapers that engaged with war in their editorials with some intellectual seriousness utilized a perspective where political, moral and legal questions of Israel/Palestine and the ongoing war were addressed only from the point of view of who, essentially, is innocent and whom is to blame. It was not questions of responsibility and the exercise of critical judgment that was called for but to decide who, ultimately, constitutes the problem and who does not. And as such, the ultimate framework through which the newspapers approached war was not that of politics or morality or legality, but that of pure (i.e., meaningless) violence, and equally pure and unaccountable innocence.

As noted in Chapter 8, the issue with such a perspective is not simply the proportion in which it allocates blame and innocence in the right proportions. The real dilemma is not whether Israel/Hamas was *as good/bad as* they were depicted to be. Rather, it was that such constructions of rigid and mutually exclusive dichotomies excluded even the theoretical possibility of dialogue and engagement. Thus, they excluded the possibility of pursuing the political solution that *all* newspapers advocate: a two-state solution based on negotiation and compromises.

This book has so far adamantly, perhaps to the point of irritation, refrained from adjudicating over truth and falsehood. It refused to jump at conclusions about which newspaper(s) reported the conflict in the right way and which were wrong. Yet, by way of conclusion, some profound wrong must be accounted for. Namely, *it cannot be right* that newspapers addressing human affairs uniformly take recourse in and are motivated by non-human concepts of Good and Evil. It leads not to critical judgment, but to (conservative) fear and (liberal) anger. Nothing good can come out of this, certainly not in a conflict (whether that of the actual war or of the peace process in general) that is crying out for political solution. It cannot be right that whilst the broadsheets all advocate a negotiated solution, the framework they construct makes it all but impossible.

Therefore, the upshot of the empirical analysis of this book is that the discourse with which the conflict of Israel/Palestine is accounted for needs to be changed. But to do so, one first has to understand why such a framework emerged in the first place and what motivates its perseverance. These will be the tasks of our last sections.

The world is a very narrow bridge...

Violence tears people apart. In the place of shades of grey, it carries black and white. In the place of responsibility, it brings blame. In the place of understanding, it offers fear and anger. Violence, in itself, leads to nothing but more violence. It was this logic of violence that ultimately motivated the accounts of conservative and liberal newspapers' coverage of the armed conflict and, correspondingly, it did not lead to critical judgment and reflections on responsibility. To *understand* violence is the ultimate way of countering it. But to do so is an enormous task because violence tears precisely those human relations apart which would make its understanding possible (Böhm & Kaplan, 2011; Harding, 2006; Lawrence, 2012).[3]

The conceptual framework the international community came up with to contain and counter political violence is that of human rights and humanitarian law (cf. Mettraux, 2008; Robertson, 2006; Smith, 1977). The horrors of the Second World War led to a consensus that certain events of inter- and intra-state violence must be confronted and accounted for not only within the established system of laws within any given state's sovereignty, but in front of *humanity as such*. Both in legal and moral discourse, the language of humanitarian law, with its basic distinction between combatants and civilians, has become the *lingua franca* of assessing war and state oppression.[4] Unsurprisingly, in accounting for the tragedy that is war, it was this vocabulary that the newspapers drew upon in critically assessing the events and the agents.

However, this language – developed in the place of and in opposition to past utopias that had some ultimate goal in mind other than that of the life of particular human beings – was used in a rather peculiar way in the newspapers. To be precise, it was either conspicuously *not* used even when made relevant; or used with some religious fervour. Israel was either *not* assessed critically in terms of humanitarian law or immediately condemned without much thought. With the occasional exception in the *Financial Times*, editorials conveying the perspectives of British broadsheets habitually occasioned the language of human rights in a way that suggested a *sacred* discourse, rather than one of political/moral/legal responsibility of judgment.

What could also be empirically established was that, conceptually speaking, this sacralization of the discourse of critical judgment derived from the broadsheets' peculiar concept of responsibility. As the newspapers attended to the issue of possible Israeli war crimes, the conception of moral or legal responsibility was reduced to the question of pure destructive intention: that is, whether those who happened to have killed civilians *willed* to kill civilians. This was paralleled by the assessment of Hamas rockets. They were *either* reduced to the pure intention they embodied *or* to the (relatively speaking) little material consequence they caused. No other conceptualization of the rockets than this radical schism between intention and effect featured in any of the newspapers.

Yet the moment that such a reductive and subjectivist conception of responsibility is used, one is once again left with only two options. Those who kill civilians are either *evil*, or essentially *innocent* and guilty only of mistakes. Correspondingly, if the matter of moral or legal responsibility is raised, it will immediately bring the spectre *not* of moral or legal responsibility, but that of evil. In the place of moral or legal responsibility and critical judgment, what we were left with was a choice between the *sacred* and the *sacrilege*.

Why was this the case? Why was a discourse of responsibility and critical judgment occasioned which then either effectively outlawed any attempt at criticism or rendered those judged as damned? There is no conceptual reason for this. Not only is a broader conception of responsibility than that of a direct wish to kill civilians clearly possible, it is normally used widely in legal and moral disputes (cf. Margalit & Walzer, 2009; Walzer, 2009b) – and glimpses of such a conception were actually there to be seen on occasion in the broadsheets' coverage of the war as well. Yet they were never followed up as, where it was attended to, responsibility ultimately became that of the reductive dilemma of a purely *subjective will to kill.*

Again, why was this the case? What made the broadsheets resort to such an unreasonable and unviable concept of responsibility?

As documented by intellectual historian Samuel Moyn, the language developed to counter and prevent excesses of past utopias that found human lives dispensable in pursuit of the ultimate goal has *itself* become humanity's (or, at any rate, the Western half of it) last utopia (Moyn, 2011; cf. Ignatieff, 2003; Walzer, 2009b, pp. 42–43).[5] Indeed, as mentioned above, notions such as 'war crimes' or 'crimes against humanity' were uttered (or resolutely not uttered) in the broadsheets precisely with some kind of quasi-religious fervour.[6] Yet if we try to answer the question of *why* exactly it occurs when issues of Israel/Palestine are discussed, another scene may be mentioned. Namely, the images of absolute separation between Good versus Evil, and Innocence versus Destruction may derive from the Western civilization's last epic and essentially uncontroversial war. It may be that it is the image of an event of metaphysical proportions in the imagination that motivate the discourse over Israel/Palestine: that, of course, of the Second World War. And, in the disguise of humanitarian law, it is the framework of 'Us versus the Nazis' that is enacted in the place of common and consensual political, moral or legal standards across the broadsheets (cf. Judt, 2010).

Be that as it may, the most important finding of this book is that the 22-day event the British broadsheets covered, commented on, and analysed was not one involving human agents. Rather, it was a scene of essentially *metaphysical* nature, with Good pitched against Evil. As such, the terms of evaluations became those of pure and impure, allowing no distinction in degrees, only ever in kind.

Whilst this book sees no option but to conclude that the coverage and critical assessment of any conflict between humans must be done according to a discourse and framework developed accounting for human affairs and not according to a mythical one for gods, we must also acknowledge how far from an easy task it is to disentangle these affairs from violence, from racism, from a humanitarian discourse that is increasingly sacralized, and from the image of the last epic battle where, on a fundamental level, right and wrong could clearly, definitely and unapologetically be established. As argued above, all these factors easily ensue in a radical and absolute separation between the active and the passive, agents of destruction and those innocent or acting on behalf of innocents. The possibility of understanding, critical judgment as well as engagement is far from evident and needs enormous work.

Having said all this, there *is* at least one historical example when someone encountered violence, ultimate manifestations of racism, crimes against humanity, genocide and all this in the context of the Second World War – and nonetheless managed to tackle one of the oldest questions:

> O chestnut-tree, great-rooted blossomer,
> Are you the leaf, the blossom or the bole?
> O body swayed to music, O brightening glance,
> How can we know the dancer from the dance?
>
> (W.B. Yeats, 'Among School Children')

It is Hannah Arendt's encounter with the Evil in Jerusalem that the last section of this book will engage with.[7]

...but we must not fear

In 1960, the Israeli government decided to abduct from Argentina former SS lieutenant colonel Adolf Eichmann who, despite his relatively lowly rank, had been responsible for the logistics of the Final Solution (cf. Cesarani, 2004). Concluding a trial held in Jerusalem that lasted for eight months, Eichmann was found guilty by the Jerusalem District Court on all 15 counts of the indictment, amongst them crimes against humanity and war crimes. Following appeal, the Supreme Court upheld the verdict and the President of Israel rejected a plea for clemency. Adolf Eichmann was hung and cremated on 31 May 1962 with his ashes being subsequently dispersed in the Mediterranean sea. To this day, he remains the only criminal executed in the State of Israel (Yablonka, 2004).

It has never been questioned that a main part of the reason for Israel's undertaking the dangerous operation of abducting a person from the terrain of another sovereign (subsequently incurring the wrath of Argentina and risking sanctions imposed by the UN Security Council) was that this elusive figure appeared to symbolize the entire collective that perpetrated the Final Solution (Cesarani, 2004; Segev, 2000). In fact, he appeared to symbolize the entire collective that perpetrated atrocities against the Jewish people throughout the ages (cf. Bilsky, 2004; Cesarani, 2004; Douglas, 2001; Landsman, 2006; Zertal, 2005).

Accordingly, at the Jerusalem trial of 'the State of Israel v Adolf Eichmann', the Attorney General presented a defendant who was a criminal 'more extreme than the evil man Hitler himself' (quoted in Cesarani, 2004, p. 304). In the opening oration of the trial, those attending witnessed the whole of the story of antisemitism canvassed, leading naturally to the Holocaust with Eichmann being the 'central pillar of the whole wicked system' (quoted in Cesarani, 2004, p. 300).

Not surprisingly, the Counsel for the Defence was of an altogether different opinion. For him, Eichmann was a mere 'cog' in the machine, executing simply the orders of his then superiors, and now a scapegoat for virtually all the crimes perpetrated against the Jewish people throughout the ages.

German-Jewish-American political theorist Hannah Arendt was present at some parts of the proceedings, read the transcript of the trial as well as publications dealing both with the Eichmann case and with international law in general (Arendt, 1994). Her account certainly differed from those of the Attorney and the Counsel for the Defence in terms of historical detail and historical perspective (cf. Mommsen, 1991). However, what is of crucial importance is that she decided that whom she saw and read (about) was a completely different person from the one presented by either party at the proceedings. More precisely, she decided that whom she saw in the glass booth was, indeed, a *person* (cf. Arendt, 1978, pp. 3–5, 2003a, 2003c).

From the point of view of the present book, historical inaccuracies, misunderstandings, even gross personal failings on Arendt's part are of no real interest (cf. Laqueur, 1983, 2001). What is of interest is her extraordinarily simple (and yet still, for many, practically impossible) act of intuiting that if an agent is understood as being either a monster, the devil himself, or a cog, then something crucial has gone missing. Obviously, the simple fact that Arendt saw and understood Eichmann as human did not mean that she would have liked him: being human does not automatically entail being *humane*. And it most certainly did not mean that Arendt would not have fully endorsed the District Court judges' finding Eichmann guilty on all counts. It was just that she approached the man and his conduct not in terms of non- or inhuman qualities, but of the relationships this man had with other (wo)men at the time. The question of responsibility became dependent on ways of relating to other humans and not the equivalent of non-human essences. By definition, and different from the question of what Eichmann actually did, neither the Evil nor cogs have conscience and, as such, political, moral or legal responsibility (Arendt, 1994, 2003a, 2003b, 2003c).[8] Monsters, the Evil and cogs have no choice but to do what they are predisposed or designed to do. They may be fought, killed, replaced or thrown away. But, lacking conscience and choice, they cannot be understood and held accountable as they are not human beings relating in one way or other to other human beings.

Thus, to investigate his responsibility, Arendt made a virtually unprecedented attempt to understand the point of view of Eichmann, and the sets of human relationships within which he lived whilst turning into a *genocidaire*. As such, Arendt exercised what she later termed 'enlarged mentality' (Arendt, 1978a, p. 94; cf. Arendt, 2003b)[9] in revisiting the scenes Eichmann went through during his career, the situations he found himself in, and the people he had contact with. In her reconstruction, Eichmann had ample reasons and opportunities to mute his conscience and feel 'like Pontius Pilate' (cf. Arendt, 1994, p. 135). Encountering the social-political context of the Third Reich as he had, killing Jews – or at any rate, arranging and organizing the killing of Jews – was all but *natural* and, after a very short period of doubting, these things did indeed come *naturally* for the lieutenant colonel.[10] *Naturally*, that is, inasmuch as the person in question is incapable of or does not arrogate *judging independently* from this evaluative context what is in fact going on, and if the person in question exhibits an 'almost total inability to look at anything from the other's point of view.' (Arendt, 1994, pp. 47–48) 'At that moment', Arendt starts by quoting Eichmann on the Wannsee conference, '"I sensed a kind of Pontius Pilate feeling, for I felt free of all guilt." *Who was he to judge*? Who was he "to have [his] own thoughts in this matter"? Well, he was neither the first nor the last to be ruined by modesty' (Arendt, 1994, p. 117 – emphasis in the original).

As is well known, Arendt's critical judgment flew in the face not only of the political-moral-legal framework of the attorney (and the Counsel for the Defence) but of virtually every other observer (distal or proximal) of the events (cf. Cohen, 1993; Rabinbach, 2004). The publication of her account of the trial prompted more than a thousand published polemical responses in English alone, and a situation amongst intellectual circles that was later metaphorized as a 'civil war' (Howe, 1983, p. 270; cf. Braham, 1969). No surprise. For as Eichmann turned out to be a human being emerging out of social relationships, and as the central characteristic of the person at the centre of the logistics of the Holocaust became not merely domination but negotiation, the hitherto straight and absolute lines between the forces of Evil and Good took on a more problematic face then previously assumed. To make an agent human means to point to other humans of agency – hence, of responsibility. As such, Arendt's report inevitably brought up the issue of Jewish responsibility and started to ponder what role Jewish functionaries played in the destruction of the Jewish people.

And here came the most terrible aspect of the scene Arendt set. Questions of responsibility and intention regarding Good and Evil are unproblematic. As they are essences, they *embody* intention: both are beyond the possibility of critical judgment as they *embody* the acts they do or do not do. Acts of humans, however, may be unintended in any strict sense yet fall within their responsibility. And if so, both Eichmann and the Jewish functionaries found themselves to be in the grey zone (Arendt, 1994, p. 120; cf. Levi, 1989) – if, obviously, of radically different shades of grey.

Indeed, the moral guilt of the Jewish functionaries in Arendt's account derived from the same source as that of the criminal guilt of Adolf Eichmann. Responsibility in both cases concerned what Arendt in relation to Eichmann dubbed '*he never realized what he was doing*' (Arendt, 1994, p. 287, cf. pp. 21–35, 49, 252 – emphasis in the original). Without necessarily *intending* straightforwardly the acts (of terrible consequence), they carried them out nonetheless. They did of course know what they did, but did not grasp its meaning and significance; and even though they did not actively want to contribute to the mass murder, they made no real attempt to extricate themselves either. They did things, but did not *think* about doing those things. They were not dancers, but they did do the dance.

Not only did Jewish functionaries become responsible and accountable in this framework; as they were part of the social context within which Eichmann acted and his conscience operated, the functionaries acquired a role, and thus responsibility concerning the very crimes the lieutenant colonel perpetrated.

> As Eichmann told it, the most potent factor in the soothing of his own conscience was the simple factor that he could see no one, no one at all, who actually was against the Final Solution.... Of course, he did not expect the Jews to share the general enthusiasm over their destruction, but he did expect more than compliance, he expected – and received, to a truly extraordinary degree – their cooperation.[11] (Arendt, 1994, pp. 116–117)

And if so, then the cooperation of Jewish functionaries (that is to say, the representatives of the victims) was the last element of a context where Eichmann, too humble to exercise independent judgment, felt convinced that what he was doing was, indeed, normal, natural and right:

> His conscience was indeed set at rest when he saw the zeal and eagerness with which 'good society' everywhere reacted as it did. He did not need to 'close his ears to the voice of conscience', as the judgment has it, not because he had none, but because his conscience spoke with a 'respectable voice', with the voice of respectable society around him.[12] (Arendt, 1994, p. 126)

Seeing human agents in contradistinction to Evil and Innocence, Hannah Arendt was not the disinterested observer she liked to claim herself to be, however (cf. Arendt, 1993, p. 227, 2003c, p. 159). Her book is one written in outrage at a scandal. As far as Eichmann was concerned, surprisingly perhaps, this outrage did not overly affect the accuracy of her historical and character judgment, as can be ascertained from recent scholarship on the lieutenant colonel.[13] It 'only' affected her tone, which throughout the book remained acerbic in the extreme.[14] This, of course, may in itself be taken as a failure to exercise the 'enlarged mentality' she did when trying to understand Eichmann, as the subsequent wrath of intellectuals may have stemmed from the inability to understand biting irony where no one ever has dared to use such kind of rhetoric. But, in retrospect, irony in Arendt's book may simply be taken as a tool to contain outrage as well as to rob someone committing the gravest possible crimes off his *greatness*.[15]

However, justifiable and inevitable outrage did seriously distort Arendt's account when it came to assessing the responsibility of the

Jewish Councils (cf. Arendt, 1994, pp. 115–126). As her subsequent clarification of the issue in an exchange with Gershom Scholem indicates, Arendt tended in fact to judge the *entire institution of the Jewish Councils morally guilty* (Arendt, 1978b; cf. Kaposi, 2008, pp. 102–112). The assumptions underpinning such assessment, as subsequent scholarship has shown, are indefensible on sociological and historical grounds (Bauer, 2002, Chapters 4 and 7; Trunk, 1972).[16] But, equally beyond doubt, an unequivocal (and faulty) collective judgment of a Jewish institution concerning the Holocaust must also to this present day be assessed as most insensitive and hurtful.

Yet, to point out problematic (and, we may say, almost *necessarily* problematic) aspects in Arendt's critical judgment should not blind us to the enormous achievements of her contribution that are deeply relevant to the present book. In accounting for the Eichmann case, Hannah Arendt's overriding characteristic was the courage to dispose of taboos – received 'metaphysical' juxtapositions – and to face the vast emotional investment with which these were imbued. Staring *evil* in the face yet concluding that both those perpetrating the acts constituting evil and those suffering from those acts were *humans* requires an extraordinary measure of independence and commitment. What is more, it offers the reward that is the establishment of the conditions for understanding and, ultimately, peace and reconciliation.

This, then, is the task that awaits those concerned with the discourse on Israel/Palestine and violence. In place of the black and white of violent acts, the human shades of grey shall be put. In place of blame and innocence, that of responsibility. In place of isolated identities, that of relationships. And, ultimately, in place of (physical or rhetorical) fighting, that of dialogical understanding.

Understanding, of course, is not all that there is. It does not *at all* mean the utopian scenario of complete absence of violence and some divinely inspired capacity to forgive anything and everything at once. It is merely the precondition of any alternative to aggression. The possibility of negotiations will not mean that their potential will always be realized or that we must not fight wars. It will only mean that people with thorough and enormous disagreements will have a *chance* to settle their differences in ways other than (rhetorically or physically) eliminating each other.

Understanding is not a magic torch of divine proportions, only a flicker of light in a dark room. Not necessarily able to bring the room to light at once, but the only means by which the room does not look very, very dark indeed.

Appendix – Conservative and Liberal Editorials

The titles of conservative editorials

Date	No	*Daily Telegraph*	No	*The (Sunday) Times*
28 December 2008			173	This bloody stalemate in Gaza must be broken
29 December 2008	7	Hamas and Iran pose a threat to the world	187	Bitter harvest
30 December 2008	17	Peace in Gaza is in the hands of Hamas		
31 December 2008			202	Security dilemmas in Gaza
5 January 2009	43	Israel needs to be quick and clear in Gaza	244	Clueless in Gaza
10 January 2009	76	A ceasefire would be in Israel's interests	278	In defence of Israel
16 January 2009			331	Smoke screen

The titles of (left-)liberal editorials

Date	No	*Guardian/Observer*	No	*Independent (on Sunday)*	No	*Financial Times*
28 December 2008	424	Talking, not force, is the only solution in Gaza	838	Gaza: The cycle can be broken		
29 December 2008	441	Killing a two-state solution: Gaza air strikes	849	The bombardment of Gaza will destroy lives, not Hamas	1039	Bombing Gaza is not a solution
30 December 2008			858	We must not let despair dash hopes of peace in Gaza		
31 December 2008	464	Gaza: Quiet of the grave				
04 January 2009	496	Israel must withdraw from Gaza				
05 January 2009	520	Gaza ground assault: When victory is a hollow word	896	Gaza will not find peace until Hamas ceases to be a threat	1226	A dangerous gamble in Gaza
07 January 2009	552	Gaza: No shelter				
08 January 2009			920	A ceasefire that promises hope, but must deliver	1239	Diplomacy must include Hamas
10 January 2009	577	Gaza: More, but worse	939	Israel's security will come only through dialogue		
14 January 2009	618	Gaza: Israel and the family of nations				
15 January 2009					1247	Endgame in Gaza
18 January 2009	641	A pointless war has led to a moral defeat for Israel				
19 January 2009	661	Gaza: Brutal lessons	987	Welcome but fragile, this ceasefire must be only a start		
22 January 2009					1256	The ruins of Gaza
23 January 2009			1005	Gaza: the way forward?		

Notes

1 Introduction: Violence and Understanding in the Armed Conflict of Gaza

1. The historical account that is to follow is based on the Goldstone Report (2011), Operation in Gaza (2009), Philo and Berry (2011).
2. Of course, these were only some of the restrictions upon the autonomy of the authorities in Gaza. Military (as opposed to civilian) developments were supposed to remain solely within the authority of Israel, in accordance with the Oslo framework.
3. 18 Israeli civilians were killed between June 2004 and the start of the Gaza war (Amnesty International, 2009, p. 66). Between 2000 and 2008, 12,000 such rockets or mortars landed in Southern Israel. In 2008 alone, 3,000 of them were fired (Operation in Gaza, 2009).
4. On 21 December, Hamas made a statement to the effect that it might renew the ceasefire if Israel stopped its aggression against the Strip and opened its border crossings. On the very same day, Hamas also fired 70 rockets into Israeli civilian territory. Likewise, Israeli words of reconciliation were coupled with airstrikes within the Strip on 24 December.
5. It is for this reason that some commentators explicitly refuse to call the armed conflict a 'war', claiming that the use of such a term would imply a balance of forces that was nowhere to be seen on the ground (Gaita, 2010).
6. Which, of course, is in itself of rather questionable value as it leads to the intensification of Israeli militancy and thus to more Palestinian suffering.
7. B'Tselem could not determine the relevant identity of 36 people.
8. The source of figures on fatalities is the Goldstone Report (2011, pp. 49–51).
9. For Israeli statistics, the age below which one was categorized as a child was 16. Elsewhere it was 18.
10. The brief of the UN Board of Inquiry investigation is available here: www.innersitypress.com/banrep1gaza.pdf
11. Critics did not hesitate to point out that what they considered the one-sided nature of the Commission's findings was already implied by the fact that it would have originally ignored the conduct of Hamas.
12. Even more controversially, the Goldstone Report found that taking Palestinians as human shields was a fairly standard procedure followed by the *Israeli* forces (Goldstone Report, 2011, pp. 165–177).
13. Cf. 'The IDF [...] made extensive efforts to avoid civilian casualties and limit damage to private property, as well as to ensure that Israeli military activities were conducted in compliance with the Law of Armed Conflict and Israel's own stringent ethical and legal requirements' (Gaza operation: second update, 2010, p. 32).
14. White phosphorous is a highly incendiary, self-igniting chemical material that, upon exposure to air, continues to burn until it is deprived of oxygen. Consequently, it is very dangerous to humans as even a comparatively

low percentage of burn (10–20 per cent) often results in death (Amnesty International, 2009, p. 29). In the war, the IDF mostly used it as obscurant (in open field as well as built-up areas), air-bursting 155mm artillery shells which exploded mid-air, ejecting 116 felt wedges impregnated with white phosphorous. The wedges ignited on contact with oxygen and cascaded down over a large area of approximately 250 metres in diameter (Human Rights Watch, 2009). Burning in air, white phosphorous released a thick white smoke, providing smokescreen for Israeli tanks.

15. This state of affairs seems to have been misunderstood somewhat by the final report of the UN Human Rights Council's panel of independent experts, as they commended Israel on the one hand on the 'significant resources [dedicated] to investigate over 400 allegations of operational misconduct' (Report of the committee of independent experts, 2011, p. 21) yet criticized it because 'there is no indication that Israel has opened investigations into the actions of those who designed, planned, ordered and oversaw Operation Cast Lead' (Report of the committee of independent experts, 2011, p. 22).

    Likewise, Richard Goldstone's recantation of some of the most important conclusions of his commission in an op-ed piece for the *Washington Post* may have been equally misguided in its argumentation:

    > The allegations of intentionality by Israel were based on the deaths of and injuries to civilians in situations where our fact-finding mission had no evidence on which to draw any other reasonable conclusion. While the investigations published by the Israeli military and recognized in the UN committee's report have established the validity of some incidents that we investigated in cases involving individual soldiers, they also indicate that civilians were not intentionally targeted as a matter of policy. (Goldstone, 2011)

16. For considerably more measured pondering of these issues with care and intellect, see Brian Klug's work (Klug, 2003, 2005, 2008, 2009; see also Fine, 2009; Hirsh, 2007, 2010; Myers, 2006; Peace, 2009).

2 Method of the Analysis and General Characteristics of the Newspapers

1. This database has its faults: some obvious, some less so. Evidently, to base one's research on an electronic text-database means missing out on visual aspects of the coverage. This means pictures and cartoons, as well as the general visual ordering of articles. There can be no doubt that these contribute to the general sense and meaning of the coverage and, as such, offer a non-negligible limitation of the book (cf. Loughborough University, 2006).

    However, Nexis's archive is also known (and proved in this case) to be less comprehensive than would be expected, even as far as textual material is concerned (cf. Deacon, 2007). In general, non-narrative types of articles (e.g., framed timelines, or other fragmented additional explanatory material) are only randomly archived. The decision therefore was made to ignore even those of them that were available.

    This is not deemed to be such a considerable limitation, as attention may justifiably be paid to factual, narrative and argumentative types of information. More troubling was to find (as the spreadsheet was assessed) apparent 'gaps'. For instance, there appeared to be no articles containing the search term published in the *Guardian* on any Thursday during the sample, and there seemed to be a relative paucity of material containing the search term in the *Financial Times*. Furthermore, no readers' letters in the *Independent* and no editorials in the *Sunday Telegraph* were found. In the case of such anomalous absences, secondary sources were consulted: firstly, the InfoTrac database, secondly the publication website. In the case of the *Guardian*, subsequent searches performed for specific dates (Thursdays) on Nexis and InfoTrac produced no results, but searches of the *Guardian* website identified several. Likewise with the *Financial Times* and the *Independent*. In the case of the *Sunday Telegraph*, however, none of the searches highlighted further editorial material.

Having performed such searches in these cases where data were feared missing, it was felt that all data that could reasonably be identified has been included, that any omissions are not systematic but randomly produced by the source databases, and thus that claims can safely be made regarding patterns in the data.

2. The difference between weighted divergence and simple divergence is that the former takes into account not just the magnitude of divergence but the empirical importance of the code as well. Weighted (rather than simple) divergence was used for a reason that can be easily demonstrated. Only one paragraph referred to the Camp David negotiations between Israel and Egypt in 1979 in the entire database. That one occasion happened to be in the *Independent*. Thus, the *Independent*'s share of the code is 100 per cent, well above the expected 20.4 per cent (cf. Table 2.3). Yet accounting for the next to total unimportance of the code when considering the entire database, the weighted divergence will be 0 per cent (cf. Tables 4.1 and 4.3).
3. The only information that later chapters will utilize whilst this one does not is the empirical importance a newspaper attributes to a conceptual area (say, to historical context). This is because whilst *every* single paragraph was coded regarding the type of article in which it appeared, it was evidently not so regarding the conceptual area of historical context. Thus, it makes sense to talk about the empirical importance of the conceptual area of historical context for individual newspapers – not that of the general characteristics of the newspapers' coverage, however.
4. Circulation figures of 2008: *Guardian*: 378.394; *Independent*: 250.641; *Telegraph*: 890.086; *The Times*: 633.718; *Financial Times*: 452.488.
5. *Guardian*: 930.849.240; *Independent*: 399.772.395; *Telegraph*: 1.135.749.74; *The Times*: 808.624.168; *Financial Times*: 533.392.824.
6. See footnote 2 above.
7. Philo and Berry (2004, 2011) argue that lack of contextualization will, in itself and in general, favour the Israeli position in the conflict. Whether this is so in a war that resulted in the known casualty figures may well be contested. Besides, it will also be important to see what, precisely, that context or those facts and events for each newspaper consisted of.
8. It has to be noted that the *Guardian* published the most letters during the conflict, according to any standard. Given that letters to the editor have a tendency to be rather partisan, this fact may also have some significance.
9. It must be noted that not only did the *Independent* feature vastly more comments than any other newspaper, and more comments even than news

articles, but an incomparably high proportion of them was written by Robert Fisk. In fact, 16 out of 43 comment-type articles were written by the controversial columnist. This is only one article less than *all* the comment pieces *The Times* devoted to the war. No other author came to anywhere near such proportion in any of the other newspapers. (The second most prevalent columnist in the entire sample was the *Daily Telegraph*'s Con Coughlin who published 3 comment pieces.) The *Independent*'s entire coverage of the war, in this sense, is very heavily dominated by one author. Not just any author, of course, but one with a very distinct voice. A paragraph that may be deemed characteristic of his style will have to suffice here. The extract will be analysed in Chapter 6:

> But watching the news shows, you'd think that history began yesterday, that a bunch of bearded anti-Semitic Islamist lunatics suddenly popped up in the slums of Gaza – a rubbish dump of destitute people of no origin – and began firing missiles into peace-loving, democratic Israel, only to meet with the righteous vengeance of the Israeli air force. The fact that the five sisters killed in Jabalya camp had grandparents who came from the very land whose more recent owners have now bombed them to death simply does not appear in the story. (*Independent*, 851)

3 Action and Death in War

1. Distribution of fatalities on the dimension of nationality and moral-legal status in the full database (on the basis of Table 3.1):

	Occurrences	% within all daily paragraphs (7830)	% within all fatalities occurrences (1359)
Palestinian	1113	14.2	81.9
Israeli	217	2.8	16.0
Other	29	0.4	2.1
SUMMA	1359	–	100

	Occurrences	% within all daily paragraphs (7830)	% within all fatalities occurrences (1359)
Civilian	699	8.9	51.4
Combatant	186	2.4	13.7
Other	474	6.1	34.9
SUMMA	1359	–	100

2. It is deceptive that whilst 34.9 per cent of fatalities were not categorized explicitly by the newspapers according to their humanitarian status, only 2.1 per cent of them were left without nationality (mainly UN workers or humanitarian volunteers). For what this vast disparity indicates is less the gross neglect of humanitarian status, and more the fact that fatalities were often reported in a format where a lump sum was succeeded by a breakdown according to more exact categories.

3. The one newspaper standing out is the *Financial Times*. In the liberal publication, both categories of Palestinian fatalities (i.e., civilian and combatant) were mentioned considerably less than in other newspapers and Israeli ones more. The *Financial Times* appears to stand out amongst newspapers on two grounds: it attributed by far the least empirical significance to the topic of fatalities, and it mostly occasioned uncategorized fatalities, be they Israeli or Palestinian.
4. This is further emphasized by the fact that it also wrote a lot, relatively speaking, about other fatalities of the war.
5. It would appear that contrasting, for instance, Israeli civilian with Israeli uncategorized, Palestinian civilian with Palestinian uncategorized, Israeli combatant with Israeli uncategorized fatalities gives us no information as to which side is 'preferred' by the ratio. Incidentally, the coverage of the *Financial Times* is overwhelmingly characterized by the predominance of uncategorized fatalities.
6. *The Times*: 3 pro-Palestinian, 1 pro-Israeli top two ratios. *Independent*: 2 pro-Israeli, 1 pro-Palestinian top two ratios. *Financial Times*: 2 pro-Palestinian and 2 pro-Israeli top two ratios.
7. *Financial Times*: 6; *Daily Telegraph*: 16; *The Times*: 4.
8. 15.5 per cent in the *Guardian* and 16.0 per cent in the *Independent*.
9. There is still the possibility, of course, that *The Times* occasioned 'Israeli war crimes' in *subsequent paragraphs* following the occasioning of 'white phosphorous'. The hypothesis was not tested within the present enquiry.

4 Engagements with History

1. This tendency can be further illustrated by the example of a pair of codes of certain theoretical interest. If it is accepted that reference to the Palestinian legislative elections of 2006 implies the democratic mandate of Hamas, and as such is somewhat of a pro-Hamas argument, and that reference to the Palestinian civil war of 2007 implies the violent and uncompromising nature of Hamas and as such is an anti-Hamas argument, then we would expect conservative newspapers to allude more to the latter. And this of course is what happens when the newspapers are taken in themselves. Yet, again, if we consider the broader picture and the newspapers' coverage of these issues relative to other newspapers, we find that the *Telegraph* underreports the Palestinian civil war by 0.2 per cent and *The Times*'s weighted divergence is around 0.0 per cent.
2. In the arguments of the Glasgow media group, underreporting context in itself may be considered a 'pro-Israeli' coverage (Philo & Berry, 2004, 2011).
3. What is more, the political-moral perspective of a newspaper as expressed in newspaper editorials may not 'conform' to the implicit perspective expressed in news articles. This feature will be more closely examined in Chapters 7 and 8.

5 Engagements with Criticism

1. Clearly, the subsample thus created will not tell us everything about issues of criticism/support as far as the Israeli-Palestinian conflict is concerned. Yet to aim at a more comprehensive analysis, virtually everything commentators

wrote could have been included, as there are practically no utterances in the conflict that one side or the other would not take as an instance of criticism. As a result, an unmanageable sub-sample would have been assembled. Issues of implicit criticism/support will be examined closely in the last two empirical chapters, dealing with arguments about war.

2. The pattern in the *Financial Times* (a liberal but not *left*-liberal newspaper) resembles more the conservative end of the spectrum.
3. For other, relatively transparent, non-genuine overlaps between perspectives, see the following examples:

> So, always excepting [Melanie] Phillips, Israel has had little support even from usually reliable quarters. Stephen Glover, while endorsing nearly all arguments in Israel's favour, also insisted in the Mail: 'We cannot ... defend what is happening. The disproportionality is too great.' In the Mail on Sunday, Peter Hitchens, describing himself as 'a consistent hardline supporter of the Jewish state', argued that *there was 'no important way' in which Israel's bombing and shelling differed from Arab murders of Israeli women and children.* (*Guardian*, 601 – emphasis added)

The overlap in the italicized part does indeed seem genuine, in that equivalence is made between the Israeli bombing and the 'Arab murders of Israeli women and children'. Yet it is important to note that this statement is not a confession from the author's part. It is a quotation. And the person that is quoted is (self-)described as a 'consistent hardline supporter of the Jewish state'. In other words, the source of this opinion is himself already partial: a *supporter* instead of a balanced *arbiter*. Clearly, then, the suggestion might be that if it is possible or indeed compelling from even such a subject position to arrive at the conclusion that Israeli and Arab crimes are equally detestable, a conclusion arrived at from a neutral position should be even less flattering regarding the conduct of Israel.

> Twelve years earlier, another Israeli helicopter attacked an ambulance carrying civilians from a neighbouring village – again after they were ordered to leave by Israel – and killed three children and two women. The Israelis claimed that a Hizbollah fighter was in the ambulance. It was untrue. I covered all these atrocities; I investigated them all, talked to the survivors. So did a number of my colleagues. Our fate, of course, was that most slanderous of libels: we were accused of being antisemitic.
>
> And I write the following without the slightest doubt: we'll hear all these scandalous fabrications again. We'll have the Hamas-to-blame lie – *heaven knows, there is enough to blame them for without adding this crime* – and we may well have the bodies-from-the-cemetery lie and we'll almost certainly have the Hamas-was-in-the-UN-school lie and we will very definitely have the antisemitism lie. (*Independent*, 918 – emphasis added)

Independent columnist Robert Fisk clearly phrases his endorsement of the criticism of Hamas: 'heaven knows, there is enough to blame them for without adding this crime.' The utterance, however, not so much overlaps with positions critical of Israel where the author's perspective is synoptic, as it is absolutely overwhelmed by them: 'Our fate, of course, was that most slanderous of libels: we were accused of being anti-Semitic'; 'we'll hear all these scandalous fabrications again'; '[w]e'll have the Hamas-to-blame lie'; 'we will very definitely have the anti-Semitism lie'. Taking this broader context in regard (let alone the even broader context of the entire article), Fisk's endorsement of a position critical of Hamas is little more than an aside – especially that whilst Israeli machinations deserve scrutiny throughout the entire article, the utterance about Hamas is never followed up and its consequences never extrapolated even by a tiny bit.

4. A similar type of argument from the other direction occurred here:

   > 'I have always defended Israel's right to be but cannot extend unconditional support and immunity from censure in perpetuity. Nor can countless, conscientious Jewish men and women who publicly condemn Israel's abominations. The Israeli academic Oren Yiftachel, who has long defended Palestine, has said his country "turned Gaza into a massive prison and is choosing to prolong the cycle of state terror and prison resistance that goes with that". In other words, Israel wants to keep the conflict alive.' (*Independent*, 986)

5. Extract 5.5 by Sally Hunt was of course not dissimilar to this kind of genuine overlap between non-genuine perspectives.
6. For a somewhat similar argument and positioning: 'But why speak about such things when we can hold up placards equating Jews with Nazis, emote over dead babies or talk tough about defending Israeli citizens?' (*The Times*, 190)
7. For example, *Daily Telegraph*, 37; *The Times*, 190; *Guardian*, 592; *Independent*, 834.
8. Cf.

   > Let's have a pointless discussion about Gaza and begin it by talking about whether Israel's bombing is 'disproportionate'. To illustrate the meaninglessness of such a debate let us attempt to agree what 'proportionate' would look like. Would it be best if Israel were to manufacture a thousand or so wildly inaccurate missiles and then fire them off in the general direction of Gaza City? There is a chance, though, that since Gaza is more densely packed than Israel, casualties might be much the same as they are now, so although the ordnance would be proportionate, the deaths would not. Of course, if one of Gaza's rockets did manage to hit an Israeli nursery school at the wrong time (or the right time, depending upon how you look at it), then the proportionality issue would be solved in one explosion. Would you be happy then? (*The Times*, 190).

9. Of course, football fans are wise enough to know that when their team puts one behind Ferencváros or AC Milan, this state of affairs does not allow them to claim political-moral superiority. Bragging rights must in no circumstances be confused with political-moral rights or wrongs.

6 Engagements with antisemitism

1. Given the nature of debates on 'new antisemitism', the otherwise obvious statement has to be made here that *none of these positions* allows for actual acts of violence committed directly or indirectly against any Jewish person. The latter issue does not concern political ideology but 'just war theory'. Whatever European Jews are and whatever their perceived or actual commitments are towards the State of Israel – they are non-combatants, full stop (cf. Margalit & Walzer, 2009; Walzer, 2000).

2. Note that this kind of explanation is common on the 'left' side of the academic spectrum as well (cf. Finkelstein, 2005, p. 66).
3. For a typical example:

   > Peace is not within Hamas's vocabulary, which is characterized by the rabid antisemitism of its charter. It makes use of the Protocols of the Elders of Zion – one of the most notorious antisemitic forgeries of the last century – continues with the incantations that turn jihad against the Zionists into every Muslim's duty, and ends with suicide terrorism. (*Guardian*, 555)

4. Based on other parts of the articles as well as other pieces by the contributor (Robert Fisk), it is probably the second interpretation that is valid.
5. Interestingly, this is partly achieved because of reporting of B'Tselem in a synoptic mode and, arguably, quoting them indirectly. Thus, judging something as antisemitic does not even have to be countered in objective terms of reality. It can also be made appear counter-factual by relying on a respected opinion.
6. Significantly, as mentioned in Chapter 2 (cf. footnote 9), the dominant role of Fisk, as far as the *Independent*'s comment articles were concerned, was exceptional amongst the newspapers. He authored more than one in three comment articles in the left-liberal newspaper. No other publication came anywhere near this ratio.

7 War – Purity of Arms and Souls in the Conservative Press

1. For the full list of conservative editorials, consult the Appendix.
2. Cf. *The Times' third* editorial of the war: 'At least 70 such rockets were launched from Gaza into Israel in December. This was the criminal act that triggered the current crisis [...]' (*The Times*, 278); '[...] it must be remembered that 8,000 rockets have been fired at their territory in recent years. Without these attacks by Hamas, the Israelis would not be bombarding Gaza.' (*Daily Telegraph*, 17)
3. Cf. 'Ron Prosor, the Israeli ambassador to London, asked yesterday what we would do if our sovereign territory were under daily attack. It is a good question; the answer must be that we would seek to protect our people.' (*Daily Telegraph*, 17)
4. It was only in *The Sunday Times*'s argument that ceasefire was constructed as substantial and as such offering alternatives to war:

   > We appear to be back at square one. It is 18 months since Israel imposed its blockade on Gaza with the aim of isolating Hamas and preventing its supporters launching rocket attacks. The six-month ceasefire, although often breached, at least suggested the possibility of dialogue. Now, as so often in the region, we are back to bloodshed and loss of life. (*The Sunday Times*, 173)

5. Cf. '[...] Hamas ceasefire expired [...]' (*The Sunday Times*, 173).
6. Slightly differing from other publications, in the account of *The Times*, the ceasefire's end was brought about by 'unravelling' or 'expiration'. That is, the factor of human action is dismissed in separating the sphere of death (rockets) from the sphere of life (ceasefire). It is not human action that is accountable for the transition from one to the other. It just *happened*.

7. Cf.

   > Like its principal state sponsor, Iran, Hamas's rallying cry is not the creation of a Palestinian state but the destruction of the Jewish one. This is why, when a ceasefire ended last month with an onslaught of Hamas *rockets aimed at civilian Israeli targets*, Israel had no choice but to prosecute this war. But the need to strike back does not excuse the mistakes that Israel has made in doing so. (*The Times*, 331 – emphasis added)
   >
   > [...] they [i.e., Hamas] *deliberately target civilians with their own rockets.* At least 70 such rockets were launched from Gaza into Israel in December. This was the criminal act that triggered the current crisis; every time that bewildered Gazans are corralled by Hamas fighters into a human shield, it is compounded by rank cowardice. (*The Times*, 278 – emphasis added)

   The Times also refers to the 'relentless shelling of its [i.e., Israel's] civilians' (*The Times*, 202). Interestingly, the feature of the rockets that they intend to kill civilians is never explicitly pointed out by the *Telegraph.*
8. A similar argument to that of the *Telegraph* appeared in *The Sunday Times'* first editorial on the war: 'The bigger question is how to get out of this bloody stalemate. Israel's response will seem disproportionate to many but it was made in response to extreme provocation, compounded by Hamas's refusal to recognize Israel's right to exist.' (*The Sunday Times*, 173)
9. This consideration is further elaborated in the first paragraph of the article:

   > After eight days of rocket attacks from Gaza the Palestinian group Hamas seemed to have left Israel with little choice but to retaliate. On Saturday it did so by launching one of the deadliest series of air assaults in the history of the 60-year old conflict. As a result, innocent lives are being destroyed. The Middle East peace plan was already dog-eared. It now looks threadbare. (*The Times*, 187)

10. Cf.

    > Israel has a right to defend itself but criticism from some European governments that disproportionate force is being used might soon become more persuasive in these circumstances. (The Times, 202)

11. Likewise, the historical-political event the that *The Times* editorial in question chooses to contextualize the war is no longer the economic blockade on Gaza, but Israel's withdrawal from Gaza in 2005 and the rocket-fire it resulted in.
12. The argument was basically repeated in the *Telegraph*'s second (but not in the third and fourth) editorial on the war:

    > The Israel Defense Forces has been condemned around the world for a disproportionate use of force in Gaza, though it must be remembered that 8,000 rockets have been fired at their territory in recent years. Without these attacks by Hamas, the Israelis would not be bombarding Gaza. Ron Prosor, the Israeli ambassador to London, asked yesterday what we would do if our sovereign territory were under daily attack. It is a good question; the answer must be that we would seek to protect our people.A resolution to the calamity lies, therefore, principally in the hands of Hamas, whose anti-Semitic leaders seem to regard the family in our picture as expendable in pursuit of their bigger ambition, which is to break Israel. For as long as Hamas refuses to contemplate the only possible answer to this conundrum – a two-state solution – there is little chance of peace. It is clear that the Israelis are not going to negotiate while their security

> is constantly under threat, which means that even the restoration of a ceasefire that can easily be broken may not suffice. (*Daily Telegraph*, 17)

13. That is, inasmuch as Israel was left with no choice it simply cannot feature in any political-moral deliberations – as those deliberations depend on the freedom of choice.
14. This, of course, does not mean that civilians cannot die in war but that there must always be attempts made to prevent this to happen.
15. The duality of these discourses surfaces elsewhere in the newspaper as well:

    > The humanitarian crisis in Gaza is so severe that a ceasefire is essential, irrespective of whether Israel feels it has achieved its military objectives. It goes without saying that there will always be civilian casualties in urban warfare; but the deaths of hundreds of people, including scores of children, cannot be countenanced. [...] It cannot be right to seek to protect the innocent victims of southern Israel by the killing of the innocents of Gaza. (*Daily Telegraph*, 76)

    The considerations here are explicitly labelled as humanitarian and the point of focus is, again, clearly the death of civilians as a wrong in itself. Equally, the standard to which Israel's conduct is measured is what is morally/legally right. Yet if we continue reading the editorial, the pragmatic argument immediately surfaces:

    > For those, including this newspaper, who sympathize with Israel's predicament and understand the motivation for the Gaza offensive, it has become increasingly difficult to watch the unfolding catastrophe with any degree of equanimity. If Israel appears to ignore the suffering of ordinary Palestinians, its enemies benefit. In all humanity, it must facilitate the movement of sufficient food and medical relief to the people of Gaza. (*Daily Telegraph*, 76)

16. The only way for it to be possible is if some deluded Israeli leader did not recognize his/her own self-interest.
17. A variation of the similar theme may be found here:

    > It bears repeating that the crime that *triggered* this war was last month's Hamas rocket barrage; vivid proof of its defining dread of peace. Hamas knew then that only its refusal to acknowledge Israel's right to exist stood in the way of a resumption of the peace process. It knows now that only its refusal to end the rocket attacks and stop rearming through tunnels under Gaza's Egyptian border stands in the way of a ceasefire. (*The Times*, 331 – emphasis added)

    The dilemmatic nature of Israeli war conduct once again becomes resolved in the question of why there is war in the first place.
18. As persuasively argued by the pioneering philosopher of just war theory Michael Walzer and moral philosopher Avishai Margalit, the question of 'intention' in war is not merely comprised of a narrow definition that one actually actively *wants* to kill as many as possible. It also pertains to reasonable efforts made to minimize the number or proportion of those being killed (cf. Margalit & Walzer, 2009).
19. The reference here is not just to the conservative newspapers' metaphysical (rather than secular) conception of responsibility. It is also intended as an ironic commentary on such a state of affairs, by (somewhat cryptically,

perhaps) alluding to a Talmudic interpretation/utilization of the biblical passage: 'It is *not in Heaven*, that you should say, "Who will go up to Heaven for us, and get it for us so that we may hear it and observe it?"' (Deut, 30:12, emphasis mine).

Namely, the tractate Baba Metzia reports Rabbi Eliezer ben Hurkanos attempting to settle a debate with fellow rabbis, by starting to perform miracles in support of his argument. His peers are not convinced, however, by acts like making a channel of water flow backwards, or making a carob tree uproot itself and move a couple of hundred meters. As a last resort, therefore, Rabbi Eliezer appeals to the Heaven to back up his argument. Whereupon the heavenly voice is duly heard: 'Why do you dispute with Rabbi Eliezer? The Halakhah [i.e., Jewish religious law] always agrees with him.' One would think the divine voice is enough to convince the rabbis, but it is at this point that Rabbi Joshua stands up and protests in the form of quoting from the above passage of the Bible: 'It is not in Heaven' (Deut, 30:12); and Rabbi Jeremiah expounds: 'The Torah has already been given at Mount Sinai [and is thus not in Heaven]. We pay no attention to any heavenly voice'.

That is it that settles it; it is human interpretation and the authority of the interpretative community that matters, not unmediated heavenly intention. And why would this be an ironic comment on the newspapers' metaphysical conception of responsibility? Note that it is a *sacred* intention that is beaten on a *sacred* (i.e., Halakhic) issue with a *sacred* (i.e., biblical) passage in a *sacred* (i.e., Talmudic) rendering – by the *secular* act of interpretation/understanding.

As a coda, and courtesy of the prophet Elijah, we also learn what the Almighty thought of these affairs at the time. 'God smiled and said: "My children have defeated Me, My children have defeated Me."' (cf. Scholem, 1995b, pp. 291–292)

20. As has been seen, the acknowledgment of the six-months ceasefire between Israel and Hamas was either downplayed in its significance or phrased as a unilateral ceasefire by Hamas.

8 War – Purity of Arms and Souls in the Liberal Press

1. For the full list of liberal editorials on the war, consult the Appendix.
2. One other exception being:

> There is, meanwhile, no mechanism to negotiate a way out of this impasse. It is not just Israel that does not talk to Hamas. The EU and US also refuse contact.
>
> That is because Hamas is a terrorist organisation. Its founding charter claims the Holy Land exclusively for Islam and calls for the complete annihilation of Israel. For all that the international community might wish for Israeli restraint, no government in the world would tolerate an enclave on its border run by an organisation ideologically motivated and heavily armed to kill its citizens. From the Israeli perspective, painful compromises already made – pulling down Jewish settlements in Gaza – resulted in less, not more security. That feels like a betrayal. (*Observer*, 424)

3. For example, 'Hamas's leadership also now has the conditions for which it has strived. They boycotted the talks offered by Egypt in November, built a

tunnel through which they intended to attack an Israeli border post, and fired hundreds of rockets into Israel.' (*Guardian*, 441) This passage from the *Guardian* depicts a less than favourable image of Hamas, not completely unlike the one found in the conservative press. At the same time, rockets, even 'hundred of rockets' feature *not* as a *casus belli*. The statement about the rockets is not followed up by occasioning the idea of 'no choice'. In fact, the very notion of counter-productivity is implied in that Hamas has 'now' the condition 'for which it has strived'. In other words, Hamas's undesirable characteristics notwithstanding, it is Israel that (co-)created this condition.

4. Interestingly, this dynamic is the exact opposite of the one witnessed in the case of conservative newspapers. There, it was questions of law *in* war that were occasionally approached with recourse to law *to* war.
5. Cf.

   > But what lesson has Hamas been taught? Has the bloodshed re-established the deterrence that Israel lost in Lebanon two and half years ago? Has it dramatically increased the penalty that Hamas and other militant groups incur for continuing to fire rockets at the civilian population in southern Israel? Israel makes great claims for the military blow Hamas has suffered, but as yet has produced little concrete evidence. Hamas's arsenal of rockets may be depleted but still exists, as does its ability to fire them. At least 13 were fired after Israel's unilateral ceasefire in the early hours yesterday. (*Guardian*, 661)

6. 'Hamas is more than just a guerrilla army. It is a political movement as well. As such, Hamas will have been seen to have borne the brunt of the occupier's might and Hamas's claim to assume the leadership of the Palestinian national movement will have been enhanced as a result.' (*Guardian*, 520) The apparent feature of this passage – the *Guardian*'s characterization of Hamas as a 'political movement' *in addition* to it being a 'guerrilla army' – has already been remarked on. Yet, the real point is not simply to ponder whether this is a somewhat rose-tinted idea of Hamas. The point is what kind of 'political movement' it is. That we do not learn from these sentences. What we do learn is that whatever characterizes Hamas as a political movement is partly the effect of it bearing the brunt of 'the occupier's might'. There is, then, an ongoing occupation, constitutive of Hamas's conduct.
7. Cf.

   > [...] Israel has mounted probably its most extensive public relations offensive, which includes keeping journalists out of Gaza. This is not just to avoid the sort of images that did so much damage in 2006 – of children being pulled like broken dolls from the ruins of their homes – from getting out. The aim is to place sole blame for this crisis on Hamas and slot it into the global 'war on terror'.
   >
   > But the claim that the Islamists' extremism is the main cause of Gaza's misery, after Israel offered Palestinians freedom by pulling out of the Mediterranean enclave in 2005, is less than a half-truth.
   >
   > Gazans have been under blockade since Palestinians had the temerity to elect Hamas three years ago, while Israel has significantly expanded its occupation of the West Bank and Arab east Jerusalem. This is a conflict that can end only if an independent Palestinian state is created on all that occupied land. (*Financial Times*, 1226)

8. Cf. 'The deadly paradox is that while Hamas has nothing but failure to show for its tactics, the conciliatory strategy of President Mahmoud Abbas and Fatah has failed too, allowing Israel to expand its occupation of the West Bank and presenting the Islamists with an alibi' (*Financial Times*, 1256).
9. It was the consequence of this, of course, that *The Times* stopped referring to the blockade when doubts were raised about the conduct and indeed the very character of Israel.
10. This does not mean that, by some sort of necessity, it will have to be realized. It only means that it becomes possible.
11. As has been seen in Extract 8.8, the *Observer*'s coverage did feature one paragraph implying the constitutive nature of context as to what Hamas does. It is not the only one of the kind: 'But the reality is that the status of Hamas as the preferred vehicle for Palestinian resistance to Israeli occupation has been enhanced by the indiscriminate brutality of the military assault.' (*Observer*, 641)

    However, this perspective was by no means systematically utilized by the *Observer*:

    > It is a depressingly familiar scenario, a cycle of provocation and reprisal that periodically escalates into full-blown war. There is no simple account of events leading up to the current confrontation that does justice to the amassed sense of grievance on both sides. But two specific events have played a decisive role: the decision earlier this month by Hamas to end a six-month ceasefire and elections in Israel due in February.
    >
    > In reality, the 'ceasefire' was a tempering of aggression on both sides rather than a cessation of hostilities. Israeli foreign minister Tzipi Livni has declared the rocket attacks 'unbearable' and asserted that the Hamas administration in Gaza must be 'toppled'. (*Observer*, 424)

    In this extract, the decision to end ceasefire is not enjoined by any reasoning. Equally, its reality is undermined by the next sentence.

    > There is, meanwhile, no mechanism to negotiate a way out of this impasse. It is not just Israel that does not talk to Hamas. The EU and US also refuse contact.
    >
    > That is because Hamas is a terrorist organisation. Its founding charter claims the Holy Land exclusively for Islam and calls for the complete annihilation of Israel. For all that the international community might wish for Israeli restraint, no government in the world would tolerate an enclave on its border run by an organisation ideologically motivated and heavily armed to kill its citizens. From the Israeli perspective, painful compromises already made – pulling down Jewish settlements in Gaza – resulted in less, not more security. That feels like a betrayal. (*Observer*, 424)

    Hamas is depicted here from a perspective that closely resembles that of the conservative press: an entity of some terrible essence.
12. To remember, it was the case even when the *Guardian* itself occasioned a radically different alternative to its account of rockets. Namely, that they *aim* 'at the civilian population in southern Israel'.
13. One use is a quotation, of course, but a synoptic one where no distance is indicated from the source.
14. Policemen do carry guns, but are supposed to use them for civilian purposes.

15. It is the definite article ('the') before the noun 'targets' suggesting that it was police stations and police stations only/mainly that were targeted: '*The* targets were not the training camps of Hamas's military wing, which were empty when the jets struck, but rather police stations.' (emphasis added)
16. Cf.

    Nowhere in Gaza has been off limits, *least of all the shelters run by the United Nations Relief and Works Agency*, which have been repeatedly hit by Israeli shells and missiles. More than 5,400 Palestinians have been injured, sometimes by *weapons designed to maim and terrorise*. If the Israeli prime minister considered himself absolved for the sins of the ill-prepared invasion of Lebanon, Gaza has paid a grotesque price for Olmert's salvation. (*Guardian*, 661 – emphasis added)

    Again, the valid question of Israeli responsibility is simply addressed here by way of a (surely indefensible) extreme formulation. Suggesting that the shelters of the UNRWA were actually one of the prime targets of the Israeli attacks means that the direct aim of those attacks was precisely the death of civilians. Likewise with weapons that are 'designed to maim and terrorise'.
17. Exactly how many of them was a question that featured strongly in investigations into the participants' conduct in the war. Whilst a blanket equation is clearly untrue, blanket exemption likewise is not appropriate (cf. Goldstone Report, 2011, pp. 60–70).
18. Cf. '[...] a country which *truly rejects* the collective concerns of the international community leaves its friends, never mind its enemies, running out of road.' (*Guardian*, 618 – emphasis added)
19. The fact that Israelis are not simply 'animals' in this construction stems from the following fact: they are a country that claims 'higher moral standards than its neighbours'. If this is done in the face of such overwhelming consensus, coming both from inside and outside, we may conclude that Israelis are not just violent but deceitful as well.
20. Suffice it to say that the densely populated area that is Gaza is certainly not the densely populated area that is the Old Trafford stadium on a match-day.
21. In fact, the notion of the 'iron wall' was explicitly mentioned in a similar context in a weekly newspaper whose publisher is the same as that of the *Financial Times* (*Economist*, 738).
22. As noted above, the complexity of the situation surfaces in the *Guardian* as well – though only at one point and being virtually negated by the rest of the newspaper's coverage: 'Hamas and other militant groups [...] continu[e] to fire rockets at the civilian population in southern Israel.' (*Guardian*, 661)
23. The *Independent*'s basically incoherent and insubstantial account of the war may well be gauged from its reflection on the war's conclusion:

    More positively, [three weeks of harrowing combat] have pushed the Middle East up the international agenda. The impressive turn-out presided over by President Mubarak in Sharm el-Sheikh yesterday – which included the Palestinian President, and leaders of Britain, France, Germany, Italy, Spain, Turkey and Jordan – was clearly designed to banish the impression of international hesitation and division that followed the start of Israel's air campaign three weeks ago and establish a new sense of common purpose.

> That is good – or at least an improvement on what went before. The need for a lasting Middle East settlement has again been demonstrated. (*Independent*, 987)

'Three weeks of harrowing combat' with human(itarian) consequences well documented by the newspaper led to a positive outcome: 'That is good. The need for a lasting Middle East settlement has once again been demonstrated.' The logic whereby people's deaths simply and exclusively lead to the optimistic conclusion of the need for lasting peace having been demonstrated is certainly puzzling, to say the least.

24. Wife and mother are obviously not. This is why, eventually, they are able to talk, in one way or another. That this may take considerable time and energy is both quite irrelevant theoretically and a huge obstacle practically.
25. This is especially true if hate towards one had already materialized in the past as genocide.
26. Or, in fact, the activity of the *defenders or liberators of those victims.*

9 Conclusion: Beyond Good and Evil

1. To some extent, depictions of Hamas reflected this turnaround. In the *Telegraph*, it was the embodiment of Evil. In the *Guardian*, it was found rather unproblematic – relatively speaking, of course. It never reached the moral heights afforded to Israel in the *Telegraph* and *The Times*. But whilst the organization was the essential, unavoidable and un-engagable problem in the *Telegraph*, it was not depicted as a major obstacle in the *Guardian*. As such, given the circumstances, it is perhaps permissible to speak of a near-complete turnaround between the two newspapers with respect to Hamas as well.
2. As analysed, the *Independent* (*on Sunday*) incorporated elements of both the conservative discourse and that of the *Guardian*. Yet merely juxtaposing otherwise contradictory elements would not do for integration. As such, the *Independent*, from the perspective of the newspapers' editorials analysed in Chapters 7 and 8, offered an incoherent line of argumentation.
3. Such a state of affairs is even more complicated when the spectre of racism (and violent acts deriving from it) is raised. The dominant understanding of racism (not only in the newspapers but, arguably, in academia as well) still implies irrationality as racism's dominant character. Understandably, perhaps, given the historical catastrophes committed in the name of racism, one tends to think of the victim of racism as innocent, and the advocate of racism as the irrational agent of evil. Just as there are no shades in violence, there are no shades of racism either. It is very rarely conceptualized in terms of (hurtful and terrible) patterns of human relationships and, as such, rarely understood in terms of responsibility rather than blame/innocence. Even to raise the question of how racism may be accounted for with regard to relationships carries the (understandable) risk of 'blaming the victim' and 'exonerating the racist'. (As far as the history of antisemitism goes, seminal exceptions to this may be found in Arendt [1966] and Beller [2007a]).
4. The convergence of the development and popularization of human rights discourse (cf. Moyn, 2011; Weizman, 2012) and that of just war theory (Walzer, 2000, 2006) must also be pointed out here.

5. Moyn's account is very much contested by the work of Eyal Weizman, who claims that it is precisely the fragmentation of the humanitarian discourse into technical details that characterizes our age (Weizman, 2012). Though Weizman's argument is certainly a cogent one, his concerns are not reflected in the way British broadsheets reported and assessed the armed conflict.
6. A practical aspect of international humanitarian law that may lead to such sacralization should also be mentioned. Namely, the application of international law very much depends on practical political factors and as a result, it is very often the case that 'quasi-monsters' (e.g., Slobodan Milosevic, Charles Taylor, Saddam Hussein) of rogue states fallen out of the favour of the entire human community are seen in the dock.
7. As a consequence of debates and emotions over issues of Palestine/Israel, the caveat needs to be made here that the reason for what follows, a longish treatise on Arendt and *Eichmann in Jerusalem* (Arendt, 1994), is *not* because the historical events surrounding it would have borne any substantial similarity to those of Gaza (i.e., the Gaza war or Operation Cast Lead was no instance of genocide). It is simply because hers was an exemplary exercise of real understanding in the face of violence.
8. Cf. what Arendt disparagingly calls the 'cog-theory' (Arendt, 2003a, p. 29; cf. 1994, pp. 57, 289).
9. The term originally comes from Immanuel Kant.
10. 'Eichmann, much less intelligent and without any education to speak of, at least dimly realized that it was not an order but a law which had turned them all into criminals. The distinction between an order and the Führer's word was that the latter's validity was not limited in time and space, which is the outstanding characteristic of the former.' (Arendt, 1994, p. 149) Cf. '[...] Eichmann acted fully within the framework of the kind of judgment required of him: he acted in accordance with the rule, examined the order issued to him for its "manifest" legality, namely regularity; he did not have to fall back upon his "conscience" for he was not one of those who were unfamiliar with the laws of his country.' (Arendt, 1994, p. 293)
11. The context of the utterance in the book makes it absolutely clear that what Arendt means by 'the Jews' here is not the people as such but their administrative arm. Indeed, Arendt was always careful to point out the difference between functionaries and the rest of the people she elsewhere revealingly called the 'simple Jews' (Arendt, 1978b, p. 248; cf. Kaposi, 2008, p. 35).
12. It is important to add here that Arendt did not see the cooperation of Jewish functionaries as coming from some sort of essence, i.e., ghetto mentality. As she put it:

    > I have dwelt on this chapter of the story, which the Jerusalem trial failed to put before the eyes of the world in its true dimensions, because it offers the most striking insight into *the totality of the moral collapse the Nazis caused in respectable European society* – not only in Germany but in almost all countries, not only amongst the persecutors but also amongst the victims. (Arendt, 1994, pp. 125–126 – emphasis added)

13. Even though in his authoritative biography on Eichmann David Cesarani often distances himself from Arendt's narrative (Cesarani, 2004), the overall image he gives of Eichmann is actually one that is very much congenial to the image of *Eichmann in Jerusalem* (Laqueur, 2004).

14. To give just one example, this is how Arendt renders Eichmann's farewell before he is hung:

    Adolf Eichmann went to the gallows with great dignity. He had asked for a bottle of red wine and had drunk half of it. He refused the help of the Protestant minister... who offered to read the Bible with him: he had only two more hours to live and therefore no 'time to waste'. He walked the fifty yards from his cell to the execution chamber calm and erect, with his hands bound behind him.... 'I don't need that', he said when the hood was offered him. He was in complete command of himself, nay, he was more: he was completely himself. Nothing could have demonstrated this more than the grotesque silliness of his last words. He began with stating emphatically that he was a *Gottgläubiger*, to express in common Nazi fashion that he was no Christian and did not believe in life after death. He then proceeded: 'After a short while, gentlemen, *we shall all meet again*. Such is the fate of all men. Long live Germany, long live Argentina, long live Austria. *I shall never forget them.*' In the face of them, he had found the cliché used in funeral oratory. Under the gallows, his memory played him the last trick; he was 'elated' and he forgot that it was his own funeral.

    It was as though in those last minutes he was summing up the lesson this long course of human wickedness had taught us – the lesson of the fearsome, word-and-thought-defying *banality of evil*. (Arendt, 1994: 252 – emphasis in the original)

15. Other than the tool of irony, another overriding rhetorical characteristic of *Eichmann in Jerusalem* that clearly confuses its readers is Arendt's profuse use of indirect quotation. If one realized the absurd content of some of Eichmann's contentions in Arendt's rendering or her vitriolic take on them, this rhetorical tool in which those contentions were *formally* attributed to the narrator (i.e., Arendt) further strengthened the absurd character of the book. If not, however, one could, for instance, believe that the narrator in fact presents Eichmann as a Zionist (cf. Abel, 1963; Scholem in Arendt, 1978b, pp. 244–245; Robinson, 1965, p. 48; Wolin, 1996, 2001).

    Of importance for us is not so much the somewhat unbelievable characteristic that the discourse on Arendt's book had taken and to some extent still takes. Rather, it is to see that by its nature *indirect quotation* demolishes the categorical boundaries between agents.

16. There are two assumptions underpinning Arendt's collective judgment. First, that by cooperating the Jewish Councils did essentially nothing else but further the killings. Second, that they had full freedom of choice at their disposal; not to resist (which Arendt thought next to impossible) but to *do nothing*:

    And in order to do nothing, one did not need to be a saint, one needed only to say: 'I am just a simple Jew, and I have no desire to play any other role.'... Since we are dealing in politics with men, and not with heroes or saints, it is the possibility of '*nonparticipation*' (Kirchheimer) that is decisive if we begin to judge, not the system, but the individual, his choices and his arguments. (Arendt, 1978a, pp. 248–249; cf. Kaposi, 2008, pp. 102–112)

Sources

Independent

834. Oliver Miles. Gaza has to be part of any Middle East peace. 23 December, p. 26.
849. Editorial: The bombardment of Gaza will destroy lives, not Hamas. 29 December, p. 28.
850. Mary Dejevsky. Don't overlook Israel's vulnerability. 30 December, p. 30.
851. Robert Fisk. Why bombing Ashkelon is the most tragic irony. 30 December, p. 6.
858. Editorial: We must not let despair dash hopes of peace in Gaza. 30 December, p. 30.
862. Robert Fisk. The self delusion that plagues both sides in this bloody conflict. 31 December, p. 6.
912. Robert Fisk. Bring in the peacekeepers? It's not as easy as it sounds. 6 January, p. 6.
918. Robert Fisk. Why do they hate the West so much, we will ask. 7 January, p. 4.
939. Editorial: Israel's security will come only through dialogue. 10 January, p. 38.
972. Alvaro de Soto. Few will thank UN when this war ends. 16 January, p. 24.
986. Yasmin Alibhai Brown. Israel's friends cannot justify this slaughter. 19 January, p. 30.
987. Editorial: Welcome but fragile, this ceasefire must be only a start. 19 January, p. 26.
1005. Editorial: Gaza: the way forward? 23 January, p. 36.

Independent on Sunday

838. Editorial: Gaza: the cycle can be broken. 28 December, p. 30.
918. Robert Fisk. Why do they hate the West so much, we will ask. 7 January, p. 4.
981. British Jews attacked for pro-Gaza solidarity. 18 January, p. 2.
1014. Pope readmits Holocaust-denying priest to the church. 25 January, p. 38.

Guardian

441. Editorial: Killing a two-state solution: Gaza air strikes. 29 December, p. 26.
473. Tariq Ramadan. An alliance of values: while governments stand mute, Muslims must unite the majority to resist the violence done to Gaza. 2 January, p. 31.
482. Jonathan Freedland. Israel has plenty of tactics for war, but none for peace: a leadership dazzled by its own military might ignores the political reality and believes the only solutions lie in force. 3 January, p. 33.

520. Editorial: Gaza ground assault: when victory is a hollow word. 5 January, p. 30.
523. Khalid Mish'al. Gaza: this brutality will never break our will to be free. 6 January, p. 26.
544. Avi Shlaim. How Israel bought Gaza to the brink of humanitarian catastrophe: Oxford professor of international relations. 7 January, p. 2.
555. Carlo Stenger. Why Israel is united: Disdain for the tactics and ideology of Hamas has led to wide support for the Gaza operation. 29 January, p. 34.
576. British Jews: We must make sure these things don't reach our shores. 10 January, p. 8.
577. Editorial: Gaza: more, but worse. 10 January, p. 34.
592. Peter Beaumont. Supreme emergency: the Gaza crisis compels us to interrogate when, if ever, we consider armed resistance acceptable. 12 January, p. 26.
601. Peter Wilby. Why we have to let pictures tell the real story. 12 January, p. 2.
603. Colin Shindler. Why the silence over attacks on Israeli campuses? 13 January, p. 10 (Education supplement).
618. Editorial: Gaza: Israel and the family of nations. 14 January, p. 32.
655. Gaza Crisis: fragile truce, fragile future amid ruins. 19 January, p. 1.
661. Editorial: Gaza: brutal lessons. 19 January, p. 30.
665. Sally Hunt. Academics do have a role in resolving conflict. 20 January, p. 10 (Education supplement).

Observer

424. Editorial: Talking, not force, is the only solution in Gaza. 28 December, p. 22.
506. Thousands join march to protest against Israeli action. January 4, p. 3.
583. Ed Husain. How Gaza is alienating Britain's Jews and Muslims: as a British Muslim, it is so frustrating that no one seems to understand our anger. 11 January, p. 29.
584. Francesca Segal. How Gaza is alienating Britain's Jews and Muslims: as a British Jew, growing antisemitisms makes me feel that I am no longer safe. 11 January, p. 29.
641. Editorial: A pointless war has led to a moral defeat for Israel. 18 January, p. 36.
699. Pope allows Holocaust denier back into fold. 25 January, p. 19.

Daily Telegraph

7. Editorial: Hamas and Iran pose a threat to the world. 29 December, p. 17.
17. Editorial: Peace in Gaza is in the hands of Hamas. 30 December, p. 17.
37. David Blair. Even Obama can't solve this problem. 3 January, p. 29.
43. Editorial: Israel needs to be quick and clear in Gaza. 5 January, p. 23.
54. Surge in attacks on Jewish sites. 7 January, p. 11.
76. Editorial: A ceasefire would be in Israel's interests. 10 January, p. 23.
84. Jews urge EU to act against anti-Semitism. 14 January, p. 16.

Sunday Telegraph

134. Simon Scott Plummer. Who is to blame for this stunning blow to Israeli Arab relations? 28 December, p. 19.
159. Matt Rees: B'tselem: views to kill. 18 January, p. 16.

The Times

180. Mick Hume. Gaza is more than a simplistic morality play. 29 December, p. 21.
187. Editorial: Bitter Harvest. 29 December, p. 2.
190. David Aaronovitch. That's enough pointless outrage about Gaza. 30 December, p. 18.
202. Editorial: Security dilemmas in Gaza. 31 December, p. 2.
212. Gerard Baker. Don't expect Obama to get tough with Israel. 2 January, p. 26.
244. Editorial: Clueless in Gaza. 5 January, p. 2.
254. Security stepped up after attack on synagogue. 6 January, p. 3.
268. Police warn British Jews of revenge attack danger. 8 January, p. 6.
278. Editorial: In defense of Israel. 10 January, p. 2.
331. Editorial: Israel's cause is just but some of its tactics are self-defeating. 16 January, p. 2.

The Sunday Times

172. Editorial: This bloody stalemate in Gaza must be broken. 28 December, p. 12.
286. Fierce words over 'Nazi link' to Gaza. 11 January, p. 12.

Financial Times

1039. UN backs global calls for truce renewal. 29 December, p. 4.
1194. France fears backlash of ethnic tension from Gaza attack. 17 January, p. 8.
1212. Editorial: Bombing Gaza is not a solution. 29 December, p. 8.
1226. Editorial: A dangerous gamble in Gaza. 5 January, p. 10.
1256. Editorial: The ruins of Gaza. 22 January, p. 10.

Economist

738. Editorial: The hundred years' war. 10 January, p. 8.

List of references

Abel, L. (1963). The Aesthetics of Evil. *Partisan Review, 30(Summer)*, 210–230.

Amnesty International (2009). *Israel/Gaza: Operation 'Cast Lead': 22 Days of Death and Destruction* (Index: MDE 15/015/2009).

Arendt, H. (1966). *The Origins of Totalitarianism*. London: Harcourt, Inc.

Arendt, H. (1978a). *The Life of the Mind*. London: Harcourt, Inc.

Arendt, H. (1978b). 'Eichmann in Jerusalem': An Exchange of Letters Between Gershom Scholem and Hannah Arendt. In *The Jew as pariah* (pp. 240–251). New York, NY: The Grove Press.

Arendt, H. (1993). Truth and Politics. In *Between past and future: eight exercises in political thought* (pp. 227–264). New York: Penguin Books.

Arendt, H. (1994). *Eichmann in Jerusalem.* London, England: Penguin Books.
Arendt, H. (2003a). Personal Responsibility Under Dictatorship. In *Responsibility and judgment* (pp. 17–48). New York: Schocken Books.
Arendt, H. (2003b). Some Questions of Moral Philosophy. In *Responsibility and judgment* (pp. 49–116). New York: Schocken Books.
Arendt, H. (2003c). Thinking and Moral Considerations. In *Responsibility and judgment* (pp. 159–189). New York: Schocken Books.
Baram, D. (2004). *Disenchantment: The Guardian and Israel.* London: Guardian Books.
Bauer, Y. (2002). *Rethinking the Holocaust.* London: Yale UP.
Beller, S. (2007a). *Antisemitism: A Very Short Introduction.* London: Oxford UP.
Beller, S. (2007b). In Zion's Hall of Mirrors: A Comment on Neuer Antisemitismus? *Patterns of Prejudice, 41(2),* 215–238.
Ben-Ami, S. (2006). *Scars of War, Wounds of Peace : The Israeli-Arab Tragedy.* London: Oxford UP.
Billig, M. (1996). *Arguing and Thinking* (2nd edition). London: Cambridge UP.
Billig, M. (1999). *Freudian Repression: Conversation Creating the Unconscious.* London: Cambridge UP.
Bilsky, L. (2004). *Transformative Justice: Israeli Identity on Trial.* London: The University of Michigan Press.
Bourne, J. (2006). Anti-Semitism or Anti-Criticism? *Race & Class, 46(1),* 126–140.
Böhm, T. & Kaplan, S. (2011). *Revenge: On the Dynamics of a Frightening Urge and Its Taming.* London: Karnac.
Braham, R. L. (1969). *The Eichmann Case: A Source Book.* New York: World Federation of Hungarian Jews.
Bryman, A. (2008). *Social Research Methods.* Oxford: Oxford University Press.
Bunzl, M. (2007). *Anti-Semitism and Islamophobia: Hatreds Old and New in Europe.* Chicago: Prickly Paradigm Press.
Cesarani, D. (2004). *Eichmann: His Life and His Crimes.* London: William Heinemann.
Cesarani, D. (2006). Anti-Zionism in Britain, 1922–2002: Continuities and Discontinuities. *Journal of Israeli History, 25(1),* 131–160.
Chesler, P. (2003). *The New Anti-Semitism: The Current Crisis and What We Must Do about It.* San Francisco: Jossey-Bass.
Cockburn, A. & Clair, St., C. (eds). (2003). *The Politics of Anti-Semitism.* Petrolia: CounterPunch and AK Press.
Cohen, R. I. (1993). Breaking the Code: Hannah Arendt's Eichmann in Jerusalem and the Public Polemic: Myth, Memory and Historical Imagination. In D. Porat & S. Simonsohn (eds). *Michael: on the history of the Jews in the diaspora* (Vol. XIII, pp. 36–60). Tel Aviv: The Diaspora Research Institute.
Cordesman, A. H. (2009). *The 'Gaza War': A Strategic Analysis.* Washington: Center for Strategic and International Studies.
Deacon, D. (2007). Yesterday's Papers and Today's Technology: Digital Newspaper Archives and 'Push Button' Content Analysis. *European Journal of Communication, 22(1),* 5–25.
Davis, D. (2003). Hatred in the Air: the BBC, Israel and Antisemitism. In P. Iganski & B. Kosmin (eds). *A new antisemitism? Debating Judeophobia in 21st-century Britain* (pp. 113–147). London: Profile Books.

Dershowitz, A. (2006). *The Case for Peace: How the Arab-Israeli Conflict Can Be Resolved*. London: Wiley and Sons.

Dershowitz, A. (2008). *The Case against Israel's Enemies: Exposing Jimmy Carter and Others Who Stand in the Way of Peace*. London: Wiley and Sons.

Douglas, L. (2001). *The Memory of Judgment: Making Law and History in the Trials of the Holocaust*. New Haven: Yale UP.

Edwards, D. (1995). Two to Tango: Script Formulations, Dispositions, and Rhetorical Symmetry in Relationship Troubles Talk. *Research on Language and Social Interaction, 28(4)*, 319–350.

Engel, S. (2000). *Context is Everything: The Nature of Memory*. New York: W.H. Freeman.

Engelbert, J. & McCurdy, P. (2012). A Threat to Impartiality: Reconstructing and Situating the BBC's Denial of the 2009 DEC Appeal for Gaza. *Media, War & Conflict, 5(2)*, 101–117.

Fine, R. (2009). Fighting with Phantoms: A Contribution to the Debate on Antisemitism in Europe. *Patterns of Prejudice, 43(5)*, 459–479.

Finkelstein, N. (2005). *Beyond Chutzpah: On the Misuse of Anti-Semitism and the Abuse of History*. London: Verso.

Fish, S. (1980). *Is There a Text in this Class? The Authority of Interpretive Communities*. London: Harvard UP.

Foster, A. & Epstein, B. R. (1974). *The New Anti-Semitism*. New York: McGraw Hill Book Company.

Foxman, A. (2007). *The Deadliest Lies: The Israel Lobby and the Myth of Jewish Control*. New York: Palgrave Macmillan.

Foxman, A. (2004). *Never Again? The Threat of the New Anti-Semitism*. New York: HarperCollins.

Gaita, R. (ed). (2010). *Gaza: Morality, Law and Politics*. Crawley: UWA Publishing.

Gaza Operation investigations: Update. (2010). Downloaded on 17 September 2013:http://www.mfa.gov.il/MFA_Graphics/MFA%20Gallery/Documents/Gaza OperationInvestigationsUpdate.pdf

Gaza Operation investigations: Second Update. (2010). Downloaded on 17 September 2013: http://www.mfa.gov.il/MFA_Graphics/MFA%20Gallery/Documents/Gaza UpdateJuly2010.pdf

Geertz, C. (2001). *Available Light: Anthropological Reflections on Philosophical Topics*. Princeton: Princeton University Press.

Gibson, J. J. (1979). *The Ecological Approach to Visual Perception*. Boston: Houghton Mifflin.

The Goldstone Report (2011). Horwitz, A., Ratner, L. & Weiss, P. (eds). New York: Nation Books.

Goldstone, R. (2011). Reconsidering the Goldstone Report on Israel and War Crimes. *Washington Post,* 1 April. Downloaded on 17 September 2013: http://articles.washingtonpost.com/2011-04-01/opinions/35207016_1_drone-image-goldstone-report-israeli-evidence.

Gutmann, A. (2003). *Identity in Democracy*. Oxford, England: Princeton UP.

Halper, J. (2008). *An Israeli in Palestine: Resisting Dispossession, Redeeming Israel*. London: Pluto Press.

Harding, C. (ed). (2006). *Aggression and Destructiveness: Psychoanalytic Perspectives*. London: Routledge.

Harrison, B. (2006). *The Resurgence of Anti-Semitism: Jews, Israel, and Liberal Opinion*. New York: Rowman & Littlefield Publishers.
Hirsh, D. (2007). *Anti-Zionism and Antisemitism: Cosmopolitan Reflections*. The Yale Initiative for the Interdisciplinary Study of Antisemitism. Working Paper Series #1, New Haven.
Hirsh, D. (2010). Accusations of Malicious Intent in Debates about the Palestine-Israel Conflict and about Antisemitism. *Transversal, 1*, 47–77.
Howe, I. (1983). *A Margin of Hope: An Intellectual Autobiography*. London: Martin Secker and Warburg Limited.
Human Rights Watch. (2009). *Rain of Fire: Israel's Unlawful Use of White Phosphorous in Gaza*. New York: Human Rights Watch.
Human Rights Watch. (2013). Israel: High Court Rejects Legal Ban on White Phosphorous. Downloaded on 17 September 2013: http://www.hrw.org/news/2013/07/12/israel-high-court-rejects-legal-ban-white-phosphorus.
Ignatieff, M. (2003). *Human Right as Politics or Idolatry*. London: Princeton UP.
Judaken, J. (2008). So What's New? Rethinking the 'New Antisemitism' in a Global Age'. *Patterns of Prejudice, 42(4)*, 531–560.
Judt, T. (2010). From the House of Death: An Essay on Modern European Memory. In *Postwar: a history of Europe since 1945* (pp. 803–832). London: Vintage Books.
Julius, A. (2010). *Trials of the Diaspora: A History of Anti-Semitism in England*. London: Oxford UP.
Kaposi, D. (2008). To Judge or Not to Judge: The Clash of Perspectives in the Scholem–Arendt Exchange. *Holocaust Studies: A Journal of Culture and History, 14*(1), 95–119.
Karpf, A., Klug, B., Rose, J. & Rosenbaum, B. (eds). (2008). *Time to Speak Out: Independent Jewish Voices on Israel, Zionism and Jewish Identity*. London: Verso.
Klug, B. (2003). The Collective Jew: Israel and the New Antisemitism. *Patterns of Prejudice, 37(2)*, 117–138.
Klug, B. (2005). Is Europe a Lost Cause? The European Debate on Antisemitism and the Middle East Conflict. *Patterns of Prejudice, 39(1)*, 47–59.
Klug, B. (2008). A Time to Move On. In A. Karpf, B. Klug, J. Rose, & B. Rosenbaum (eds). *Time to speak out: independent Jewish voices on Israel, Zionism and Jewish identity* (pp. 286–296). London: Verso.
Klug, B. (2009). *Offence: The Jewish Case*. London: Seagull Books.
Kustow, M. (2008). Last Straws. In A. Karpf, B. Klug, J. Rose, & B. Rosenbaum (eds). *Time to speak out: independent Jewish voices on Israel, Zionism and Jewish identity* (pp. 210–219). London: Verso.
Kymlicka, W. (1989). *Liberalism, Community and Culture*. Oxford, England: Oxford University Press.
Landsman, S. (2005). *Crimes of the Holocaust: The Law Confronts Hard Cases*. Philadelphia: University of Pennsylvania Press.
Laqueur, T. (2004). Four Pfennige Per Track km. *London Review of Books, 26(21)*.
Laqueur, W. (1983). Hannah Arendt in Jerusalem: The Controversy Revisited. In L. H. Legters (ed). *Western society after the Holocaust* (pp. 106–120). Colorado: Westview Press/Boulder.

Laqueur, W. (2001). The Arendt Cult: Hannah Arendt as Political Commentator. In S. E. Aschheim (ed). *Hannah arendt in Jerusalem* (pp. 47–64). London: University of California Press.

Laqueur, W. (2006). *The Changing Face of Anti-Semitism: From Ancient Times to the Present Day.* London: Oxford UP.

Lawrence, J. (2012). *Deconstructing Therapists' Understandings of Domestic Violence and Abuse: Implications for Practice and Supervision.* Unpublished PhD dissertation, University of East London.

Lerman, A. (2003). Sense on Antisemitism. In P. Iganski & B. Kosmin (eds). *A new antisemitism? Debating Judeophobia in 21st century Britain* (pp. 54–67). London: Profile Books.

Lerman, A. (2008). Touching a Raw Nerve. In A. Karpf, B. Klug, J. Rose & B. Rosenbaum (eds). *Time to speak out: independent Jewish voices on Israel, Zionism and Jewish identity* (pp. 154–164). London: Verso.

Levi, P. (1989). *The Drowned and the Saved.* London: Vintage.

Loughborough University, Communications Research Centre. (2006). The BBC's Reporting of the Israeli-Palestinian Conflict (1 August 2005–31 January 2006) http://www.bbc.co.uk/bbctrust/assets/files/pdf/our_work/govs/loughborough_final.pdf (accessed on 13 October 2011).

Margalit, A. & Walzer, M. (2009). Israel: Civilians and Combatants. *New York Review of Books, 56(8),* 21–22.

Markovits, A. S. (2006). An Inseparable Tandem of European Identity? Anti-Americanism and Anti-Semitism in the Short and Long Run. *Journal of Israeli History, 25(1),* 85–105.

Mearsheimer, J. J. & Walt, S. M. (2008). *The Israel Lobby and US Foreign Policy.* London: Penguin.

Mettraux, G. (ed). (2008). *Perspectives on the Nuremberg Trial.* Oxford: Oxford UP.

Mommsen, H. (1991). Hannah Arendt and the Eichmann Trial. In *From Weimar to Auschwitz: essays in German history* (pp. 254–278). Cambridge: Polity Press.

Morris, B. (1999). *Righteous Victims: A History of the Zionist-Arab Conflict, 1881–1998.* London: Knopf Doubleday Publishing Group.

Myers, D. (2006). Can There be Principled Anti-Zionism? On the Nexus Between Anti-Historicism and Anti-Zionism in Modern Jewish Thought. *Journal of Israeli History, 25(1),* 33–50.

Moyn, S. (2011). *The Last Utopia: Human Rights in History.* London: Harvard UP.

The Operation in Gaza: Factual and Legal Aspects (2009). Downloaded on 17 September 2013: http://www.mfa.gov.il/NR/rdonlyres/E89E699D-A435-491B-B2D0-017675DAFEF7/0/GazaOperation.pdf.

Peace, T. (2009). Un antisémitisme nouveau? The Debate about a 'New Antisemitism' in France. *Patterns of Prejudice, 43(2),* 103–121.

Philo, G. & Berry, M. (2004). *Bad News from Israel.* London: Pluto Press.

Philo, G. & Berry, M. (2011). *More Bad News from Israel.* London: Pluto Press.

Rabinbach, A. (2004). Eichmann in New York: The New York Intellectuals and the Hannah Arendt Controversy. *October, 108,* 97–111.

Report of the Committee of Independent Experts in International Humanitarian and Human Rights Law Established Pursuant to Council Resolution 13/9.

Downloaded on 17 September 2013: http://www2.ohchr.org/english/bodies/hrcouncil/docs/16session/A.HRC.16.24_AUV.pdf.

Report of the Independent Panel for the BBC Governors in Impartiality of BBC Coverage of the Israeli-Palestinian Conflict. (2006). Downloaded on 17 September 2013: http://downloads.bbc.co.uk/bbctrust/assets/files/pdf/our_work/govs/panel_report_final.pdf.

The Report of the United Nations Headquarters Board of Inquiry (2009). Downloaded on 17 September 2013: www.innersitypress.com/banrep1gaza.pdf

Richardson, J. E. (2007). *Analysing Newspapers: An Approach from Critical Discourse Analysis*. London: Palgrave Macmillan.

Richardson, J. E. & Barkho, L. (2009). Reporting Israel/Palestine: Ethnographic Insights into the Verbal and Visual Rhetoric of BBC Journalism. *Journalism Studies, 15(5)*, 594–622.

Robertson, G. (2006). *Crimes against Humanity: The Struggle for Global Justice* (3rd edition). London: Penguin Books.

Robinson, J. (1965). *And the Crooked Shall Be Made Straight: The Eichmann Trial, the Jewish Catastrophe, and Hannah Arendt's Narrative*. New York: Macmillan.

Rorty, R. (1999). The Pragmatist's Progress: Umberto Eco on Interpretation. In *Philosophy and social hope* (pp. 131–147). London: Penguin Books.

Rosenfeld, A. (2006). *'Progressive' Jewish Thought and the New Anti-Semitism*. American Jewish Committee.

Said, E. (2004). *From Oslo to Iraq and the Road Map*. London: Bloomsbury.

Schank, R. (1999). *Dynamic Memory Revisited*. London: Cambridge UP.

Scholem, G. (1995a). The Tradition of the Thirty-six Hidden Just Men. In *The messianic idea in Judaism and other essays on Jewish spirituality* (pp. 251–257). New York: Schocken Books.

Scholem, G. (1995b). Revelation and Tradition as Religious Categories in Judaism. In *The messianic idea in Judaism and other essays in Jewish spirituality* (pp. 282–303). New York: Schocken Books.

Segev, T. (2000). *The Seventh Million: The Israelis and the Holocaust*. New York: Henry Holt and Company.

Shlaim, A. (2004). *The Iron Wall: Israel and the Arab World*. London: Penguin.

Slater, J. (2011). The Attacks on the Goldstone Report. In A. Horowitz, L. Ratner & P. Weiss (eds). *The Goldstone Report: The Legacy of the Landmark Investigation of the Gaza Conflict* (pp. 360–368). New York: Nation Books

Smith, B. (1977). *Reaching Judgment at Nuremberg*. London: Basic Books.

Taguieff, P.A. (2004). *Rising from the Muck: The New Anti-Semitism in Europe*. Chicago: Ivan R. Dee.

Trunk, I. (1972). *Judenrat: The Jewish Councils in Eastern Europe under Nazi Occupation*. New York: Macmillan Company.

Walzer, M. (2000). *Just and Unjust Wars: A Moral Argument with Historical Illustrations* (3rd edition). New York: Basic Books.

Walzer, M. (2006). *Arguing about War*. New York: Yale UP.

Walzer, M. (2009a). On Proportionality: How Much is Too Much in War? *The New Republic, 8 January*. 12.

Walzer, M. (2009b). Responsibility and Disproportionality in State and Nonstate Wars. *Parameters, 39(1)*, 40–52.

Weizman, E. (2012). *The Least of All Possible Evils: Humanitarian Violence from Arendt to Gaza*. London: Verso.

White, H. (2010). *The Fiction of Narrative: Essays on History, Literature, and Theory.* New York: The John Hopkins UP.
Wistrich, R. (2011). *From Blood Libel to Boycott: Changing Face of British Antisemitism.* Jerusalem: Vidal Sassoon International Center for the Study of Antisemitism.
Wolin, R. (1996). The Ambivalences of German-Jewish Identity: Hannah Arendt in Jerusalem. *History and Memory, 8(2),* 9–35.
Wolin, R. (2001). *Heidegger's Children – Hannah Arendt, Karl Löwith, Hans Jonas and Herbert Marcuse.* Oxford: Princeton UP.
Yablonka, H. (2004). *The State of Israel vs. Adolf Eichmann.* New York: Schocken Books.
Zertal, I. (2005). *Israel's Holocaust and the Politics of Nationhood.* London: Cambridge UP.

Index